W9-CGQ-186

A Pastor's Challenge

A Pastor's Challenge

Parish Leadership
in an Age of
Division, Doubt, and
Spiritual Hunger

George A. Kelly

Our Sunday Visitor Publishing Division
Our Sunday Visitor, Inc.
Huntington, Indiana 46750

ISBN: 0-87973-738-7
LCCCN: 94-66027

Cover design by Rebecca J. Heaston

PRINTED IN THE UNITED STATES OF AMERICA

738

Contents

Acknowledgments

A book, any book, even one with modest ambitions, is never really the work of one writer, although one name appears on the cover. In the normal course of publication, many people contribute remotely or proximately by relating experiences, making suggestions, criticizing, sometimes negatively, or simply by being a close friend who talks a lot about subjects dear to the heart of a potential author. Since this book is about priests, it is priests above all others who have shaped this or that aspect of the subject under discussion, men who have helped shape my life and the thinking that has gone into this book. Although their views were often different than mine, still I wish to thank each and every one of them both for friendship and for the learning:

Father Kenneth Baker, S.J. (New York, NY)
Father Joseph Cahill, C.M. (Queens, NY)
Father Frank Canavan, S.J. (New York, NY)
Monsignor Francis M. Costello (Venice, FL)
Monsignor Irving A. DeBlanc (Lake Charles, LA)
Monsignor William B. Delaney (New Milford, CT)
Father Joseph Dirvin, C.M. (Queens, NY)
Monsignor Charles Diviney (Brooklyn, NY)
Monsignor Charles Dollen (Poway, CA)
Monsignor Peter Finn (Staten Island, NY)
Monsignor Robert A. Ford (White Plains, NY)
Father John Gallagher (Yonkers, NY)
Monsignor George Graham (Levittown, NY)
Monsignor Daniel Hamilton (Lindenhurst, NY)
Father Donald Keefe, S.J, (Denver, CO)
Monsignor John Keogh (Hampton Bays, NY)
Father Ronald Lawler, O.F.M. Cap. (Pittsburgh, PA)
Monsignor Edgar McCarren (San Jose, CA)
Monsignor John Mulroy (White Plains, NY)
Monsignor William O'Brien (Bronx, NY)

Father Robert Silverman (San Antonio, TX)
Father Kenneth Sullivan (Los Angeles, CA)
Monsignor Kevin Toomey (Melbourne, Australia)
Monsignor Michael Wrenn (New York, NY)

Mrs. Terry Archer, formerly my assistant at St. John's University, and Miss Patricia Hand, who worked with me on other books, notably on *Inside My Father's House* and *Keeping the Church Catholic*, were in on this project, too, as it unfolded. The one who did most of the tedious work, however, on the wordprocessor through draft after draft, was Mr. William J. Kimmig, whose expertise and tireless dedication was extraordinary, and his wife Bernadette, who did the copyediting and related work. The Kimmigs were part of my staff as youngsters in my first parish assignment just about fifty years ago.

Finally, Our Sunday Visitor's publisher, Mr. Robert Lockwood, and OSV's acquisitions editor, Ms. Jacquelyn Murphy, deserve appreciation for entertaining the idea underlying the book and then encouraging its completion. OSV published my first book after arriving at Saint John's University, *Who Should Run the Catholic Church?*, and the publisher then, Father Albert Nevins, M.M., a friend thereafter, laboriously read through the present manuscript in its entirety several times and made many valuable suggestions. To him, and to all who have gone before, I can only say thanks, freeing all of them from responsibility of whatever imperfections they find in this book.

"I Will Give You Shepherds":

An Introduction

This book has a strange genesis. I began to think about it around the time (1990) when the world's bishops were assembling in Rome to worry out loud about their priests. Then, when John Paul II used the words of Jeremiah (3:15), in *Pastores Dabo Vobis* (Latin for "I Will Give You Shepherds"), his 1992 apostolic exhortation on priestly formation, to define precisely what the Vatican II priesthood was all about, he struck a chord in the hearts of priests like myself who, for all of our half-century of holy orders, never looked upon ourselves as anything but *pastores*. We had been weaned on the ideas of another scholar-pope, Pius XI, whose 1935 encyclical *Ad Catholici Sacerdotii* shaped our seminary training. Few of us ever lost sight of our identity as parish priests. Indeed, prior to World War II, bishops had a hard time luring parish priests into special work. Now, a new pontiff comes along to assure the Catholic community that without such priests the Church would not live, a sentiment the old Italian mountain climber would share. So, as far as the Catholic Church is concerned, old or new, there is no substitute for the ordained priesthood. Cardinal William O'Connell's ordination hymn thrilled us in 1992 as completely as it did in 1942: *Juravit Dominus et non poenitebit; Tu es sacerdos in eternum secundum ordinam Melchisedech.*

A seminarian-in-training from Pius XI's time, fortunate enough to serve out his priesthood through the pontificate of John Paul II, may perhaps be excused for noting that these two popes thought alike about the priesthood; not about the incidentals (because Western culture has changed radically since 1936), but about its substance. For Karol Wojtyla (as much as he was for Achille Ratti), the priest remains Christ's special minister and his instrument for mankind's redemption. All priests ordained in 1942 believed that premise, while many *ordinati* today have been taught, perhaps in their seminaries, that they are to see themselves more as community-organizers for human betterment rather than as vicars of Christ for the kingdom of heaven.

To men of my generation, however, being a priest meant standing in Christ's place among people for his eternal purposes. An awesome definition, to be sure, but also a Catholic reality, the unworthiness of the subject notwithstanding.

Because the issue of priestly identity has become a matter of controversy in our day, made so, says John Paul II in *Pastores Dabo Vobis*, by a "conscious bias," against the very notion of priesthood, and a distortion of Vatican II, some purpose may be served by assessing this vocation through the eyes of one battle-scarred but upbeat witness. The word "priest" suggests to most Catholics a man's mission within the *ecclesiola* (the parish) to fashion a Christ-like way of thinking and acting among God's people (Philippians 2:5). The priest, therefore, like the father of a family, has done his work well when he leaves behind him a generous share of sons and daughters who live faithfully in the Lord. It makes no difference where his parish is; he will know, if he stays at it long enough, whether or not he himself has been a good shepherd.

An Author's Expectations

I doubt very much whether anyone can learn the details of how to be a good parish priest in a classroom or from a book. But those who do effective parish work, in their own style, have usually been inspired by someone else's good example, or by living out someone else's ideas. Beloved parish priests, at least the ones I have admired most, had special qualities that transcended anything they learned in school. Certainly no seminary rector I know, looking at his latest ordination class, can identify the future "good shepherds." Only by funeral time will this be clear to an informed and honest eulogist, and to the parishioners who pass on the stories about the great priest who has gone from their midst.

We all have come across so-so priests, of course, and occasionally a bad one. But what is surprising today is how little interest elites, including historians, have in the doings of parish priests, or in how so many of them become neighborhood legends in their lifetimes. Surprising, I say, because parochial life, beginning with Peter, is still the rock on which the Church is built, whether in Rome or in Kokomo. Teachers, intellectuals, health and welfare workers, chancery officials all play vital Catholic roles, but their services are intended to enrich the Church's home life — that is, the parish. It is the outstanding parish priests who create and maintain the Catholic community.

This kind of priest is more realistic about "the possible" in parish life than he was in 1942. God gives the increase, of course, yet a priest on the front line of the apostolic enterprise may follow in the footsteps of a legendary predecessor, or perhaps walks into a parish that has been falling apart for years. It is easier to look good when a recent predecessor was less than good, but the human test for any shepherd is a simple one: Is the parish better off — does he leave his flock better Christians — for his being there?

The condition of his social surroundings, even of his diocese, helps or hurts. On his arrival a local scandal may have agitated "the little ones"; he may inherit a large debt, a difficult curate, a fussy congregation, a confused diocese, and so forth. What is becoming a real problem is the breakdown of general consensus about what the "ideal" parish should be. Many priests, after the recent Vatican Council, lost interest in what the Church had to say about norms of Catholic parish conduct, or even about the accomplishments of the Church in the United States. After 1965, a sudden rush began to change parish structures, and even to find substitutes for the parish itself. Priests and religious sometimes began to have doubts, inculcated in their own classroom settings, that Christ had anything specific in mind about the Church itself, except to see that his followers were decent human beings.

As this book moves from chapter to chapter, we will explore just how realistic the Church's hopes, and today's doubts, are. One young bishop installs new pastors with a ritual that includes a profession of faith and an oath of fidelity to the mind of Christ as this is known through the *magisterium* of the Church. It is in kindred spirit with him that we proceed with this book.

George A. Kelly

11

Part One

The Parish Priesthood —

Past and Present

Chapter One

Priesthood Before Ministry

By the Sacrament of Orders priests are formed
in the image of Christ the Priest, to be ministers
of Christ the Head in constructing and building
up his whole body, the Church.

— Vatican II, *Presbyterorum Ordinis*

The ordained priest, according to John Paul II, participates in a "specific," "authoritative," and "consecrated" way in the mission of Christ (Luke 4:18, 19), and he states this before he defines what that mission is. It seems appropriate, therefore, to explain what a priest is before we exegete his ministry. And, while we could do this by lengthy citations from Saint Paul to Saint John Vianney, as good a start as any can be made, given the circumstances of our time, by simply quoting the pungent remarks of a modern American novelist.

Many years ago, Flannery O'Connor attended a supper at the home of Mary McCarthy, a fallen-away Catholic writer who, in the course of table talk, described the Holy Eucharist as a "pretty good symbol." To which the pious Flannery replied, "Well, if it's a symbol, to hell with it!" This less-than-elegant riposte reflected her annoyance with McCarthy's effort to reinterpret the Church's chief sacrament differently from its defined reality. O'Connor went beyond annoyance. She exploded: "It is the center of existence for me; all the rest of life is expendable!"

What Flannery O'Connor was defending, of course, was the reality underlining a Catholic definition of revealed truth. To a woman with her faith convictions it was insensible to let go unchallenged an assertion of the Eucharist's subjective value, which, by inference at least, denied its objective meaning. "To hell with it" may have startled Mary McCarthy at her own dinner table, but, in the mind of Miss O'Connor, eviscerating a revealed truth of its proper meaning was the greater indignity.

Whenever I think of what is being said about the priesthood today, this little upper-class contretemps of years ago comes to mind.

As obvious as the true meaning of the Eucharist was to O'Connor, it is also evident that any authentic discussion of the ordained priesthood must be carried on within the parameters set by the convictions of the Church. Every priest, even one who no longer lives the life, is free to write a personal commentary on his experience in holy orders; but what Vatican II called "Christ's priestly office," in this vale of tears, at least, determines whether a particular priest is a success or a failure.

State of the Contemporary Question

Many opinion molders regularly speak about the morale problem of contemporary priests. One priest-convert thinks it is more serious than anything else that concerns Catholic laity. The annual number of priestly ordinations in the United States is below par, we have begun to accept the notion of "priestless parishes," and we talk openly at breakfast about clerical scandals. This is a new phenomenon in our religious experience, one whose explanation goes beyond a bad press. In some elite circles, the tradition of the Church, even the testimony of the New Testament, is considered irrelevant to what modern Catholic Christianity should be; assertions are commonplace that bishops in union with the pope cannot any longer, or with finality, speak about what Christ actually intended for the Eucharist or the priesthood. On the other hand, if the Catholic Church from its earliest days has been inaccurate, even wrong, in its definitions of apostolic succession, priesthood, Eucharist, and Church government, why is anyone surprised at the dearth of priestly vocations? Conversely, can low seminary enrollments be called evidence of renewed Catholicity à la Vatican II expectations?

Social scientists like to think the priests' morale problems can be mitigated by improved pay scales, better understanding of people's new needs and wants, by less heavy-handed bishops, by female or married priests, and by greater attention to personal choices, self-fulfillment, and theological pluralism. However, religious orders, which first followed this advice, are still in short supply of priests. Indeed, the sociologists, who explain the low esteem for the priesthood among young upwardly mobile Catholics in the same way they explain the absence of educated white Anglo-Saxons in today's prizefighting business, may be part of the modern problem. Proposed change in social circumstances leaves unexplained the important and radical Catholic questions: Why would anyone seriously wish to be a Catholic priest if one is no longer, thereby, an *Alter Christus*? Or, if he must be open-ended about his faith convictions? Or, if his chief role is to act as a Catholic facilitator, a pop psychologist, a social worker, or a community organizer? Or, if the Church to which he consigns himself for life is merely a congregation of people who say they believe in Christ, but not necessarily the Mystical Body of Christ? A potential aspirant might do better looking elsewhere.

What occurs, therefore, in today's dining rooms of "the best and the brightest," may indeed be a better gauge of the state of the *sacerdotium* than what goes on in Greeley polls. Flannery O'Connor definitely felt like an odd-Catholic-woman-out in Mary McCarthy's home, simply because she believed in the Real Presence. The parlous state of the contemporary priesthood may also be due to less than clear faith convictions in elite circles, widely circulated. One priest (according to *Origins*, February 4, 1988) alleges that the decline in the number of priests, and their present ennui, "are the natural and perhaps even inevitable result of the documents of the Second Vatican Council," and to the fact that the council demoted the priest from his status as *another Christ* to something else. At one national meeting of bishops, where the extraordinary use of a "priestless Communion service" was approved, several minor USCC observers in the background reacted immediately: "This is a great breakthrough!" For what? one might ask. Bishop Raymond Lucker of New Ulm acknowledges the question of the future: whether parishioners are to attend Mass or a Communion service.[1] Headlines in journals like the *National Catholic Reporter* read: "Priestless Parishes Are Riding A High Tide," "Laicized Church Could Solve Priest Shortage," "The Eucharist: A Threatened Species." A world-preaching pope may inveigh against the laicization of the clergy (and the clericalization of the laity), yet violations of liturgical norms are commonplace — from celebration of Mass in secular clothes to regular distribution of Communion by laity in the presence of sitting priests, or by laity to concelebrating priests!

David Power, onetime theologian at the Catholic University of America, takes declericalization one step further. His volume, *The Sacrifice We Offer*, contains this sentence: "The Roman Church indulges in a misrepresentation of its own earliest tradition when in the composition of the new Eucharistic prayers it presents the section after the supper narrative as the offering of Christ himself, or of his body and blood."[2]

Only a few years ago Notre Dame's Jay P. Dolan's *Transforming Parish Ministry* presented this conundrum to John Paul II: "In the past quarter century the traditional understanding of the priesthood has been reshaped in a very substantial manner. Nevertheless a satisfactory definition of ordained priesthood still remains as elusive as a fistful of water."[3]

I have no doubt what Flannery O'Connor would say to that.

In the Catholic world, the priesthood is one of two things: either the institutionalized shadow of Christ himself, with all the human individuality this presupposes; or simple role-playing by a Church member, striving to make life on this earth meaningful for himself and his flock, without indebtedness to what the Church's *magisterium* describes as necessary to the priesthood. Pursuing the latter course incautiously has built-in dangers for the Church, many of which are already evident twenty-five years after Vatican II. Demythologizing the triumphal aspects of the priesthood, or enlarging the role of the laity in the Church's public prayer life or its governing procedures, may be harmless nibblings at priests' *modus operandi* in any century. But denying or denigrating the priest's essential nature is one of the more substantial threats to the uniqueness of the Catholic Church.

The Priesthood Is Christ's and Sacrificial

The important thing to remember about Christ's priesthood is that it involved dying. His life, of its nature, was sacrificial. Within twenty-five years of the first Easter Sunday, Saint Paul was teaching his Roman listeners: "[We] are justified through the free gift of his grace by being redeemed in Christ Jesus who was appointed by God to sacrifice his life ..." (Romans 3:24-25).

The Second Vatican Council paired this priesthood of Christ with that of those who celebrate the Eucharist today. At the late council's end (1965) the assembled bishops, in union with Paul VI, affirmed that priests exercising their sacred functions act in the Person of Christ and, from generation to generation, continue to apply the fruits of the Lord's unique sacrifice to the spiritual benefit of God's people. We may be dealing here with God's mysterious movement among his people, one not fully understood this side of eternity. Yet anyone who believes what the Church teaches about redemption knows that the death of Jesus Christ, and his subsequent Resurrection, alone restored mankind to the friendship of God. This reconciliation is continued daily through the ministry of the ordained priest, and in his role as celebrant of the Eucharist. These doctrines of the sacrificing Christ and the sacrificial priesthood of the New Testament are what distinguish the Catholic Church, both East and West, from other Christian communities.

Intrinsic to the Catholic faith, therefore, is the understanding that the saving power of Christ's redemptive sacrifice makes his Church a priestly Church, through which God's living presence (grace) is conveyed, a foreshadowing, too, of the eternal salvation he promises will follow. The normal channels for the dispensation of this grace are the Church's sacraments, each of which have been instituted by Christ in their original form, all of which, save baptism and marriage, require for validity the ministry of the ordained priesthood. (However, Church law, promulgated by *magisterium*, is specific about the conditions necessary for the valid and licit administration of baptism and marriage by non-priests.) The power to celebrate the Eucharist, and to offer the Sacrifice of the Mass, resides in the ordained priesthood exclusively. The authority to teach, rule, and sanctify in Christ's name, first bestowed on the apostles, belongs to bishops and to those who, though of lower rank, share in their priesthood.

All of the above assertions are *de fide* teachings of the Catholic Church.

Priests As Suffering Servants

Throughout history, God has revealed himself through people — starting with Adam and Eve, through Moses and Mary, at times through converted scoundrels, but last of all through Jesus. The Lord's unique saving mission called upon him to empty himself of signs of his glory, to humble himself, to accept death on the cross as the price the Father wished him to pay to accomplish mankind's redemption (see Philippians 2:6-11). Catholic priests are also destined to be God's suffering servants and, if need be, to be martyrs for the Catholic faith. The servant role, however, does not mean that priests are people of no account, or that they lack special status in the Church. As Saint Paul made clear about the humbled Christ, "God raised him high." Similarly, the Catholic priest was ordained to be a sacred person with the dignity appropriate to his unique responsibilities. Walking in the footsteps of the obedient Christ, he receives from the Master the teaching, ruling, and sanctifying powers over those matters that pertain to the salvation promised by the Lord. Like the prophets, priests, and anointed kings before him, it is the priest of the New Testament who has been chosen by God through the Church to keep Christ's revelation alive among God's people and to maintain God's very life among them.

"O Lord, I Am Not Worthy" — A Priest Nonetheless

Considering this sacred function, it is not surprising that the Church has the priest say at daily Mass: *"Domine, non sum dignus."*

Every priest brings his human limitations to the altar of ordination. The ordaining bishop cannot be sure in advance which one of the *ordinandi* kneeling before him is capable of causing the kind of scandals that have been perpetrated in Church history by weak, incompetent, unbelieving, lustful priests. Even so, those shortcomings do not vitiate the charisma of the priest. Was it not once said of Jesus by his enemies: "From Nazareth? ... Can anything good come from that place?" (John 1:46). The Palestinian leadership might not have revered him, but they respected his holiness and his influence with the people. The apostles surely held him in high regard, as did those early Christian presbyters and bishops who created the apostolic Church that Saint Augustine admired so much. Even Oliver Goldsmith of a much later date wrote epigrammatically, "I take my religion from the priest."

Prominent public figures, and priests are surely that, can be domineering and unlikable at times. The anticlericalism in so-called Catholic countries is also ample evidence of this. Yet empiricists, in the United States particularly, are usually short on suitable explanations for the veneration showered upon those traditional neighborhood heroes who go by the name "Father." Devout people had no difficulty in conveying honor on men whom they name Padre, Pater, Abbé, Abba, Papa — in recognition of the role and the responsibility priesthood imposes.

The new 1983 *Code of Canon Law*,[4] a fruit of Vatican II if anything is, reinforces the honorable place of priests in the Church by making clear the burdens they are expected to carry: to provide Catholic catechesis, to supervise the Church's liturgical and sacramental life, to be the chief organizer of the Christian community and the parish treasurer, to be the parochial registrar and the Church's legal representative, in charge of the neighborhood's Catholic social works, and the presiding officer over pastoral council affairs. The local pastor, like the bishop in a diocese, is held responsible by Church authority for the correction of error and of other abuses that may beset his ministry; for making decisions that, while aimed at seeing that the laws of the Church and state are observed, also frustrate the will of those elites who array themselves against public authority of any kind.

Nor must we presume that the priest's position of honor in the Church is due simply to the functions he performs. It is the priestly character itself the Church holds in high esteem. As Henri De Lubac has said so eloquently and so often, every priest is delegated by no less than God himself to "participate in the Church's mission to engender and maintain the Divine life in us." Whether he be hale and hearty or confined to a wheelchair, or lives in a fine house or a cloister, whether he enjoys prominence or suffers in a gulag, the ordained cleric participates in Christ's dignity as priest, prophet, and shepherd of the flock. And providing he keeps the faith and observes the priestly discipline, the priest speaks for God, offers sacrifice to God, and governs some part of God's kingdom in Christ's name. He does this in spite of the unworthiness of the best and the scandalmongering of the worst among his kind.

Saint Francis of Assisi, who considered himself unworthy of the office, confessed his "great faith in priests who live according to the laws of the Holy Church of Rome because of their dignity." So much so, he added, "I am determined to reverence, love, and honor priests." And again: "I refuse to consider their sins because I can see the Son of God in them."

Francis' respect merely reflects the mind of the Church, which long before the thirteenth century called upon priests to be virtuous exemplars of Christ. If one leafs through the post-Vatican II liturgy celebrating the Catholic priesthood, he or she will be staggered by the number and quality of the virtues considered to be the essentials of priestly life — faith, courage, chastity, detachment, sobriety, hospitality, piety, holiness, prayerfulness, as well as soundness in doctrine and obedience, with apostolic fervor for the pastoral care of the faithful. We also tend to overlook the significance of the daily prayer of the Mass that the priest is told by the Church to offer "quietly," as if between himself and God alone: "Lord Jesus Christ, Son of the Living God, by the will of the Father and the work of the Holy Spirit your death brought life to the world. By your Holy Body and Blood free me from all my sins and from every evil. Keep me faithful to your teaching and never let me be parted from you."

Vocation to Holiness

Why does a priest, especially a veteran, look uncomfortable whenever someone calls him "holy"? He may take "man of God" in stride, but "holy man" somehow embarrasses the typical priest. Although "spiritual life" and "interior life" have been code words for his state since seminary days, somehow, if he is a "secular priest" particularly, he thinks these words apply more to Carthusians, maybe to Capuchins, than to him. Even Saint Augustine made holiness seem ordinary: "For you I am a bishop, with you I am a Christian." The Second Vatican Council's *Lumen Gentium*, too, makes the "call to holiness" the responsibility of the whole Church, so why should a priest think of himself any differently.[5] Yet, John Paul II is of the mind that any priest who acts in the name of Christ is obligated to think like Christ and act like Christ, and this alone spells a special kind of holiness. Why priests, especially diocesan priests, shy away from the nomenclature may say something about the way they were trained, or about their expectations. Still, in *Pastores Dabo Vobis*, the present pope identifies holiness as the priest's "specific" vocation.

Should this not be so? Every form of Judeo-Christianity involves a personal relationship with God, easy enough for Christ to whom the Father was immanent, but still available to an earthbound priest who cultivates the relationship. For the priest the Church is the mediatrix, the home where he first learned about Christ, about God's word, about Mass and the sacraments, and through Church discipline that taught him how to do priestly things correctly. The Church is his framework within which God vivifies him with his presence, otherwise called sanctifying grace, itself holiness pure and simple.

Holiness can also be defined as the absence of serious sinfulness, a legitimate enough explanation as long as the priest realizes that holiness is presence more than absence, and that it is vitally important to ordinary priests of the Church, not just to the heroes. The laity depend on good priests, and when they speak of someone as "a good priest," they really are attributing holiness to him. Scandalmongering priests have been rare in the history of the American Church, and whatever their moral weaknesses were, even these failed to inflict mortal wounds on the ecclesial body.

Catholic vitality was the result of the quality of Church discipline in the priesthood. Daily Mass for priests, like frequent Communion for churchgoers, was not always the rule, but it became so in recent centuries, particularly in the United States. One old priest, asked on his golden jubilee to explain his success, replied simply: "I have been able to say Mass, sick or well, every day of my fifty years." Few priests can make that claim, although most American priests were so imbued with the ideal that it became their general norm. If one truly believes that the Paschal Mystery is re-presented in the Mass, the central act of Christ's life, why should it be otherwise?

Similarly "the Divine Office" — now called "the Liturgy of the Hours," the daily recitation of psalms, hymns, patristic readings, and selected prayers to which priests are daily bound to say for the whole Church — dominates priests' prayer life. When said, even routinely without fervor, this daily prayer calls the priest back, again and again, to God. We forget how meaningful routine acts, multiplied over and over again, can be (like signs of the cross, genuflections, in the old days by tips of the hat), even though a given individual act seems to be of minor significance. Cynics often laugh at, sometimes scorn, what are called senseless rules; but when the formation takes hold, the result is ingrained reverence, for God surely, and for sacred things in general. An old teaching axiom applies here: "Give me the body, I'll get the mind later." Even when the priest hardly notices, saying Mass regularly — and reciting the Office — does lift his heart to God. It surely reminds him of who God is.

Consequently, the trend among earthbound skeptics to miss Mass regularly, to violate its sacredness by coldness, vulgarity, disregard of rubrics or neglect, contempt, diminishes holiness. Byzantine priests may think that Mass is not sacred unless it lasts an hour and a half, but Roman priests can manifest devotion half that time. Accidents of culture are of little account.

But *"Hoc est enim corpus meum"* (this is truly my body) remains for the priest his entrance into the "Holy of Holies." In like fashion, the sight in olden days of priests on vacation scurrying to various corners of someone's room simply to "finish the Office," like the act of teenagers on a Sunday morning before they go home, running for the first Mass after an all-night spree on the town, are real acts of piety, however imperfect. The tendency to treat these matters lightly, or to omit them unless the prayer is perfectly said, represents coldness of heart toward God, and, in many cases, involves sin. Good prayer remains fundamentally in the intention, and may involve a simple juggling act before a tabernacle or a Christmas crib. The opening line of a meditation in a religious house, "Let us place ourselves in the presence of God," is often prayer enough. An old priest in a hospital, sick to death, mumbling his beads, with hardly a thought of the words, pleases God immensely.

John Paul II rounds out the requirements of priestly holiness when, besides these essentials, he insists on frequent confession: "If a priest were no longer to go to confession or properly confess his sins, his priestly being and his priestly action would feel its effects very soon, and this would also be noticed by the community of which he was the pastor." To this admonition the pontiff adds the enjoiner that for holiness the priest must develop the virtue of obedience, "submission to those invested with ecclesial authority"; "only the persona who knows how to obey in Christ is really able to require obedience from others in accordance with the gospel." Few things are so countercultural in our time as acknowledgment of sin and obedience to superiors, yet without both a priest is in trouble with himself almost from the beginning, because both virtues are necessary conditions of priestly apostolic service. Parishioners do not get to know the priests who are rarely available, who are hard to find on a Sunday, are never in the confessional, at wakes or on rides to the cemetery, who never bless the homes of newcomers or old-timers, whose sermons are devoid of sense or meaning, who are disagreeable, end up little remembered.

The prophet Jeremiah did say, "I will give you shepherds" (3:15), but shepherds, he said, "after my own heart." And that heart, as we know, is as *sacred* as the Lord expects his priests to be.

23

But reverence for the sacred, even by priests, is not inborn. It must be cultivated. Vatican II speaks the obvious when it teaches that priests grow in holiness by doing their duty, especially by offering sacrifice for their people (*Lumen Gentium*, No. 41). "Rendering to God what belongs to God" is the special obligation of priests and, following Christ's example, this means they must go aside from time to time ("for a while") and commune personally and directly with God. This is why much emphasis is laid on priests' retreats and days of recollection, and why in former days they were mandated, sometimes bringing together large congresses of diocesan or religious confreres. The quality of these exercises always remained uneven, as far as individual receptivity was concerned; but the lessons were not totally lost on even spiritually tepid clergy. And they reminded the diocese, or the religious community, what priestly priorities really were. "So could you not stay awake with me one hour?" was not simply Christ's challenge to a sleeping Peter (Matthew 26:40). It confronts every priest every day. The fall from grace of many clerics begins when the spiritual exercises (e.g., of Saint Ignatius), with their stress on perfection in one's relationship with God, fall out of fashion in favor of psychological uplift in small groups. Since it is easy to be profane in a totally secular environment, bishops and superiors may wish to reevaluate the relationship between diocesan and community exercises and the worldliness of their clergy.

The Prophetic Value of Celibacy

He was hardly seated in Paul VI's papal chair when the present pope on his first Holy Thursday (April 9, 1979) addressed the challenge of priestly celibacy: "The priest, by renouncing this fatherhood proper to the married man, seeks another fatherhood and, as it were, even another motherhood, recalling the words of the Apostle about the children whom he begets in suffering. These are the children of his spirit, people entrusted to his solicitude by the Good Shepherd. These people are many, more numerous than an ordinary human family can embrace. The pastoral vocation of priests is great, and the Council teaches that it is universal; it is directed to the whole Church."

In the Church's view, therefore, a priest, like Christ, shares in God's fatherhood, finds his fruitfulness in the Church, and is its witness before the world of the promise and reality of God's kingdom. Within a quarter century of Christ's resurrection (*c*. 56 A.D.), Saint Paul is declaring what became very early a Church norm: "...The unmarried man is anxious about the things of the Lord, how to please the Lord; But the married man is anxious about affairs of the world, how to please his wife." (1 Corinthians 7:32-33). For the Church, celibacy is the sign of the priest's individual love of God and of God's people, evidence itself of his holiness. In his recent study, *Clerical Celibacy in East and West* (published in London in 1989), Roman Cholij establishes celibacy as the apostolic norm, the practice of a married clergy in the East being a departure from that norm.

Much is made these days of the complaint that celibacy is the most difficult part of the priesthood. Saint Augustine surely had his trouble with celibacy. Though driven to the priesthood by the impulse of a newly acquired faith, he remained withdrawn for a time from taking the step because (as he later confessed) "of my need of woman." Less gifted priests surely need not be embarrassed by the challenge inherent in the commitment to celibacy that goes with the priesthood. That they are not fully converted Augustines on their ordination day should surprise no one.

Still, even if the human instinct for congress with the opposite sex is potent, God's mind on how those faculties are to be used by all Christians is clear enough — revealed in Genesis, reaffirmed and amplified by Christ himself, and constantly reiterated by the Church ever since. Commitment to chastity in and out of marriage is the norm, and the Church, from its earliest days, has associated celibacy with the priestly state of life. Paul VI wrote the encyclical "*Sacerdotalis Caelibatus*" ("Priestly Celibacy") in 1967, which only recapitulated the mind of Pius XII whose 1954 encyclical "*Sacra Virginitas*" ("On Holy Virginity") listed Fathers of the Church and early apologists, going back to Ignatius of Antioch and Justin Martyr, for their endorsement of virginity and celibacy.

At various stages of history it must be granted that the Western Church experienced difficulty enforcing Christian sexual norms on both laity and clergy, especially when kings and prelates themselves were known to be profligate. Within weeks of my ordination in 1942, for example, I was assigned to work with an American Dominican recently returned home after many years in South America. There he had served (with Dominican friars) in a diocese that had been placed under censure by Rome for the concubinage of its diocesan clergy and of their bishop.

In modern times, however, the clergy of the West, certainly in the United States, have been remarkably celibate. The reforms of the Council of Trent made it so. The ideal was always there, attested by the celibate lives of those saintly missioners we venerate on our altars, from

Paul to Patrick to Boniface to Francis Xavier with Cyril and Methodius, to Isaac Jogues and the Jesuit martyrs in our country. But the effectiveness of the Tridentine discipline was everywhere reflected in the lives of those dedicated parish priests and teaching clergy whom Mr. and Mrs. U.S. Catholic held in high esteem, not only for the services they performed, but in large part for the purity of their lives. (Priests who lived rectory life in those days would be the best witnesses.) Saint Paul was correct in identifying fully committed service to Christ with the freedom of the celibate to provide an undistracted ministry. When Augustine's faith was up to it, he took the step. And so did most of the American priests in our time without their giving the matter more than a second thought. They fully recognized the connection between Christ's priesthood and their celibacy.

Of course, the discipline of chastity — in marriage, in the priesthood and religious life, or the single state — becomes easier when the Church, which makes these demands, supports the lifestyle it says a religious vocation of any kind requires. Not only does this mean, for the priesthood at least, careful selection and training, but priestly fraternity also in and out of rectories, a full life of priestly endeavors, ecclesial rewards for their achievements, and appropriate censure of public misconduct. The Church's mission and the care of souls are the dominant priorities. Celibacy frees the priest to embrace those objectives without divided loyalties.

Were all priests great successes? Of course not. Did not Church authorities discover the misfits in the priestly ranks too late? If they did not, the Catholic people surely did. But, by and large, my friend Monsignor Robert Ford was quite right when he toasted a gathering of priests: "Here's to the greatest fraternity in the world!"

In contradiction, Church authorities sow the seeds of disillusion, if not disintegration, when the wants and needs of individual priests, especially of the disgruntled or the self-willed, occupy greater attention from them than those who contribute to the effectiveness of the Church's mission.

Of course, attacks on celibacy, recurrent throughout history, as Pius XII noted, have picked up since Vatican II, many of which blame the hierarchy for its failure to realize how important sexual fulfillment is to human development, and for its stern insistence on the outdated exaltation of virginity.[5] But the effort by Catholic scholars to isolate the recent Vatican council from the bimillennial Church tradition, or to identify

Church progress with conformity to a sex-saturated modern world, is destined to failure, even when it makes the celibate life more difficult for young men reared in the present culture.

I have never met a bishop who did not realize the gravity of the modern temptations to priests nor care for a priest really in need. But, then, during most of my years the Church's mission itself was not sacrificed, neither to the self-willed nor to recalcitrant priests, alone or in combination. This does not mean that every policy decision of a prelate was of a higher order. Still, the proper priorities of the Church were held in balance.

Priests obviously need elbow room to do what they do best, if this fits nicely into the reasons for which Christ established a Church. They need privacy, too, to lick their wounds after they encounter frustration and failure. Still, priests are not private persons. They are the Church's first officers.

They need direction and support from the ecclesiastic responsible, before all others, for the integrity of the priestly mission. If they are encouraged by the system to think that their own wishes, or felt needs, transcend the priestly apostolate, the Body of Christ will suffer, and eventually the priest himself. I once heard a pastor tell a young priest to maintain his priesthood because "people's faith in Christ depends on their faith in you." If Christian spouses usually place the good of their children above their own pleasures, the Catholic priest ought to be expected to do no less.

Samuel Johnson once remarked, "Celibacy has no pleasures," his assumption being that man's chief delight, or woman's, is heterosexual association or copulation. However, the committed priest normally has pleasures few others have time or reason to enjoy. It is great to go to bed at night contemplating the good things one has done for people for the sake of Christ. How often has it occurred to the Samuel Johnsons of the world how little celibacy is discussed when everyone in the Church takes it for granted? And when the accomplishments of the priestly fraternity are recognized as little short of phenomenal? Does this mean an abatement of the struggle? Hardly. A priest-mentor of young priests once responded to the question, "At what point in life do temptations against the Sixth Commandment subside?" as follows: "I don't expect that to happen until my third day in the tomb!" That is a rule of life, for laity particularly.

Sins Against the Priesthood

Sins against the priesthood are as old as sins against marriage. Every priest, as every spouse, can draw up his own scorecard on this account. The unmentioned sin against the priesthood, often thought to be impurity, may more likely be lack of piety. And by "piety" I refer not only to the calluses that grow on a priest's knees as a result of heavy praying but also to the filial reverence and sense of duty (as Saint Thomas indicates) all Christians owe, and priests particularly, to God our Father, to Jesus Christ, his Son, and to those who in Christ's name are appointed to rule over us. Some priests demonstrate a lack of enthusiasm for the Church's "holy rule" (the definition of "hierarchy") early in their ministry. These priests become problems for the Church, as Germain Grisez explains in his commentary on the *Summa Theologica*,[6] they are unable to deal with or tolerate frustration in living out the norms and ideals of their vocation. Instead of accepting God's will as "an essential part of any vocation" — including frustration of one's self-will, of comfort or convenience, and their personal sense of direction, etc. — impious priests, asserts Grisez, take solace in any combination of the seven capital sins. After a half-century of clerical life, I find sloth, covetousness, gluttony, and envy the more common priestly sins rather than pride, anger or lust.

Priests who have an undeveloped sense of piety find it easy to blame others, especially superiors, for their own vices. If the pastor does not permit the priest to establish a boys' club, that curate sometimes invents reasons not to visit the parish school or the local hospital where he would be most welcome, even by the pastor's standards. If he is sent out to do his share of parish visitations, he does less than any others in the rectory because, he says, the people are cold or unfriendly. Some priests seemingly were never trained to see, or to learn, that obedience is a virtue, unless, of course, the given directive happens to be morally evil. Let us also keep in mind that there are people in every walk of life who seem to be born losers. The best any system can do in these cases is to shelter the losers and prevent them, insofar as it is possible, from doing more harm to the flock than to themselves. Not even Christ guaranteed happiness or success in this life, certainly not he who maintained that cross-carrying was an integral element in discipleship (see Matthew 16:1-24).

It must not be presumed, on the other hand, that only the wise and the strong are welcome to do God's priestly work or to witness his providence. The first priest I met was the most lovable drunk I ever knew. He staggered through twenty years but was always there when it counted. Many were those who wept at his funeral. Two associates (close friends) were reformed alcoholics who did more for the down-and-out than many of their enlightened peers, helping those floundering to stay close to God in their sobriety. Another, a most learned companion priest, a magnificent preacher, was a mean-spirited man who, nonetheless, proved himself to be an effective pastor.

Recently, a retired pastor with a remarkable academic record to his credit, made the following remark about the present priest shortage: "I don't know what today's crying is all about. When our rectories were lush with priests, at least a third of them were below-par performers." Maybe so, but Elizabeth Barrett Browning said it well: "A minute's success pays the failure of years." Was this not the lesson of the first Easter morn?

We must never forget what Christ said in the Upper Room to twelve men whose human failures were well known to him: "You are the men who have stood by me faithfully in my trials; and now I confer a kingdom on you, just as my Father conferred one on me; you will eat and drink at my table in my kingdom, and you will sit on the thrones to judge the twelve tribes of Israel" (Luke 22:28-30).

Endnotes

1. *National Catholic Reporter*, November 25, 1988, pp. 11ff.
2. Crossroads Publishing Co. (New York), 1986, p. 180.
3. Crossroads Publishing Co. (New York), 1986, p. 299-300.
4. Canons 528ff.
5. See Laurie Felknor, *The Crisis In Religious Vocations: An Inside View* (Mahwah, NJ: Paulist Press, 1989).
6. *Summa Theologica*, 2-2, q. 121, a. 1.

Chapter Two

The American Parish Priest: Conceived in Rome — Born in the U.S.A.

The Church is a community, but in order to be that community she is first a hierarchy. The Church which we call our mother is not some ideal and unreal Church but this hierarchical Church herself; not the Church as we might dream her but the Church as she exists in fact, here and now. Thus the obedience which we pledge her in the persons of those who rule her cannot be anything else but a filial obedience.

— Henri De Lubac, *The Splendor of the Church*

The American parish and its priests have been looked upon, even in Rome, as a wonder of the universal Church. Few comparable successes can be documented in the history of Christianity, and by the turn of the twentieth century, the accomplishment was attributed exclusively to the American priest. Church historian John Talbott Smith, for example, called the parish "the highest achievement of the American priest," whose virtues (Smith averred) were "like sweet incense to the Republic."[1] Well into modern times, bishops in such diverse sees like New Orleans, San Francisco, Salt Lake City, Rochester, Camden, even New York, came to the episcopacy directly from a neighborhood pastorship. Church historians of those early days paid attention to such pastors,[2] who played vital roles in the administration of their dioceses, usually by membership on bishops' board of consulters.

By World War I the effectiveness of the American parish system began to bear rich fruit among practicing Catholics, filling churches, monasteries, convents, and seminaries with their offspring in such numbers that during the 1950s anti-Catholic bigots began to fear that the Catholic Church was in the process of taking over what its members should have known was a Protestant country. Between 1940 and 1960 the Catholic population grew from twenty to forty million, with a high birthrate, and with seven out of ten Catholics at Mass every Sunday. By the start of World War II the parochial school system was so firmly established that a priest could have played golf five days a week without seriously harming the Church.

Following the war, by virtue of worldwide air travel, the American priest acquired a special international reputation. One day in 1960, as four American priests stood on a curbstone conversing with a group of Spanish *senoras* outside one of Madrid's large public markets, a tall Spanish priest passed through the crowd stiff-faced, turning his head neither to the right nor to the left. The priests and the ladies kept chattering, although the latter had some difficulty because of the slaughter of the Spanish tongue they were encountering. As the priests turned to depart, one of the matrons turned to the group and said: *"Adios. Sacerdotes Americanos muy simpaticos."*

Such appreciation did not come overnight. Those priests were the products of legions of American priests who had gone before.

The Poor Beginnings

A common inside joke among parish priests in earlier days was: Roman prelates make the laws, but American priests keep them. The Romanization of the hierarchy and of American Catholic religious life, during the nineteenth century, is an acknowledged fact, although recent Church historians concentrate on the virtues of "Americanism" over Romanism.[3]

Unquestionably, American bishops did adapt the Roman model as paradigm, but they also invested a substantial amount of American know-how into making the parish system work, something the Holy See did not accomplish in many parts of Catholic Europe.

In any event, to measure where we are today, or are likely to be tomorrow, it may be helpful to have some idea of whence we came.

The prized American parish, which earned high commendation from Pius XII, came into being with the establishment of the American hierarchy in 1789, after the twenty-four priests on the New World scene cried to Rome about the weak condition of the Church in young America — declining membership, a shortage of priests, unruly priests, and lack of money. Father John Carroll, who became the first American bishop, once told Rome's Congregation for the Propagation of the Faith that his practicing Catholics were few (though often wealthy), and that "you can scarcely find any among the newcomers who discharge this [Easter] duty of religion." The future bishop was shocked by "the general lack of care in instructing children," most of whom were "very dull in faith and depraved in morals." Carroll told the Roman authorities: "It can scarcely be believed how much trouble and care they gave the pastors of souls." A generation later things had not improved, as Church historian Peter Guilday describes: "The Church here during this period of its infancy was sadly hampered by priests who knew not how to obey and of laity who were interpreting their share in Catholic life by non-Catholic systems."[4]

From these meager beginnings, and in spite of (and because of) the immigrant wave which multiplied its numbers sixteen times by the Civil War ("the poorest and most wretched population that can be found in the world" according to New York's Bishop Hughes) the American Church grew to be the envy of the Catholic world everywhere.

The upward movement from mediocrity to classy parish life was a struggle all the way. John Carroll's problem was unworthy pastors, those floating and undisciplined priests who in too many cases traveled from diocese to diocese providing erratic priestly service. As the quantity of priests began to grow, questions were still asked about their quality: "Why are they not worthy now to be *Parochi* — not *quasi* parish priests, but *real* Parish priests?" asked convert James McMaster, editor of the *Freeman's Journal,* who turned his fire on bishops, in 1868.

John Tracy Ellis' work, *The Catholic Priests in the United States,*[5] recounts the emotions of that era vented in the struggle by Rome to introduce irremovable pastors to the American Church, as a means of protecting priests from capricious treatment. In 1886 the Third Council of Baltimore finally established qualifications for irremovable rectors, and the following year (on March 28, 1887) the Cardinals of the Propaganda, approving Baltimore's regulations, decreed that prior to the "removal or total deprivation of the office of rector a canonical trial must be conducted." Practice never quite followed theory, for as late as 1915 the Consistorial Congregation once more reminded bishops that pastors could be removed only for serious reasons, and with due regard for the merits of the priest concerned.

In the meantime, the Councils of Baltimore, convoked regularly after 1829, concerned themselves with the quality of priests, clerical discipline, the proper celebration of the Mass, the administration of the sacraments (especially marriage and penance), the integrity of the faith and its proper teaching, and with the faithful's problems, too, especially their poverty, drunkenness, and impiety. Priestss were told to implement Church regulations from Trent to Baltimore, and that the mind of the Church was to take root in parish centers.

The 1918 *Code of Canon Law* practically abolished removability *ad nutum episcopi.* Canon 454 said that the office of parochial rector should be permanently bestowed in what one canonical expert called "subjective perpetuity." That Code distinguished between so-called "irremovable" and "removable" rectors. All rectors were technically removable, at least in two instances. One, after a trial for an alleged crime (*delictum*); the other for lesser but serious reason. But, even in the latter case, the bishop must have reason and proceed with a certain formality. Needless to say, the old Code provided more stability for pastors than that enjoyed by their predecessors in the nineteenth century.

Until Vatican II, American pastors and their bishops, for the most part, enjoyed a peaceful relationship. Going to canonical trial over disputes was rare, in part because bishops feared Rome's support of pastors;

also because priests by virtue of their training had acquired general respect for bishops, and not a little awe. (Priestly penury was also a factor. Diocesan priests rarely had enough savings to pursue an independent course.) If priests were transferred with their consent to an easier (perhaps better) assignment, the hope was that change might improve performance. This did not always happen, of course.

The Fruit of Baltimore Councils

These canonical developments aside, the facts indicate that as a result of the vigorous implementation of the Church's pastoral decrees going back to Cardinal James Gibbons, the Church of the United States was booming by 1940.

The first large census study of fifty thousand American Catholics in Florida (completed in 1944) discovered the following:[6]

- Seventy-five percent of the married Catholics attended Mass every Sunday.
- Forty percent received Communion at least monthly.
- Eighty-five percent made their Easter Duty.
- Eighty-five percent of single people went to Mass every Sunday, regardless of whether they were 19, 29, 39, 49, or older.
- Fifty percent and more of single people received Communion monthly regardless of age. College-educated Catholics were more regular in attendance than anyone else, went to Communion more often, had the largest families.
- Native-born Catholics were more faithful to Church duties than foreign-born, including the Irish. City Catholics performed better than rural Catholics.

Not only were Americans practicing Catholics but their parishes were neighborhood centers of affection and social services. Remarkable loyalty to priests and bishops, even from the Church-created Catholic elite who poured out from our colleges, was evident.

As a *tour de force* the institutional and community accomplishments of the American Church are unsurpassed in history; some think unequalled anywhere in the world. By the millions, Catholics identified with their priests, their rituals, their symbols, their laws, their buildings. Far from being objects of contempt among the rank and file, "brick and mortar priests" were sources of pride because those priests took care of their children, their troublemakers, their sick and dying parents. The priest, though not always a Pat O'Brien, was still "*alter Christus*" to the parish. Matrimony was a "little church." Babies were "gifts of God." Mothers were blessed before and after pregnancy, during cold weather, and at Easter time. Saint Christopher rode in Catholic cars, and the "traveling" Virgin made parish rounds with the family rosary in someone's pocket. "Ethnic pride" was really "Catholic pride." Even the "fallen-aways" who lived long stretches of life without the full endorsement of the Church "came back" at the birth of a baby, in a hospital room, or when the right in-law joined the family. "Once a Catholic, always a Catholic" was the rule. Most Catholics "died with the priest" and the Catholic crowds anywhere in the country represented the Universal Church at its best.

By the end of the nineteenth century, the major credit for developing immigrant faith into a vital Catholic Church body belonged to the pioneer bishops and priests. Faithful Catholics of a later vintage credit religious — nuns and brothers — for their lifestyle and loyalties. But in the formative years of the American Church it was bishops and priests who set the tone for the people. The American hierarchy knew what it wanted and set about finding priests and religious who would help get those things accomplished. By singleness of purpose and industry they created a mood, set an example, and tolerated little nonsense from those who would have it otherwise. What Catholics of the mid-twentieth century took for granted — high standards of priestly behavior, resident pastors, good seminarians and novitiates, a clear understanding of how sacraments were to be administered and received, what was required for marriage or penance, missions and schools in places where they were needed, money to expand and economy in its use — all these strengths were the bequests of nineteenth-century bishops and priests, including imports like the Sulpicians who trained their seminarians. These were the priests who gave the Church its crowded Masses and long confessional lines, common everywhere in the United States up to and during the post-World War II period.

The Secrets and Dangers of Success

Let us examine the secrets of that success. Fundamentally they were two: (1) single-minded and determined bishops pursuing clearly defined goals; and (2) the willingness of priests to work industriously under adverse conditions to implement those goals.

In essence, it all came down to priests. The priests of the late nineteenth and early twentieth century were a remarkable group. They were not cultivated gentlemen, but they worked arduously at evangelizing, catechizing, and supporting the poor, ofttimes weak members of their constituency. Pastors managed the Church's internal affairs rather well, and became commanding public figures. For long stretches of their lives most worked alone and, even after they were privileged to have curates, maintained general respect from their congregations. However much or little they were as men of faith, they were a self-disciplined lot. Priests ordained at the turn of the century were often prayerful and did their duty, were the first in the confessional on Saturday night, and could be found at rectory meals most of the week. Their legendary feats, handed down after their death, involved more fact than fiction.

The strengths of the American priesthood — developed from the founding of Saint Mary's Seminary in Baltimore in 1825 to World War I — include the following features:

- A clearly defined doctrinal role.
- Increasingly careful selection and training of candidates.
- A priestly fraternity fostered by bishops, but inspired by priests themselves.
- Challenging Church conditions.
- Authoritative leadership and precise roles.
- High expectations for output and results.
- General following from the faithful Catholics.
- Personal esteem and status.

Success and affluence eventually came to priests around the time bishops began to be more concerned about diocesan needs than about the effectiveness of parish life. Indeed, parochial prosperity made larger diocesan agencies ever more necessary. In some respects, American priestly life fell victim to its own prosperity. Routine, monotony, and part-time service in rectory life took the place of creativity, dedication, and hard work. Well-run societies normally routinize corporate effort, establishing times and rules for rising, sleeping, working, even playing, making it possible for many things to be done easily, freeing people from time-consuming decisions. The parish priest's life, too, came to include scheduled Masses, rounds of Communion calls in the morning, wakes in the evening, regular rides to cemeteries, regular hours in the school, times for altar boy rehearsals, etc.

The reverse side of routine, however, is monotony. Routine may serve as an apprenticeship during the first flush of priesthood, but doing the same thing year after year leads to rote — and to leisure. (Civil servants and office workers often learn this, as well as priests.) In early decades of the century this was not a psychological handicap, because everyone's life then was occupied at least ten hours a day with routine. With affluence, however, came the eight, seven, even six-hour day, and the dispersal of Catholic crowds to the suburbs. Leaving the parish on days off became commonplace, and removed priests further from the lives of parishioners. It also gave them still more free time. Professional study, first encouraged by religious orders to help enrich their specialized apostolates, eventually encouraged parish priests to go back to school, too. Industrious priests acquired new interests away from their primary area of responsibility.

Bishops unwittingly nudged the process of alienating priests from parish work by creating specialists for the spreading chancery offices and making monsignors out of young bureau chiefs. Under these conditions seminary faculties were inclined to search for "brains," not necessarily priests who could turn a ride to the cemetery into an invitation to renewed Christian life.

Finally, the rectory situation changed. The paternal supervising power exercised by pastors over curates during the pre-World War I era became *laissez-faire* for all priests.

Freedom of initiative and freedom from direction, even from chancery offices, reverted to the priests themselves, some of whom came to do only what was required. The post-Vatican II rush to equate renewal with freedom from all restraint saw the basic needs of priestly life become subject to negotiation with the individual.

These latter situations were just beginning to become more common when the Church and the nation entered World War II.

Endnotes

1. John Talbott Smith, *The Catholic Church in New York*, (New York: Hall and Locke Co., 1904) vol. 2, p. 270, and vol. 1, pp. 173-174.
2. See John Gilmary Shea's *The Catholic Church in New York City* (New York: Goulding and Co., 1878).
3. A late example of this is Gerald P. Fogarty's *The Vatican and the American Hierarchy from 1870 to 1965* (Wilmington, DE: M.D. Glazier, 1985).
4. *History of the Councils of Baltimore 1791-1884*, (New York: Macmillan, 1932), p. 85.

5. This historical investigation was compiled for the NCCB and published by Saint John's University Press (Collegeville, MN), 1971.
6. George A. Kelly, *Catholics and the Practice of the Faith*, (Washington, DC: Catholic University of America Press, 1946).

Chapter Three

Diary of a Parish Priest

The records show them (priests) to have been strong men, though not cultivated on the average, as both time and means were wanting to secure a thorough education. The people supported them handsomely; confidence was not misplaced or betrayed. While the faith of the people edified their Protestant neighbors, the devotion of the priests to the people edified still more; it was seen that the plague had no overpowering terror for the priest, nor poverty of his people, nor any distressing condition. The virtues of the clergy and the people a half-century ago was like sweet incense to the Republic.

— John Talbot Smith, *The Catholic Church in New York*

Priests ordained fifty years were born during the time American parish life had come into its own, and when they ascended the altar for the first time the Church of the United States was never so richly endowed with practicing Catholics, full monasteries, convents, and rectories, with the widest network of Catholic support institutions in one country the Christian world has ever seen.

I would like to say something about what a priest was and did in those years, before making generalizations about the parish system itself. One priest's experience by itself, even if it is a Gotham City experience, does not a saga make, nor is it a learning handbook for others. But rolled into one story may be the tales of many others, and taken together explain why the Catholic Church was recognized everywhere as a phenomenal institution. It is easy now, therefore, for us to empathize with the final reel of *Goodbye, Mr. Chips*, when Robert Donat dreamed during his death scene of a parade — one school boy after another walking through his memory, those whose lives he touched radically, and those who touched him intimately. Old priests, like old parents, if they are proud of their accomplishments, enjoy the kind of nostalgia that often dies with them. Unfortunately.

In our lifetimes, we were part of many great liturgies, shared impressive pulpits, had more good teachers than bad, and an occasional first-rate mentor. Every priest who has something to talk about in his later years had a "big gun" in his youth who influenced him. Perhaps mentors like Father John Patrick Monaghan, who told young seminarians to look for the ideals of the priesthood only in their own lives and they would never be disappointed; or Father John Moylan, a simple pastor, who in his golden years inspired priests with his praying before and after Mass, being first in and last out of the confessional, working every Saturday night on his notes for the sermon next morning; or Father John Courtney Murray telling diocesan priests that they were less faithful to the Church's bishops than his fellow Jesuits; or Father John Tracy Ellis instructing priest friends to write, not just talk; or Monsignor John A. Ryan making sure that we took *Quadragesimo Anno* seriously; even Bishop J. Francis A. McIntyre who "learned" priests that they were here to serve the Church, not the other way around. Mentors are not always right, nor even a good influence, but in their best days they are idealists who reinforced young priests in their commitment, while enlarging their vision.

Then there were the great events, the apostolic movements — and the crosses, if only lack of approval — which take hold of a priest's soul, if he lets them. Perhaps it is the first assignment or the first pastorate, the sight of golden wedding jubilarians in the cathedral, the bishop's solicitude for his parents, the parish pilgrimages, the Christian Family Movement in its good days, or the truly Catholic professors who sustained the Fellowship of Catholic Scholars in one of the Church's darkest hours, and, of course, fellow priest-friends of strong faith. If the influences were all good, the priest was the beneficiary, and every priest was affected by them.

Those same aging diocesan priests, when they really become sentimental, remember that it is their parishioners who enriched their personal development, including those already gone to God, those still around and in touch, and the activists who helped teach them to be priestly. Those meaningful priest/people relationships grew slowly, but there are ways to speed up the process.

First, the easiest way early in a pastorate, is to get out of the rectory.

Many years ago, a French-Canadian fallen-away (of thirty years standing) excoriated a priest on a public street because the rectory failed to respond to a call on behalf of his wife who, earlier that morning had suffered third-degree burns when a propane tank exploded in her face. The disagreeable spouse hung around during the eventual anointing, and appeared whenever the priest visited the hospital again. When, finally, after several months, the wife left the hospital without a scar on her face, François returned to the sacraments. He surely had no idea of the *ex opere operato* effect of "extreme unction," nor that when the priest's hand reached into the oxygen tent to say *"per istam sanctam unctionem,"* he was touching raw flesh. But no less impressive was the wife, when she told the young cleric: "If that was God's price for returning my husband to the Church, it was worth it."

Another lady, this time from Boston, was icy cold during the first ten minutes she faced a priest. Then she broke into uncontrollable tears. She had not talked to a priest in fifteen years, when she had been disowned by her family because she was pregnant by a Protestant boyfriend, whom she had married civilly. After three children, she was anxious for a Catholic marriage and the restoration of her family's Catholic commitment.

In another case, two sisters were so hostile to the Church that their language to a visiting priest bordered on violence. They had been caught up while young in an intolerable man-made situation (pope-made, they said). In 1907 the Holy See declared that Catholics henceforth must be married by a priest, putting the sisters in a Catch-22 situation. Both had been married by a judge, both subsequently divorced. But the younger sister was entitled to remarry later in the Church because her first wedding occurred in 1908. The older sister, married in 1905, was not free to marry again, bound by the earlier Catholic form of marriage. In the face of understandable anger, what can a priest do but soothe savage tempers, realizing that there are problems no priest can solve this side of eternity.

Another way of getting to know people quickly is to have charge of the parochial school.

In the post-World War II period a parish school with nineteen nuns and eight hundred children was not uncommon. The American Catholic system was the fastest growing institution of its kind and Catholic parents loved it. So did pastors, beginning with bishops. That vaunted educational enterprise is now withering away, but in its heyday it did more for parish piety than any other Catholic infrastructure.

You gain a good deal of wisdom when you are appointed "acting pastor" of a parish school. A "school director," as he was officially called, was not expected to teach the ABC's, nor to promote fourteen-year-olds into Catholic high school. That was the principal's job. His task was to guarantee that the operation had a proper pastoral orientation. The school sisters shared this apostolate but, in the last analysis, it was the pastor, or his delegate, who had primary responsibility for integrating the school with parish well-being. Professional education was one thing; the inculcation of faith, piety, and parochial solidarity were ultimately the responsibility of the priest.

It was in the school building that a young priest quickly learned, as nowhere else, about his neighborhood and about the local service agencies, from nursery schools to hospitals, all around him. Fifty-nine such institutions could be found in a city like Yorkville, many of them Catholic, where a priest could go for help, if he chose, to get someone's father into a nursing home, or to deal with a baby born out of wedlock, to retrain an exceptional child, to handle a drunken mother, etc. Abundant resources like these were only the beginning of his learning.

Among the many things you learn in such a large institutional setting is that rules — enforced rules — are necessary to get anything done. When a neighborhood begins to disintegrate, and stability gives way to unpredictable change, the unruly tend to take over. To function effectively, therefore, a parish priest also had to maintain reasonable discipline within his parish or, when it was lacking, move to restore it as soon as he could. Not everyone in a neighborhood does what pleases the pastor or the pope. But a disorderly parish is something of a scandal. In this century a good deal of Catholic identity was evident in the fidelity of most parishioners to Sunday Mass, in Friday abstinence, in the chastity of most Catholic girls and boys, in the size of our families, in our public processions, even in bingo. The oft-made observation in recent years that Catholics are now like everyone else is hardly a compliment to a new Catholic order.

The School Sisters of Saint Francis, who ran our school, were ladies of German extraction from the rural mid-West, half of them holding masters' degrees, born into parishes ruled by German pastors. They were new to, and overwhelmed by, New York's East-side kids. Ragamuffins, and even an occasional thug or two, hardly made for an ideal teaching situation.

Establishing school norms was easy. Getting kids off the street at night, establishing dress and homework codes, preserving the privacy of the convent, dealing with hookey players and chronic absentees, with drunken parents, took a lot more doing. But once everyone got the message, the people fell into line, especially "the East-side Boys." The gripers griped, but most parishioners accepted the routine and the civility. They learned that it was easy to tell their youngsters *ad nauseam* "Sister says," "Father says," thus saving themselves a long argument. On the way to good order there was some good fun, like the outrage of Holy Name officers when the priests banned beer at parish events, and when an Irish mother reported: "I can get my son to do anything, he's such an obedient boy, except to get me the evening edition of the morning paper if it's after 9 P.M. at night. 'Are you crazy, Mom, expecting me to run into that priest!' "

The third way for a parish priest to extend his influence is to make sure that the parish properties are overrun with people, reasonably, of course.

Worshipers know what it means to be members of a "warm," as distinct from a "cold," parish. If you never see anyone milling in front of the church on Sunday, if the church seems bare, if you walk by the parish buildings at night and everything is dark, that means a cold and uninviting parish. Most parishioners are laid-back members of the Church, who remain non-joiners unless they like what they see. They represent "silent majority" types, but sense when priests are "open" to their presence. Many will join a mini-crowd after Sunday Mass, some will walk into a coffee hour, attend a weekend flea market, or simply develop the habit of saying "Hello" to the priest, if he's there to face. In days bygone, when Catholics identified themselves by the name of their church, rather than by neighborhood, it was " 'round the church" that they discovered "we-feeling." There, too, the clergy — at least one of them — was available to make strangers feel welcome.

Puritans, with a little touch of the Manichean in them, sometimes criticize a given parish for being too social — too many dances, plays, bingos, bus rides, and so forth. Surely, a parish ought not to be known for only fun and games. Yet conviviality is usually the natural by-product of collaboration between priests and laity in the pursuit of parochial piety. There are few better signs of a vital parish than hundreds, perhaps a thousand neighbors, at a show or on a bus ride mainly because of their church connection. Effective parish priests help families grow in smiling, as well as in praying. What's more, these little concourses are occasions for alert priests to tap lay leadership, who become hands and voices of the parish in corners where priests are rarely visible. A working index of a well-functioning parish is the participation of one such Church activist for every ten churchgoers.

Unquestionably, a parish is at its peak when a majority of its Catholic residents attend Mass every Sunday. Bodily presence may not be the ultimate sign of holiness, but regular worship normally relates to Catholic thinking and pious practice. The Sunday-go-to-church men and women keep the Catholic way of life visible in a neighborhood, even for those who momentarily may be flouting its norms. Catholics such as these, if in abundance, make it easy for priests to walk through their streets with familiarity. When a priest can do this comfortably, and even better when he greets people by name, you know "community" is present. While this may not be what the Church is all about, it is an indication that someone is doing the Lord's work. When the non-joiners, too, feel they have ready access to the rectory, to come day or night for counsel, to complain or to gain support, the Church is doing its job. When the parish records show that the sick and the aged are well tended, that the baptismal and marriage rites are well used, that conversions to the faith and validations of invalid marriages are commonplace, the parish is doing more than its duty.

We are also, hopefully, in the process of recovering a tradition that, for a while after the recent Council, looked like it might fall into desuetude — the parish devotion. The falloff was due in part to the fact that American city streets became unsafe at night, although nighttime is not the only time of the day to hold it. But the enthusiasm for centering popular attention on liturgical, rather than paraliturgical, worship, brought a temporary halt to the recitation of the Rosary, to novenas and litanies, to churching young mothers during their pregnancies and after childbirth, to benediction of the Blessed Sacrament and parish missions, to national and ethnic feast days, to nocturnal adoration, local pilgrimages, and processions. These pious practices were actually encouraged by the Second Vatican Council both in its *Constitution on the Sacred Liturgy* and later by individual popes in documents like *Familiaris Consortio*. But when going in and out of churches, chapels, and convents became less noticeable, city streets, towns, and villages lost a distinguished Catholic presence. Whether the parish has one priest or many, an inventive cleric will find ways to utilize available space. Devout parishioners, the pious prayers, if you will, have a certain claim on parish facilities, and in this age of the laity, neighborhood watchers and off-duty policemen can be very helpful. Vatican II insists that parish devotions have a special dignity, and we are bound to enhance their availability.

As the spirit of a parish with a sense of direction picks up, rectory management begins to handle more and more business. Housekeepers of old, secretaries in the new dispensation, were, or are, not amenable to erratic bother from too many phone calls or door bells. And some priests have to unlearn their fondness for privacy. Yet as more and more people come the rectory way, even the housekeepers learn to enjoy the fun, and priests meet some real human needs.

What can a priest do (as once happened) when two sisters enter the rectory late on a Saturday night to confess that a third sister gave birth that day to a baby, with her husband arriving home on the morrow. The problem? The husband had been in Europe fighting Germans for three years!

Or, what does he say to a father with an inveterate "night owl" beer-drinker on his hands — a sixteen-year-old daughter?

How does he deal with a wife-beater whose overgrown son tries strong-arm tactics on a seventh grade nun?

What should the priest do for a beautiful but sterile thirty-four-year-old, except bless her, she who is denied adoption possibilities by a Catholic foundling hospital, because her home is not roomy enough?

What does he do in a parish, where most churchgoers are Italian-American, but most parish functions are controlled by old but possessive Irishmen?

What does he do about the prominent parishioner who has been raiding the poor boxes for many years?

How can he move Saint Vincent De Paul men out into the caverns of the city to search out the poor, when they would rather force the needy to come to them, in order their weekly card game might begin without delay?

What will he do when he finds that most of the churchgoers in the new parish to which he is assigned are angry at the bishop, and do not want him either, because he is the bishop's man?

What should he do when he inherits a rebellious parish council or a curate who, by personality, is a saboteur?

Every parish priest has his good days, and his unpleasant ones, too. Every good shepherd loses some sheep, but ultimately his effectiveness depends on more than victories over problems, or on control of obstreperous parishioners. A priest may not succeed too well with a violent father or his bully son, except to put a little "fear of God" into both. If the nuns experience less trouble thereafter, this was a boon. The marriage of the returning veteran was actually saved by having the hospital move the wife out of the maternity ward, and turning the baby over to one of her married sisters for rearing. The barren housewife, properly churched (this time in advance of possibilities) went on to have four children of her own. (Indeed, so confident had she become in the power of divine intervention, that she sent word back to "turn the blessing off!") It is not possible to say that school children got more sleep from the imposition of a curfew, but they surely didn't streetwalk at night. And if their parents imbibed too much, they didn't do it on parish property. More than a little fighting occurred when the Italians finally made it into the parish hierarchy, but the ill-feeling gave way eventually in the surge of new blood into the parochial lifeline. A pastor can always tolerate a lazy or incompetent curate, but the bishop must send the saboteur elsewhere, for the pastor is better alone than as head of a divided rectory.

This recap of ancient history has little point except to reinforce the fact that most people like good order, and tranquility is necessary to get things done properly. Helter-skelter organization and *laissez-faire* administration of any kind are not signs that a parish priest cares for his parishioners' well-being. Those who argue for a "bottoms-up" church may not like a "trickle-down" view of religious formation. However, if a parish priest is not responsible for "the message" and for the common good of the sheepfold, then Christ had it all wrong from the very beginning. A parish priest who creates the environment in which Christ's message breathes and lives comfortably deserves to be the Church's shepherd.

Some Lessons Learned

Once parish priests of any day grasp fully what the Church's mission is all about, and appreciate the role the Church expects them to play, they must have their personal plan of action.

The doctrines and policies of the Church, flavored by the personality and experience of a particular priest and regulated by his immediate superior, are his *vade mecum*.

A majority of American priests function in one kind of metropolitan area or another, differently from their confreres serving rural areas and small towns. Urban priests sometimes forget that a significant Catholic migration occurred in the nineteenth century when immigrants went into country areas as Catholics, only to have their progeny turn out Protestant. Nineteenth-century bishops worked hard to urge Catholic newcomers to farm the land, while bishops on the East Coast strove to keep their people near the Atlantic shoreline, slums and all, where the priests were. The Catholic Church Extension Society, created in 1905 precisely to extend the Church's ministry into rural and small town areas, founded missions and staffed them with priests as well, who often worked alone and unnoticed by the bishop. Their parish ministries were difficult, with long distances to cover; a dominant Protestant presence; indifferent, neglected and fallen-away Catholics close at hand; few or poorly-trained priests; geographical obstacles to organized catechesis; and overt anti-Catholicism, all of which contributed significantly to clerical frustration in those outlands. The Extension Society helped, of course. As one Michigan pastor told Francis Clement Kelley, the Society's founder (and later bishop of Oklahoma City) about an Extension priest: "His light may look dim in Chicago, but 'in the sticks' he is a star of some magnitude!"

Whatever its difficulties, small town parish work, today as yesterday, is more intensely personal, more social, and likely to be more ecumenical. Some priests belong there, others do not. In many small town dioceses, however, there is more priestly fraternity than in big archdioceses.

Consequently, the lessons to be learned from personal experience vary, and what one old-time pastor has to say may not be relevant to some others. Still, the Church is a universal institution with a precise constitution, role definitions, normative procedures, and expected results. Evangelization is not salesmanship, shepherding is not managing, care of souls is not physical therapy, worshiping together is not the same as a corporate meeting. Neither is the Catholic hierarchy, nor a parish priest, in the business of collective bargaining over the meaning of revelation. The standards of a priest's success and failure have more to do with faith than with freedom, with Godliness more than cleanliness, with the city of God than the city of man. There are similarities, of course, between God's world and man's, because it is human beings this side of eternity who find the words which define both. Full faith and full economy have something in common, but so does ecclesial and corporate bankruptcy. If the modern world is in crisis, so is the post-Vatican II Church, and for reasons that are not totally dissimilar, yet oftentimes interlocking. In either situation the stages of recovery are not too clear, nor has leadership of state or Church clarified the best course, or prescribed the necessary remedy, for the ills of their respective constituencies.

All that a good parish priest can know is what the Church really expects of him, as this is reflected in the decisions of the pope and the bishops in union with him. He then does the best he can in the circumstances of his own or the bishop's choosing, at least until he is overruled by higher authority. Suggested lessons by one priest are merely intended to contribute more to thinking than to practice. Realizing, too, in the last analysis that it is God who disposes, every priest will do his own thing. Yet at least four considerations should underpin the thinking of every parish priest.

The first thing it takes to be a good parish priest is for him to recognize his central role in making Christ live in the hearts of his people.

The parish priest, by definition, is the good shepherd of the local church on whose shoulders alone rests the burden of bringing God's children to Christ and keeping them there. Other priests teach, sanctify and govern in special circumstances, but only the parish priest rules the local community of the Church. The buck of decision-making on things Catholic stops with him, especially if he is the pastor.

It is fashionable in this post-Vatican II period to speak softly about anyone being "boss," although in the real world someone always rules, frequently those who hold no office but have the political clout to frustrate law enforcement. When disorder takes over any part of the Church, who speaks with authority for the Kingdom of God?

Christ spoke of his company as wandering members and lost sheep, and a shepherd (pastor) is responsible for their safekeeping. In Christ's Church, teaching, leading, directing, governing, and correcting, all devolve on the local shepherd.

An old-time pastor once told a young chancery hotshot that there were three key people responsible for the governance of the Church: the pope, the bishop, and the parish priest, all inexorably linked, because in their hands was ultimate authority for making disciples of Christ. The old pro was right.

Notice, however, that the pastor-emeritus did not say — that the parish priest is more important, or wiser, or holier, or abler than anyone else in the Church. Only that he, not the bureaucrat, nor the professor or the saint, is the "key" to the proper governance in the Church. The shepherd of the flock, with or without portfolio, is "the boss." If Abraham Lincoln was correct in insisting that a nation could not exist half-slave/half-free, the parish priest, the pastor especially, may assert with reason that the Church body cannot have two heads any more than it can be half-Catholic and half-Protestant. Parish priests know that they are surrounded by their betters, but they, not the betters, are the ones who hold the keys to the kingdom.

Someone may ask: What about the shepherd's competence, or his fitness? Appointees or electees to office at times are misfits, who ought to be transferred to less demanding ministries. Even saints and scholars are often poor leaders/administrators. In such situations the Church relies on its bishops to intervene. In this post-Vatican II era, questions of quality are numerous, but equally important to keep in mind is the erosion that has taken place in the status and role of parish priests who must, with some exceptions, be reinforced in their rights, as often as they are reminded of their obligations (see Canons 528-537).

Granted, parish priests, like Christ, should be suffering servants. This does not mean, however, that they do not have special status or authority as fathers to God's people. No statement in the documents of Vatican II, no section of the new *Code*, no implementing decree issued by Rome after 1965, denigrates or dilutes a pastor's authority. Neither the recommendations concerning consultation, collaboration with other priests, the assistance of the laity, finance committees and parish councils, not even his obligation of obedience to pope and bishop. A parish priest's authority can be taken from him only by higher authority following duly-prescribed administrative or judicial procedures.

The first rule of parochial life should be this: a parish priest must be comfortable with who he is as he stands before his people, even before he demonstrates by deeds what Christ intends him to mean to his parish community.

Second, a good parish priest, above all else, gives witness to the Church's faith by teaching what the Church teaches and by implementing the decrees of the Holy See and those bishops in union with the pope. If he does this faithfully, he will be exercising his pastoral responsibility, although the role he plays may be a lonely, often thankless, one.

A parish priest should know, and know well, the teachings of the Church which bind him and his people in conscience. If he feels himself inadequately trained, he should seek counsel, perhaps have the United States Catholic Conference or the Daughters of Saint Paul send him their fine collection of the Constitutions, Exhortations and Addresses of John Paul II, or have Our Sunday Visitor enroll him as a subscriber to *The Pope Speaks*.

The policies of the Church, which are his to obey, are contained in the relevant sections of the *Code of Canon Law*, in the liturgical books, and in the pastoral handbook of his diocese, if it has one. It would be well for him to keep up-to-date on the latest directives and decisions from Rome by subscribing to the NCCB's documentary service, *Origins*, or the *Catholic International*, although careful to give no mind to material in those publications which from time to time undercuts, or explains away, authentic ecclesial policy.

He should be faithful not only to the letter of these official documents, but to their intended sense, careful not to take advantage of a dissenting casuistry, common in our time, by which the mind of *magisterium*, even the clear teaching of Christ, is reinterpreted to the point of meaninglessness. The conduct of the parish priest is a more powerful teacher of obedience than anything he says. Nonconforming priests usually inculcate the propriety of disobedience in matters such as prescribed rubrics, altar girls, first confession, Eucharistic ministers, general absolution, parish councils, and so forth.

Third, the good parish priest must have his own priorities in proper order, the following being a few worthy of special mention:

• A beautiful liturgy every Sunday and on great feasts, with the careful administration of each and every sacrament. While the reform of the liturgy is considered an outstanding accomplishment of Vatican II, the fact is that American parishioners worship God weekly less and less, especially those who will comprise the Catholic population of the twenty-first century. The "beauty," of course, has more to do with making the Church's sacrificial and sacramental acts awe-inspiring and reverential, than merely popular or meaningful. The liturgy is drama, seeking not so much approval from an audience, as externalizing worshipers' acknowledgment of dependence on God, and because Christ comes to His people through the priest's ministry and through the Christ-instituted symbols of his living presence.

• The preaching must be instructive and inspire a proper response from Catholics who often live in difficult situations. Preaching is being severely criticized today for its harmless, banal, and often dull moralizing. The parish priest ought to devote special attention to the homilies and sermons to which his people are regularly exposed, even if this requires from time to time introducing outside priests with talent to enliven the weekly message. It is especially important that parishioners be reminded of the need to worship God in the Eucharist every Sunday, and about remaining in the state of grace.

• Since the secular world has chosen "sex" as an instrument for weaning away "the little ones" of Christ, the good shepherd must confront these issues with conviction, clarity, and courage, leaving no doubt about what Christ has taught and about their obligations to Christ's moral norms.

• The priest must also encourage his poor to take up their own cause on behalf of family and faith, and teach the prosperous to share their goods and their energy with less-fortunate members of the parish.

• The good shepherd knows his people and loves them in Christ's name because their salvation is in his care.

• A priest is best remembered because he seemed to know — or at least have married or baptized — everybody. He often comes to know them by encountering them on Sunday mornings outside church, at coffee hours, at baptismal and wedding parties, at wakes and during rides to the cemetery, in the hospital when they were sick, having their babies, at bingos, outings, and bazaars, and from all those pious exercises (novenas, missions, retreats) which bring closer to God those most likely to volunteer for all the causes dearest to the priest's heart.

• Regular visitations to and blessings of homes have fallen into desuetude, but sacramentals, especially when administered by priests, help create a vibrant Catholic community. The shortage of priests today causes some parish priests to be overwhelmed by details. It is unfortunate, nonetheless, that so many people today confess they do not know their pastor, even if they attend church weekly. If parish priests do not know their people — and it may take five years in a large urban setting, even for a personalist — it is unlikely that they will have any impact on the character formation of the congregation or on the spirit of their neighborhood.

Presuming he manages these matters well, the chances are that the good shepherd, if he is convinced of the Church's faith and so preaches it, will find himself with more enemies than his recent predecessors. Criticism may come because dissenting elites can be found by now in every parish, and because, in many quarters, authority figures are no longer regarded as necessary. The role of "pastor" itself has been denigrated, sometimes by diocesan officials.

Early on after Vatican II, canonists proposed that pastors be forced to retire, variously from seventy to seventy-five years of age, that future pastors serve terms of office, that personnel boards take over the assignments of priests, and that evaluations of a pastor's performance be conducted in a quasi-public manner by "a committee." Any one of these suggestions of itself could be helpful — providing that the bishop remains in full charge and in personal contact with his pastors every step of the way; providing, too, that *forcing* retirements or transfers against the bishop's common sense, or against the strong wishes of a dedicated successful priest, in violation of the overriding love relationship people had with the priest, does not become an absolute everywhere. Exceptionless norms, based only on age or terms, reduce the pastor to the level of ecclesiastical functionary; a man holding just another job, some say. In many cases, automatic transfers result in the bishop himself, to whom alone the priest promises reverence and obedience, becoming a shadowy figure in the priest-personnel process. In some cases the new system becomes "the enemy" when confronted by strong-minded but good pastors who begin to think that present-day diocesan personnel policies are disrespectful of their role and good work.

The folly of certain novelties in Church administration is illustrated by what West Coast priests call "the mating game." At various times of the year, the diocesan personnel board sends younger priests out on the road to look over a group of pastors, to determine who feels comfortable with whom in a potentially new parochial arrangement. As one pastor cagily remarked:

"How can you tell a curate what to do in a parish when you have to negotiate the terms of his arrival? The whole sense of mission and commitment is being undermined bit by bit."

Of course, the withering away of fatherhood — of father as an authority figure — has been going on in secular society for a long time. It is surprising to see it happening in the Church. Bishops, popes, and fathers, one would think, ought not permit the abasement of the pastorate. The Church's well-being depends on "good shepherds" at their level. If enlightened sons on university campuses, or in seminaries, or in formation houses, willingly throw off what they consider the yoke of fatherhood, other sons, and Church mothers, soon learn to pay lip service to those still called "fathers."

Today's pastor no longer has a large base of institutional support as a faithful officer of the Church. Divisions in teaching and practice have fractured the ecclesiastical system. Our good shepherd goes before his congregation to praise the pope and the Holy See, but the pastor next door tells his people that "Cardinal Jones" is a nut who ought to be confined. One shepherd preaches the Church's sexual morality as taught by John Paul II, but east of town a contemporary advertises the view that the Church's no-nos will change when the present Vicar of Christ goes to God. "Father Smith" does not have altar girls, but a prominent prelate of the diocese has, and allows women to preach homilies, besides; he insists on the truth of the Nicene Creed, but the local university chaplain excludes it from every Sunday Mass; he holds Catholic politicians to account for their public misbehavior, even as an oft-quoted priest-activist is arrested for pederasty; and so forth.

The lightest cross the good shepherd may bear is the label "conservative," an unfounded implication, perhaps, that he rejects the changes authorized by Vatican II. A heavier burden may be the put-downs of his views by closet dissenters or fence-straddlers in the diocesan bureaucracy. "Father Smith" has no influence on the course of diocesan action, has difficulty acquiring a suitable parochial associate, or even another pastorate when his term expires. Harassment of good priests by headquarters is not uncommon.

Well-intentioned pastors, of course, may talk too much, enjoy controversy as much as Richard McBrien or Charles Curran, and may embarrass their bishops unnecessarily. Closet Lefebvreites are a particular source of annoyance. Such clerics are advised to remember that they are responsible before God only for their portion of God's people. They have every right to keep the bishop — and the pope — informed about the facts of ecclesial life and to make recommendations, but it is the Church's highest officers, not they, who must give an account of their diocesan stewardship. Let the parish shepherd worry only about his own final judgment, and leave his superiors to God.

Fourth, the good pastor should supervise a well-run parish in the Catholic mold.

In former days not all parishes were well-run, but they were reasonably Catholic. Today many parishes are well-run, but ambiguously Catholic. Why should anyone think that Christ sent his Apostles out to be failures as fishers of men; why should less be expected of modern pastors than transforming big worldlings into fully-believing Catholic Christians? Educating parishioners — the saints, the tepids, the resisters, and the fallen-aways — to think like Christ living in his Church, and having them act accordingly, is what shepherding is all about (Philippians 2:5). After two millennia one would think there is an established Catholic way of doing this.

Whether one inherits a solid parish of churchgoers or a rundown parish in need of more than better plant management, good parish priests will have three things in common: (1) a clearly-defined purpose reflected in their sacramental, catechetical, and social programs; (2) a dedicated hard-working staff committed to the Church's creed, code, and cult; and (3) the ability to support and defend the parish community against debilitating forces whether they be civic, economic, or religious. At one time the general Catholic system was so good that parishes seemed to run themselves, and some priests lived off the patrimony of their predecessors. Today, because of recent doctrinal disputes, the individual priest, like his bishop, may find himself having to start all over again, as John Paul II suggested at least once. His chief antagonist may be a lack of funds, or a hostile civic environment, or half-believing Catholic activists who would use Church institutions against good shepherds. Still, dealing with institutional difficulties is an essential element of governance. The shepherd never leaves any doubt about where he leads the sheep, and he does not allow hirelings to misdirect them. Nor rustlers to steal them.

Oh, he should be good at raising money and be careful about spending it; and if he is a great pray-er, or an idea man *par excellence*, more than an administrator, he must tap talents around him who compensate for his deficiencies. If he would build and rebuild the Body of Christ correctly, he must surround himself with people as committed to the *magisterium* as he is. He must supervise their performance, including the oversight of associate priests, of the parish council, of the liturgical ministers, of the catechetical apparatus, and of his media, such as they may be. Christ said it plainly: "A kingdom torn by strife is headed for a down fall. A town or household split into fractions cannot last for long — he who is not with me is against me" (Matthew 12:25, 29).

A good shepherd can be done in by a curate, by a school principal or CCD director, by the editor of his newsletter, even by the parish secretary. Like the servant in the Gospel, he can only serve his most important master (see Luke 16:13). What about other people's freedom? you may ask. Maria Montessori gave the best answer to that question: Freedom is best exercised in a prepared environment, and the law of any society sets the parameters of freedom. Christ specified the *norms* for his Church — disciples believing what he taught (see Luke 10:16) and life to be lived by keeping his commandments (see John 8:31, 32). Anyone who would enter his sheepfold has to choose. Christ recognized that some would leave it or be abandoned to their own devices (see Mark 6:11), or would be treated as outsiders (see Matthew 18:17). In extreme cases, excommunication would become a disciplinary measure in the Apostolic Church, centuries before there was anything like a Roman Curia (see John 9:34).

What happens if a priest walks into a bad parish? Bringing a parish out of bankruptcy, or out of the doldrums, involves changing peoples' ways of thinking and their accustomed behavior. This is not an easy thing to do, especially if it requires belt-tightening or discipline. A priest may have been the cause of difficulty, or the chancery itself may be the source of the problem, be it over-taxation, uncalled-for interference with parochial initiative, or the presence of Church law violators in high places. The new shepherd himself may be the wrong man for a reforming role, too irascible, too timid, or simply incompetent for crisis management. The situation can become acute when leading parishioners, through no fault of their own, are on the wrong side of important Catholic issues.

How does one re-Catholicize such a parish? Carefully, to say the least. To use a biblical metaphor, the priest must treat the parish as a reluctant bride, embracing her slowly, with caution, but embracing her nonetheless. The honeymoon must be successfully consummated, lest precipitous divorce be the unfortunate outcome.

If the good pastoral leader has the cooperation and clear support of the diocese he is fortunate. In this case people must know that the bishop personally endorses his efforts. Even so, he must not be impetuous, lest he initiate untimely conflict. Entrenched anti-establishmentarians are quite adept at intimidating anyone, including a new priest, who threatens their hold on a Church structure.

The new shepherd must also be discreet, keeping proper distance from those inclined to misjudge a priest or taking undue advantage of a seeming "hail-fellow-well-met." He must encourage reverence and respect more than familiarity. Friendship and friendliness will come in time, but initially he must avoid a meaningless war of words with perceived critics, allowing himself time to build his own allies in the community. The first impression he creates should be that of a pastor interested in nothing for himself, save the creation of a truly Catholic community of believers. Once he has found competent staff, he can make his own suitable appointments, quarantining troublemakers, if this is a better course than replacing them. However, he must correct serious error or immorality, wherever he finds it, privately at first, and only publicly at an appropriate moment, if this purifies the parish climate. He should be compassionate with public sinners, if this means suffering with them during the trials of reform.

Compassion does not mean, however, tolerating the evil of those who act wrongly in the Church's name. Public dissent, after all, is public sin, especially by those who use sanctions against faithful priests. By learning how to deal with the local media without becoming their whipping-boy, and by developing popular support among friends of Church teaching and policies, the pastor cements community we-feeling.

We ask a lot of parish priests. We surely do when the major threat is bankruptcy. Why not ask even more when the overriding matter is the integrity of Christ's mission in the Church? Losses of souls are not quantitatively measurable this side of eternity, but they are unconscionable because they often result from scandal or neglect. The freedom of some priests to appropriate unto themselves the "right" to question the *magisterium*, to tolerate vast amounts of evil in the Church household, to complain about but do little to correct it, to believe in parish peace at the price of loss of faith, to speak with two tongues on Catholic doctrine, slyly supporting dissent, but making life difficult for those who dissent from dissent, and priests who leave behind them a Church whose last state is worse than the first, constitute new difficulties for the ecclesia, hardly known to our predecessors.

Cockle in the field always strangles the Church's good wheat until that day of judgment when God sifts one from the other. In the meantime, however, scandal, of which Christ had much to say, must be confronted. Moral disease, like its physical counterpart, spreads rapidly. Epidemics call for disease control. It is an old Church problem, however new to the United States. Long ago the great Gregory I (pope 590-604), facing an interfering Byzantine Emperor, and a host of Eastern heretics, pointed his finger at the ecclesiastical malfeasance in his time. In a homily still used in the Daily Prayer of the Church (27 Ordinary Saturday), this pope spoke as follows:

> "I speak of our absorption in external affairs;
> We accept the duties of office
> But by our actions we show that we are attentive to other things.
> We abandon the ministry of preaching and, in my opinion, are called bishops to our detriment
> For we retain the honorable office
> But fail to practice the virtues proper to it.
> Those who have been entrusted to us abandon God
> And we are silent.
> They fall into sin
> And we do not extend a hand or rebuke."

Amen.

Chapter Four

The Parish
in a Post-Christian Era

The Church does not feel dispensed from
paying unflagging attention to those who have
received the faith and who have been in
contact with the Gospel often for generations.
Thus she seeks to deepen, consolidate, nourish
and make ever more mature the faith of those
who are already called believers.... The
phenomenon of the non-practicing is a very
ancient one in the history of Christendom; it
is the result of a natural weakness.... [among
many today, who] more so than of previous
periods, seek to explain and justify their
position in the nature of an interior religion,
of personal independence or authenticity.

— Pope Paul VI, *Evangelii Nuntiandi*

The two great obstacles to any effective work by the Church in our time are (1) widespread unbelief outside and (2) non-practicing Catholics within. Paul VI made this point, as late as 1975, in what may be the greatest piece of papal writing during his pontificate — his duly famous *Exhortation on Evangelization.* Vatican II was convoked in part because of these difficulties in large segments of the world and while the forthcoming century will tell the tale of its long-range effectiveness, these are still the Church's major problems in what many commentators now call the post-Christian era.

The problems facing American parish priests of my generation were not exactly these — at least not in the United States. Outside the Church Christian belief was widespread, mostly Protestant, and the religious practice of Catholics was extremely high. The unbelieving outside forces at work on our culture, then, were intimidated even by the Legion of Decency, and the worst irreligion you could accuse government officials of practicing was stealing and occasional adultery. Today, pollster George Gallup speaks authoritatively of Americans as a "religious people," but fails to specify what many of them believe — a vague civil religion with little Christian content. The Protestant culture has been devastated by anarchy, violence, and the breakdown of family life, while the once-vaunted Catholic community is one-third of what it was. The paganism of the European Enlightenment has filtered onto our shores with a vengeance, and today's parish priests will never have the easy time doing the Church's work that their pre-Vatican predecessors did.

The European Background

Our present predicament is not new. Fifty years ago Abbé Michonneau, speaking of Paris, and French Catholics in general, said loud and clear, "More often the parish means nothing." He placed responsibility for this sad condition not on the parish institution as such — but on priests. In his book *The Missionary Spirit in Parish Life*, Michonneau coined some remarkable sentences: "The missionary problem is a priestly problem"; "the unhappy state must be traced to priests who were not up to the mark"; "the main task is the making of good priests"; "they have not contact at all with the masses." These statements were not meant to deny that overworked priests very much about their Father's business did exist, even in France, men who were well loved by their people, administering parishes bubbling with sacred and secular activity. But by and large, he thought, they were too few.

In 1942 European priests, looking at the broken Church into which they were born, were using phrases now popular in so-called progressive American circles — the "post-Christian era" or "cultural Catholicism." They alleged that the Catholic world housed more baptized pagans than Christians, and parishes were dying on the vine for communicants, except on High Holy days. *The Sword of the Spirit* in England, the *Jocist Movement* in France, *Catholic Action* in Italy, and the *Catholic Youth Movement* in Germany were novel ties that caught from afar the imagination of young priests in the United States, who devoured these downcast but literate authors, mostly French. In spite of the alleged paganism of their Catholic congregations, on the continent and in Great Britain, those European priests had great hopes for the future of their churches, providing they learned how to evangelize properly within the modern milieu. American clerics, however, the more they became embedded in their own urban parishes, the more they recognized that the paganism charge did not apply to this country. The less they believed, too, that the American Church had need to learn from Europeans how to evangelize in the United States those who really were mostly their emigres. (This is not to say that the American Church of the World War II era lacked its own crises, not the least being a virulent anti-Catholicism outside the Church, and a certain smugness within it — best represented perhaps by priests who did not think they had to work very hard.)

It is still useful, however, to look back on the charges levelled by well-known European abbés and divines against their own congregations: negligible Sunday Mass attendance; those who did attend thinking like pagans; indifference to the Church's creeds and rebellion against her moral norms; visible Catholics were mostly women; baptismal and burial rituals which brought out more adults, but without any understanding of their significance; children who were taught for First Communion, but not for Sunday Mass; young adults, if they decided on Church marriage at all, who wanted a wedding on *their* terms. It was not possible to speak, Michonneau insisted, of apostasy because to be an apostate you had to have some convictions about the Church. His famous *Revolution in a City Parish* (1949) reported that while French Catholics had a lingering devotion to Christ, even among the paganized masses, resentment against the Church was everywhere, and anticlericalism was rampant. Parish priests there would not recognize paganized Catholics if they saw them on the street. Yet they were lulled into peace of mind by the respect, even the servility, showed them by churchgoers. Also, by the ability of the Church to draw spectacular crowds for spectacular events, like the Forty Hours procession through the streets, Christmas midnight Mass, or the visit of the bishop at Confirmation time. Under the cover of these occasional signs of perjuring Catholic life, the indifference of the masses was allowed to go unattended and unchallenged, so wrote these authors.

The downturns in European Catholicity are not too difficult to understand. The Council of Trent exhausted half of the sixteenth century before it coped with the Protestant revolt. Those years saw the beginning of the secularist movement, which eventually received the name modernism, a period when the European Church became defensive and, because of its long dependence on various national states to protect Catholicity, lost confidence in its evangelizing procedures, and the trust of its baptized masses. At the turn of the twentieth century, Pius X squelched modernism in Church-controlled institutions, but Catholic decline in Europe by this time was well on its way. "Modernism," a grandchild of Protestantism's private (subjective) interpretation of Christian faith and anti-papalism, and the child of the Enlightenment's adoration of man and its pseudo-religion called deism, invaded the corners of the Catholic sanctuary. Once Catholic opinion molders began to look at Christ mainly through Enlightenment eyes, the truths revealed by God became less precise, and remaking Christ into man's own image became the best way to keep his memory alive in smart Church circles.

Throughout the intellectual turmoil of the eighteenth and nineteenth centuries, when Modernist thinking proliferated among opinion molders, the Church in the United States was finding its place in the New World. Spanish explorers were extraordinarily good at importing their culture, unquestionably of Catholic inspiration but solidly Iberian, and it had a certain popular piety. But they hardly created a vibrant, intelligent, disciplined, educated body of churchgoing Catholics. Nor did they erect, even in Latin America, a pervasive Catholic support structure for the faith of the masses, wherever they remained in control. It was American bishops and their parish priests who did this in a very hostile Protestant environment, one which fortunately had not yet become infected with the Modernist virus. By the time this new danger to Christianity reached our shores the American Church was entering its golden age.

The Evolving American Parish

What was described by many as a general parochial condition in France after World War II may be commonplace today in the metropolitan United States: diminishing Mass attendance, virulent dissent in religious houses and on Catholic college campuses, fewer priests available to give personal attention to parishioners, a school system cut in half within one generation, grumbling about Catholic teaching, clerical misconduct and secularized religious, and more broken Catholic marriages. In the core cities, there are as many poor as ever, who are more angry at the world, and seemingly less capable than their predecessors of moving out of the ghetto. Demographically, there are large pockets of aging and aged people and more and more unattached singles. Some city parishes have as many as fifty thousand residents, a third or a half of whom are Catholic, with only a few thousand going to Mass on Sunday. Even these nuclear Catholics are rarely in touch with the church from one end of the week to the other.

There is another change to consider: the laity no longer think of their priest the way they used to, as a savior of sorts. In former days, even those who did not go to church on Sunday sent for their priests for all sorts of reasons. A priest did not have to be dragged into a home. He was called, and he went, or he went without calling. The laity hiding from the priest might have included those who were afraid they would be pulled into the confessional box before their time. Legends still exist of parish priests who could name most of the families in the parish, by lane or by street. There were priests, too, who knew every child in the school by first name, and could recall their parents' names equally well outside of church on Sunday morning.

Priests and people needed each other in those days, indeed believed in each other, and the belief was as important as the need. Immigrants usually arrived with their own priests not far behind and, before long, they begot their own native-born son priests. This source of priests was as much the effect of apostolic priests as it was of pious mothers. Priests were busy, parish life was rich, and people could not seem to get enough of their parish or their priests.

But the social conditions of the urban parish changed, and the mindset of the inhabitants likewise. Many of these exurbans, who moved by choice or by bulldozing, were the best endowed in the neighborhood faith-wise. In those times of change, the Irish, Germans, and Poles moved first, the very ones who demanded a lot of their priests, to be succeeded by Italians, Negroes, and Spanish, who were not only poorer but made fewer demands on the clergy.

Throughout these migrations, the parish operation remained fairly static, with less rush on the rectory and the sacraments. Imbedded old-timers would tell a new pastor of "the great parish this was before you came"; but the pastor had changed, too, coming to a large parish not in his forties, but in his sixties. No longer did pastors dominate their tables, assigning programs and work to their curates, nor, in too many cases, was he an impressive neighborhood figure. The good pastor became the man who did not interfere with his associates.

Diminishing numbers often meant fewer demands on priests, whose work week was shortened. "Off duty" meant out of the rectory, and that came to mean out of the parish, too. The parish system remained sturdy, but slowly eyes turned away from the rectory to the school, from the priests to the nuns. In metropolitan areas the ecclesial maxim, "Build the school first," only symbolized a popular trend. As years passed, the pastor became an administrator, and curates who were charged up with fervor and zeal took for granted that the pastor was to be bothered as little as possible. Almost simultaneously, the trends in the education of priests and nuns speeded the process of specialization, and part-time service in diocesan, not parish, causes followed.

Then there was the money factor. When prosperity found its way around the nation's corners, it found its way also into priests' lives, and into religious motherhouses, too. In this latter case millions of government dollars flowed freely into Catholic institutions, including colleges. Institutional prosperity made it a little harder to keep clerical and religious noses to the parochial grindstone. When the good life was readily available elsewhere, and when everything else in the Church seemed on the upswing, doing pedestrian things lower down in the Church became unattractive.

During all these changes in urban parish life, which so often were for the worse, chancery offices looked on, too. Diocesan officials made sure that every parish had one idealistic hard-working priest, but never exacted the same standard of performance for a pastor that they did for a chancellor. As parish life became routine, and as ecclesiastical rewards began to go to special workers and to teachers, bright young priests aspired to anything but a parish. Few prelates thought of rewarding hard-working parish priests ahead of special workers. One diocesan survey indicated that sixty percent of the parishes were not functioning properly, but nothing happened later to change the pattern. In another diocese a full-time parish priest was assigned for every fifteen hundred Catholics in one county (where many "dead" parishes existed), while the adjoining county (where all the people lived) suffered a priest/lay ratio of one to three thousand. Little attention was paid either to the observable fact that parishes staffed by religious enjoyed better performance records and a more popular acceptance in the same neighborhood than so-called "secular" parishes. Nor did prelates bother to find out why. Urban parishes suffered economically, not exclusively because the people were poor, but because they reached fewer people and provided fewer useful services. The Mass priest or the sacristy priest, who once hardly ever existed in America, came into being. As urban parishes sometimes grew to be arid plains of pious Christianity, parish priests, more and more, merely looked on.

The Impact of Vatican II

The American bishops governing, as they did, a prospering Church, were unable to comprehend, let alone cope with, what French and German bishops were doing at Vatican II in 1962 to bring new energy to their ancient but half-dead institutions. Those bastions of the old faith may still have possessed most of the Church's grand traditions, including its beauty; but less and less did they have a hold on the Church's people (old or young) or their cultures. Ralph Wiltgen has colorfully called it "the Unknown Council," an example of "the Rhine flowing into the Tiber," that is, the victory of the German hierarchy over the Italian pope. But, if the Rhine flowed into the Tiber as early as 1966 (when his book was published), it was not long before it also found its way up the Hudson, down the Mississippi, and over Sacramento way.

Pope John XXIII certainly did not have the Church in the United States in mind when he convoked Vatican II, and many of the structural changes inaugurated by the Council were not only long overdue, but welcomed on this side of the ocean. But, in the process of *aggiornamento* the *magisterium of the academe* ran away with *magisterium of the hierarchy*, much to the surprise of Angelo Giuseppi Roncalli (Pope John XXIII), but not without the collusion of some bishops in National Conferences and within the Roman Curia.

There is little need here to rehash the tiring and oft bitter controversies that ensued, except to say that they have laid heavy burdens on the Church's parish priests. Those who have failed officially to win a different Church than the one *magisterium* formally specifies, and those who take *magisterium* at its word, are equally troubled. An ex-religious, who rued his days as a dissenter, but reconverted in time to enjoy the faith into which he had been baptized, summarized the contemporary Catholic situation this way: "The Church is in for the fight of her life!" She surely is! And there is no new Messiah to cure her ills overnight. The old One will have to do, and the voice of Peter who still speaks in his Name.

Whatever else can be said about the impact of the Council on Europe and the Third World, the fact is that our Church has been shrinking in piety ever since, even as the baptized Catholic population continues to grow by natural increase and new immigration. We cannot fall from seventy-five percent regular Sunday Mass attendance to twenty-five percent without realizing that we now veer more toward the downside of present European Catholicity, than to our own historic standards. Standing on a predella today, beholding their Sunday congregation, many parish priests with imagination are already asking: "What will my Church look like twenty-five years from now when all these 'whiteheads' go to God?" This is a fair, but critical, question. Those who keep in step with the Catholic literature of elites might be musing as did the editor of *Commonweal* in August, 1984: "the End of Catholicism?"

So, pastors of tomorrow, those with direct links to the Catholic belief system that is today, might be asking themselves the same question about the "paganism" of their flock ("secularism" is the preferred word in this country) that Abbé Michonneau asked about French Catholics a half-century ago. The long-range impact of "pick-and-choose Catholicism" on the piety of parishioners who have cut themselves off from Sunday worship is somewhat ominous. In his 1987 address to the American bishops in Los Angeles, John Paul II reminded the entire world that it is "a grave error" to think that selective faith does not disqualify its adherents as "good Catholics," nor inhibit their worthy reception of the Eucharist. Furthermore, he added, "pick-and-choose Catholicism" undercuts the teaching office of bishops, and at the grass roots level it turns its devotees into other-than-Catholic. Optional Catholics have always existed in the closet of the Church, of course, but were never heralded as "good Catholics." This is what is being legitimized today by errant priests as Vatican II policy.

So, today parish priests, young and old, are experiencing the revolution that has disrupted the Catholic way of life at the street level. Theological squabbles, which would have hitherto taken place in rarified circles and under Catholic rules, now occur in many diocesan headquarters and in parish auditoriums, led often by priests and religious. And pastors are frequently denied the right to decide what is indeed legitimately Catholic. In the process, parish life has been radically altered and Catholic worship attenuated. Personal choice has replaced religious obligation, egalitarianism in government is substituted for hierarchical rule of the Church, and subjective feelings about things Catholic are in many minds the established norms of truth and right. As *aggiornamento* unfolded from these principles, the parish priest found himself redefined as a facilitator for reconciling religious differences, a therapist for psyches he was told had been wounded, a community organizer for a flock hitherto thought to be one. No longer was he to be the institutional leader the Church describes so thoroughly in the 1983 *Code of Canon Law*.

What Moderns Say About the Vatican II Parish

All parish priests, therefore, must know at this time that current opinion-molders of the Church are saying two important things: (1) priests are no longer the Church's dominant authority figures, and (2) private conscience is the primary *magisterium*. The *Notre Dame Study of Catholic Life Since Vatican II* (Harper and Row, 1987), summarizes the contemporary situation as follows: "Vatican II engendered sense of lay ownership of the Church is reflected in the growing reliance by Core Catholics on their own conscience instead of Church teaching in deciding what is moral and what is best for the Church" (p. 199).

From time immemorial, those who did not fully profess the Catholic faith have rejected the Catholic notion of the priesthood and of the Church. The Gnostics, the "know-it-alls" of the first and second century, denied that priests or bishops were the legitimate interpreters of the meaning of Christianity. A thousand years later, a theologian named Berengarius denied, at least until corrected, that Christ was really present in the Eucharist. In the sixteenth century Protestant reformers categorically rejected the notion of a sacrificial priesthood at all, and of the need after Christ of any other mediator between God and man. Post-Vatican II dissenters also maintain that priesthood, and the defining role of the Catholic hierarchy itself, is the result of a takeover by Church officeholders, not of anything that could be called divine revelation. They argue that modern theological research is reflected in the documents of Vatican II, requiring new approaches to the roots of Christianity itself, such as:

1. Jesus Christ himself must be reinterpreted. Revisionists see Jesus primarily as a teacher (rabbi), a worker of mercy, and a cultic (worshiping) figure only at the end of his life. He was not a priest, as Catholics have been taught to understand the term, nor did he intend the priesthood to be a special or ruling class within the Christian community. The Catholic priest should be understood as a merciful healer meeting human needs, helping to change political structures to achieve humanistic ends.

A study on the history and nature of the priesthood commissioned by the U.S. bishops — rejected by them in 1971, but not suppressed — was later published by former priest Bernard Cooke as *Ministry to Word and Sacraments*.[1] Cooke denied that priests "stand between Christ and community" or derive their role "from the more basic role of the community," or that "they function for the sake of the community priesthood," and "in a sense (their priesthood) is a specialized or intensified expression of that common priesthood (of the people of God)."

2. The Catholic Church must be reconstructed. That same study downgraded the bishops as successors to the apostles, and justified the priesthood, not by an intrinsic quality of its own, but by the function that it performs, and by the service it renders within the Christian community. Twenty years later, Bernard Cooke, by then a president of The Catholic Theological Society of America, reasserted the same: "We have become so accustomed to the notion that the ordained celebrant, and he alone, is the agent in the Mass that we have forgotten that it is the community gathered as the Body of Christ which enables the risen Lord to be present as the principal agent." The institutionalized Church's prejudice against women, the married and the laity, and the long-standing assumption that priesthood must be a full-time professional occupation, explains the Vatican's modern control of liturgical practice universally (see the *National Catholic Reporter*, May 11, 1990).

Whatever notice these views have acquired among today's Catholic youth derives from the widely publicized speculations of modern biblical critics who consider the traditional functions of the priesthood to be historical accretions without any foundation in the New Testament. As Cooke was underway with his study (1970), biblical theorist Raymond Brown wrote *Priest and Bishop: Biblical Reflections*,[2] which insisted that we must modify our understanding of the claim that Jesus historically instituted the priesthood at the Last Supper. "This statement," he alleges, "is true to the same real nuanced extent as the statement that the historical Jesus instituted the Church." Brown continues: "By selecting followers to take part in the proclamation of God's kingdom, Jesus formed the nucleus of what would develop into a community, and ultimately into the Church. By giving special significance to the elements of the (Passover?) meal that He ate with His disciples on the night before He died, Jesus supplied His followers with a community rite that would ultimately be seen as a sacrifice, and whose celebrants would hence be understood as priests." Brown's final word on the subject: the formal priesthood emerges in the course of the second century.

The Council of Trent anathematized everyone "who says there is no priesthood in the New Testament." According to the same Council, Holy Orders is "a true and proper sacrament instituted by Christ," not merely "a rite of sorts for choosing ministers of the Word of God and of the Sacraments."[3] Four hundred years later Vatican II taught: "(Priests are) consecrated in order to preach the Gospel and shepherd the faithful, as well as to celebrate divine worship as true priests of the New Testament" (*Lumen Gentium*, No. 28).

3. The priesthood is neither a higher calling, nor is its traditional role in the Church relevant to contemporary needs. As theologians like Edward Schillebeeckx, Hans Kung or Bernard Cooke would have it, the priest is simply another member of the Christian community, one better advised in these days to exchange his special status, which no longer satisfies modern mankind's needs, in favor of a joint ministry with other believers for the betterment of human life.

The thinking which underlays this recommendation reflects less an understanding of the Church's priestly patrimony, than a rejection of the very notion of priesthood, and indeed of Catholic hierarchy itself. Cooke and his group candidly admit that they are not interpreting Vatican II authentically, but are working to create a new Church. Insisting that monopoly of the liturgy by ordained priests can no longer be maintained, they assert that the Church's classic distinction between the sacred and the secular is not valid. Indeed, the real Christian vocation, they aver, is to reform the secular life, a state in which the priest ranks no higher than the shoemaker or the political leader. (Henry VIII would have agreed.)

Many catechetical centers take this perspective for granted. The doffing of clerical attire, less insistence on the respect associated with "Father," the takeover of once considered sacred functions by laity, and the ferocious drive to compel the ordination of women priests may, in the long run, do no great harm. Indeed, they may be serving God's mysterious purposes.

More serious, however, are efforts to wear down second-level Church leaders into believing that collegial government means the inevitable downgrading of hierarchy in the Church — that doctrinal pluralism, once institutionalized in Catholic circles, will eliminate the need of oaths of fidelity to simplistic creeds and absolute norms, and signal the birth of "the people of God" Church. In recent years, priests have often been made to feel like futuristic second-level Church leaders. Some of them, as a result of their seminary training, are already unclear about the precisions of Catholic doctrine or are reluctant to preach it on the *magisterium's* terms. Some bishops have admitted, too, that they are unable to get their priests to preach *Humanae Vitae.* Yet the Church of the twenty-first century will depend on the faith commitment of those priests who are presently being trained. Revisionists are more interested in redirecting present-day seminary training toward a generalized ministry, than toward the sacrificial priesthood defined in Church documents. Not long ago the Congregation for Religious criticized an American seminary in the nation's capitol whose programs, it said, were "characterized more by an undifferentiated concept of ministry in general than by a theologically informed idea of the ordained priesthood in particular."[4] Opposing this unauthorized drive toward general ministry is unappreciated, even in Catholic circles.

Recently, a research director of the United States Catholic Conference aired his concerns: "In the most recent study on seminarians, a good number tend to be less activist oriented than in the past and they see the primary task of the Church as encouraging its members to live the Christian life rather than to reform the world. They tend to stress the essential and unchanging aspects of Catholic doctrine. They see themselves responsible for ministering primarily to those who are closely affiliated with the Church within fixed geographical boundaries. Social justice and the missionary outreach it implies are low on their list of priorities." The speaker concludes: "One cannot seriously fault seminarians for wanting to provide the Mass and sacraments. This has legitimacy. However, the attitudes found by the study raise an alarming question. Do they reflect an imbalance?"[5]

Apart from the stereotyping which distorts the missionary effectiveness of earlier generations of American priests, those observations hardly reinforce the Vatican view of the Catholic priesthood. From the Council's end onward, predictions have been numerous that the Church's future depends on the changing the practice of ecclesiastical institutions, not on Catholic doctrine. The argument asks this question: If the practice changes, can change in doctrine be so far behind?[6]

Many priests in the field think these allegations are farfetched, and of little consequence to their everyday ministry. But, surely, if priests are exposed to "new" theories, the proposers must have in mind institution-alization, if only partially at the beginning. Opinion polls give some in-dication that Catholic parish life is being reconstructed in ways not con-templated by the fathers of Vatican II.

The *Notre Dame Study of Catholic Life Since Vatican II*, mentioned earlier and published under the title *The Emerging Parish*, was written by Monsignor Joseph Gremillion and Jim Castelli, two former employ-ees of Church agencies, in Rome and Washington, D.C., respectively. The book was advertised as "the first of its kind, this descriptive and interpretative survey," one which "reveals the past, present, and future of 18,500 (*sic*) Roman Catholic parishes in the United States."

The "emerging parish" is described as one, engendered by Vati-can II, where the "sense of lay ownership of the Church is reflected by the growing reliance by Core Catholics [i.e., those who are parish-con-nected] on their own consciences instead of Church teaching in decid-ing what is moral and what is best for the Church" (p. 199). In his earlier book with George Gallup, called *The American Catholic People* (Doubleday and Company, 1987), Castelli said "the only belief that separates many active and inactive Catholics is the belief by active Catholics that they are in, and the belief by inactive Catholics that they are out" (p.177).

A study of less than 1,100 parishes out of 19,500, and of 2,667 Core Catholics from thirty-six representative parishes out of a universe of 52,000,000, is hardly the last word, even if two-person teams, com-posed of a liturgist and a social scientist, made on-site visits to selected parishes. But given the book's reliance on social science normative judg-ments, it might be helpful to recall first what Church authority says about the ideal type of Catholic parish and, then, how sociologists evaluated parochial success or failure in other days.

First, John Paul II. During his September 13, 1987 visit to the His-panic Catholics in San Antonio, the pope specified the "essential factors" of parish life: "Instruction in the faith of the Apostles, the building up of a living community, the Eucharist and the other sacraments, and the life of prayer."

The parish, therefore, is the Universal Church in miniature, called upon to make disciples in a local neighborhood, and to make those disciples as good as possible. The new *Code of Canon Law* (1983) re-institutionalized these ancient Christian objectives, and parishes may be classified as "poor," "bad," or "mediocre," depending on how well or poorly these norms are implemented.

Secondly, old-time Catholic sociologists once classified Catholics with this Church nomenclature in mind: baptized Catholics were *nuclear* (i.e., the activists who performed works of supererogation for the Church beyond the call of duty); *average* (i.e., regular Sunday churchgoers, usually seventy-five percent, who were not otherwise engaged in parochial matters); or *inactive,* not surprisingly called *dormants* (i.e., those who, though baptized, rarely attended Mass, although most of these died with the sacraments), and the *apostates*, many of whom went to God with the blessing of a priest.

The "emerging parish," however, is not simply one with good and bad Catholics, but one which, allegedly as a result of Vatican II, "has already awakened Core Catholics (i.e., the old nuclears) from the sleepy myth of an unchanging Church" and who "practice the same kind of pick-and-choose Catholicism found among inactive Catholics; they follow Church teaching when they agree with it and reject it when they do not" (pp. 4-8).

As for parish priests: "Parishioners seem unaware of a silent opposition among pastors to some Church teachings. For example, in one parish in six, parishioners did not realize their pastor believes the Church's position on abortion is too rigid, fourteen of thirty-six pastors were opposed to the Church's teaching on contraception, but only one of fourteen parishes knew this. Sixteen pastors supported ordaining women" (p. 204). The book calls upon Notre Dame's Jay Dolan to explain the current Catholic trend: "The longing for order, so central a feature of the Church in the immigrant era, has given way to a longing for pluralism" (p. 24).

The largest proportion of the study's Core sample think of the Church's faith system in individualistic terms, but this (so the authors say) is "the product of four centuries of catechesis which emphasized growth in personal holiness and the individualistic nature of sin, confession and absolution." The new Communal Catholics, on the other hand, are of the mind that "the parish should give higher priority to help the poor" and "if a Church teaching does not make sense to them, they will refuse to agree" (p. 37). Two of every three oppose the Church's ban on artificial contraception, yet they "are not less faithful in Mass attendance and communion practices" (p. 44). They value independence, pluralism, and participated democracy, we are told, because they "have accepted and internalized the Second Vatican Council" (p. 51).

To gain an idea what these elites say about the local church, we present some of the book's *bon mots*:

1. "The post-Vatican II American parish is now returning to its lay roots" (p. 13). In post-Vatican language "the Church in the form of the people of God came first, and the Church in its institutionalized form followed" (p. 9). History also "has wrongly depicted the trustee system and lay trustees as detrimental to Catholic life" (p. 12).

Time and time again the book turns to the "people" Church and to dissent, the authors obviously pleased that even Core Catholics are not traditionalists. "Church leaders may regret this independence ... but they themselves have helped foster it, and it is not likely to disappear" (see p. 199, also pp. 5, 75, 196).

2. The book makes cynical gibes at the pre-Vatican II Church: "The parish where Father O'Brien took care of God, Sister Cerita ran the school, and people met their Mass obligations and said 'Holy Marys' would be a woefully inadequate stereotype of U.S. parishes in the 1980s" (p. 3). "Religious Orders were used much like the Marines" (p. 20). "For a century priests took center stage and left the laity to pay, pray, and obey" (p. 29).

The initials NCWC (the predecessor of the USCC) "were often said to stand for 'Nothing Counts West of Chicago' " (p. 22).

Contemporary pastors may not find the Castelli-Gremillion report representative of what occurs on their parish streets, but the "experts," who put books like this together are opinion-molders, and have large influence with college teachers and catechetical leaders. Furthermore, they have already influenced many seminary professors. Father Theodore Hesburgh's optimistic assessment of the data in the Foreword to this book, or Cardinal Joseph Bernardin's expectation on the book's jacket, alleging that the volume offers a "wealth of information for predicting trends and values of the future parish," need not be taken as the wave of the future. But they are significant witnesses to a trend some think is irreversible; whether it is or not remains to be seen. In either case, the pastor whose administration conforms to Canon Law has his work cut out for him — as teacher, sanctifier, and ruler. The "modern" view tends to undercut all those roles. This is the mood which filtered into diocesan seminaries and into Church bureaucracies after Vatican II, creating a situation where a pastor today may find himself working in a diocese having different Churches side by side, as if in a schizophrenic relationship.

Sources of Renewal

When Catholic renewal in the United States comes under discussion — and there is more need of it in 1994 than in 1962 — fair credit should be given to the traditional importance of the personal or emotional aspects of religious belonging. But these attributes, or the pious practices that result there from, do not separate particular groups from the universal Church community which sustains their sacramental relationship with Christ. Personal or cultural or experiential pieties, and they are legion, always remain subject to those who govern the Church under a public law based on the nature and constitution of the Mystical Body of Christ.

Whenever we speak of Christ's Church, therefore, we address the manner in which it incarnates God's words in the lives of believers, and fashions those truths within ecclesial society, under the graced guidance of that episcopal body united to the pope, to whom Christ gave all teaching and ruling power "in heaven and on earth."

Since this is the Catholic norm, a number of corollaries follow about the Catholic parish:

1. Bishops and their priests must be of one mind about the nature and role of the Catholic parish. Ways of running a particular parish will differ with personalities and cultures, but the nature of the Church remains what it is. Modern difficulties in parish life grow out of the failure of bishops and/or priests to keep that Church's nature uppermost in their minds, and to safeguard the vital mechanisms of evangelization passed on to them by their predecessors, for instance, the primacy of worship. The effort, however, to dismantle outdated instruments has led some innovators to try changing the Church itself.

However much parishes vary, they must always strive to realize the following objectives: to make Christ live in human hearts; to have believers baptized, even in infancy; to instruct them in Catholic doctrine, including the uniqueness of Christ's Mystical Body; to weld them into a worshiping community, especially at Sunday Mass and the regular reception of the sacraments; to provide human services to the unfortunate and sacred exercises to the pious; to eliminate roadblocks to people's way to salvation; to support them in their hours of difficulty and oppression; and to direct them to Christ through the portals of death.

Obstacles to renewal may include priests or religious of little faith, of idle habits, disinclined to obedience, or bureaucratic roadblocks of one kind or another. But, in a well-run Church, violations of doctrinal, moral, or canonical norms by parish priests should be rare exceptions.

2. The bishops set the policy and provide the example. It is not easy to be a "man of authority" in an era where individualism, subjectivism, and egalitarianism run riot. At the episcopal level the union between national hierarchies and the pope is far from perfect. There are competing minds within the Roman Curia, and some of the bishop's next-door neighbors may be in dissonance with stated policies of the Holy See. Still, the local bishop is "Ordinary"; that is, under the pope, he functions on his own authority within his diocese. What goes on badly in other places need not interfere with his faithful administration, even if it calls for exceptional courage.

The local pastor also has ordinary jurisdiction, and need not be intimidated by errant pastors in his diocese, while pursuing fidelity to Church norms within his own jurisdiction. His problem often is not the bishop (although in a given case it may be), but the administrative apparatus of the diocese. His curate may have been trained in a bad seminary, or be lacking a Catholic sense or disciplined habits; or diocesan agencies may want to limit his freedom to hire a religious educator or a youth minister of his own choice. As the *Code of Canon Law* requires, he is to correct error or patent evil, only to find that the offender has supporters in the chancery, who are willing to temporize unduly with bad work habits, laziness, antipapal attitudes, incorrect teaching, or worse.

Many years ago, one archbishop responded to a correction from the then Apostolic Delegate: "If you clean up the mess in Rome, I'll clean up the mess in my diocese." Whenever higher authority tries to micro-manage lower authorities, it is well that it be above reproach. Lower authority, and the parish priest is one such, cannot do what Church law expects him to do if the imperfections or defects of administration at higher levels go unattended. Or if good priests work under unnecessary tension, under less than admirable supervisors.

But even if the bishop sets the correct policy for all parish priests, he must also choose the right pastor for a given parish. Personnel boards are important for the collection and collation of data pertaining to priests and parishes, and as counsellors to the bishop. But the appointment of pastors is the personal responsibility of the bishop. When a bishop is beleaguered, often by a plethora of time-wasting meetings, there is a danger that his parishes (which are "out there") may become his poor relatives, never fully a part of his real household.

Appointing good pastors is not an exact science, to be sure. The "right man" may not be available, and a critical situation may call for a snap decision. However, if a parish needs a money-man, the bishop ought not send in a scholar whose interest is footnotes. Regardless of how the bishop handles the matter, the less he is involved personally, the more vague is his knowledge of what really goes on in the most important centers of his diocese — the parishes.

3. The pastorate must be the personal responsibility of the pastor and/or his alternate. An administrative genius of some reputation once explained how he got things done: "I organize, I deputize, I supervise." This man, who made administration look easy, was a hands-on director of operations who determined priorities and chose competent subordinates to do the actual work. Yet, like Kennesaw Mountain Landis peering from a box seat scanning home plate, he never allowed things to depart radically from the rules of the game. He was "the judge" of what was right and wrong.

In an age of pluralism, when street wisdom suggests that deputies be allowed to do their own thing, pastor-as-boss is a form of institutional heresy. Young priests may also have been well-trained to resent directives, or to demonstrate adulthood by charting their own courses without so much as a "by your leave" to their elders. Yet, good institutional leadership requires that the priest in charge determine what the parochial priorities and objectives are going to be, and to deal imaginatively with those who look like obstructionists. The vital principle of unity in any society is the leader who leads, and who knows how to obtain compliance. There is no one way to do it, but everyone knows when it has been done.

Shortly after Vatican II's Constitution on the Sacred Liturgy was approved, a number of young priests approached their superior insisting on beginning concelebration immediately. When informed that, with the bishop still in Rome and diocesan guidelines unavailable, this was not possible, the men pressed their cause with the affirmation that a conscientious decision like this did not require the bishop's permission. To which the superior replied: "I have a great regard for your conscience, but remember my conscience is running this place and, until the bishop says 'Yes,' there will be no concelebration."

There is no sensible way to run a parish, or anything else, unless someone is in charge whose word is law. To reintroduce the habit may be difficult, but the habit begins with the first act, repeated again and again. Public peace leaves ample room for sensible free play and initiative, but also demands general obedience to public law. The "characters" of any society are playboys who bend the rules, or treat them frivolously, while leaving the system intact. The good society, however, depends on good people being good most of the time. The function of constituted authority is to maintain this balance. When everyone becomes "agin the government," and acts out their hostilities, chaos reigns and the freedom to be good, even by the law-abiding, is in jeopardy.

4. The priest in charge of a parochial apostolate should be a good communicator. Parishioners should not have to guess what the priest expects of them, any more than curates must read the pastor's mind through tarot cards. The pastor, in particular, should solicit advice, but never simply as first among equals. Better to have up-front disagreement, or even conflicting recommendations, than to institutionalize ambiguity in administration. When everyone knows the rules of the game, there is a likelihood of general compliance. The leader who talks out of both sides of his mouth, or who declares himself strongly on one side of a controversial issue while tolerating disobedience, or gives bad example himself, automatically creates division in the ranks.

A priest who declares in September what he hopes to accomplish by the following August provides direction. He is able to measure the effectiveness of whatever he is about — in family life, Mass attendance, conversions, raising money — and knows what kind of report card he merits at the end.

5. Every priest in charge of a large enterprise should have an executive officer. In the old, old, old days this man was known as "the first assistant." In presidential terms he is "the chief of staff." In the Navy he is "the exec." In an archdiocese he would be "the vicar general" or "the coadjutor," the person who handles the "nuts and bolts" of administration. In a large parish the pastor should not be so bogged down in checking the plumbing that he has little time for praying or burying the dead.

Depending on the scope of the parochial enterprise, it might not hurt a pastor to have a few "chancellors," too. General H. Norman Schwarzkopf, hero of the Persian Gulf War, in his book *It Doesn't Take A Hero*, makes a point that giving important aides a share in running an enterprise can bring good results — a sense of belonging, cooperative assistance — which provides Number One with the capacity to measure the strengths of his subordinates, and see to it that they work in unison, not as opposing sideshows.

Parish priests should demonstrate how a good parish can be run. Archbishop John Mitty of San Francisco, a military-type personality, sometimes rubbed people the wrong way, but he is remembered by old-time priests for personally choosing the assignments of the newly ordained to older men whom he thought were good teachers of the real-life priesthood. The trouble with our system, as it has been inherited, is that an "assistant" can work for ten years without ever learning how to become an able chief officer. He may rarely see one in practice.

On the other hand, there is more to pastoring than leading. Pius XII had a great line about collaborators in the apostolate: "Choose them, train them, let them go." This does not mean giving away what a priest does not like, or what he does not understand, or what takes too much time. The "letting go" comes after a novitiate for someone who seems to have talent commensurate. The training of Number Twos to be Number Ones is the essence of good governance.

The hardest job for a priest-in-charge is to evaluate his own performance and to correct his shortcomings. Secular institutions, profit-making or not, survive only by reason of built-in checks and balances. When profits become losses in business, or cold wars turn into hot ones for governments, incompetence and indifference in administration is dealt with severely. The care of souls requires no less vigilance.

6. The pastor must organize parochial work in such a way that priests, even if in short supply, are available to work in a direct and personal manner with the faithful. Rectory life should be organized around "days ON," not on "days OFF." Every priest should work a five-day week. Above all, the insulation between priests and people must be eliminated. For parishioners to pursue a priest for days and rarely find him, something that occurs more in this age of telephone-answering machines, is annoying.

7. The parish should be overrun by laity and suitable associations of its best leadership. Priests are successful when a few vigorous apostolic groups run the parish. Irrelevant, archaic, and unpopular lay organizations ought to be de-chartered.

Organizations that appeal to the Catholic public — with hundreds and hundreds of active workers — are not to be discounted in a culture that prefers smallness. Karl Marx, who spoke glibly about the masses, nonetheless taught a basic principle of sound community organization: "Organize the few to influence the many." Specialized groups, led by enthusiastic leaders, usually control parish assemblies. Big labor, big business, big government, big university, though dominant social forces, are driven by a handful of dedicated and overworked enthusiasts.

Even when a parish school exists, lay organizations should be programmed as if the school did not exist. In American parish life the school has often served as a crutch for priests, one less and less available today. Parish councils must develop structures that reach into every segment of the parish, the school being only one structure, albeit an important one.

The point of this chapter is simple. Nothing is wrong with the average parish that good priests leading good people would not cure. A tree survives, particularly if it is planted in an unfriendly soil, by proper feeding and pruning. For this you need a smart gardener. If the parish did not exist, the Church would have to invent it. Parish life is always in trouble when we do not have the right kind and number of priestly gardeners.

No experienced and successful parish priest needs a Church document, not even one from Vatican II, to tell him what makes a parish do what it was created to do. The 1965 decree on *The Bishops' Pastoral Office in the Church* described the successful parish priest as the man who (1) knew his people, (2) visited them, (3) worshiped with them, (4) performed the corporal and spiritual works of mercy, and (5) organized a vital lay apostolate. Ineffective bishops may nurture bad morale among the clergy, unresponsive laity may dishearten priests; but if parish priests succeed in doing what Vatican II said they should be doing, parishes would be in business forever. Yet the priest leaders must be Christ-like. Once upon a time from a jail cell, Saint Paul warned his converts at Phillipi that troublemakers would try to ruin his handiwork. He gave them simple counsel, "Make your attitude that of Christ" (2:5), the mind which comes from the Church's teaching office. When this reminder comes up in the Priest's Daily Office, the Church calls upon Saint Polycarp, the second-century bishop-disciple of the Apostle John, to interpret this Pauline message as follows: "Our observance of what is good should be meticulous, avoiding anything that might cause another to stumble; we must shun false brothers and those who assume the Lord's name hypocritically and lead the unwary into error" (Reading for the Twenty-sixth Sunday). "Thinking with the Church" is in short supply today, and the parish priest, like Saint Paul, has difficulty trying to solve the problems created by lost sheep, and even by lost shepherds. Still, the Church places responsibility on him to guarantee, as best he can, the vitality and fidelity of "his portion of God's people." And for that effort to prevail the priest must first of all have that mind which is in Christ Jesus, our Lord, and in his vicar, the pope.

Endnotes

1. Augsburg Fortress Publishers, (Minneapolis, MN), 1976, pp. 641, 648.
2. Paulist Press (Mahwah, NJ), 1970, pp. 19-20.
3. *Enchiridion Symbolorum Definitionem et Declarationem de Rebus Fidei et Morum*, edited by Henricus Denzinger and Adolphyus Schönmetzer, Nos. 1771-1773.
4. This Roman letter was dated July 14, 1989, and signed by Cardinal Jean Jerome Hamer. It received little public attention.
5. An address (February 22, 1990) to the National Organization for the Continuing Education of the Roman Catholic Clergy. Reported in *Origins*, May 3, 1990. The study in question was sponsored by the National Catholic Education Association in 1987.
6. The logic of this kind of thinking about Catholic realities leads to inevitable conclusions. Bishop Donald Montrose of Stockton, California, directed his pastors to put an end to "row by row" reception of Holy Communion in order to avoid encouraging the unworthy reception of the Eucharist. One of his Franciscan pastors thought the bishop's emphasis was wrong — stress on the ordained priesthood and sacrifice, not on the Eucharist as a family meal. Georgetown University's theologian Monika Hellwig, responding to the Stockton directive, thinks the view that the Eucharist is a reward for good behavior should give way to an understanding that in the Eucharist Christ is encountered (*National Catholic Reporter*).

Part Two

The Parish Priest

and the Sacraments

Chapter Five

Preaching to the Pews

The pastors of the Church have the task not
only of proclaiming and explaining to the
people, directly, the deposit of faith committed
to them. They must also judge correctly the
formulations and explanations sought and
offered by the faithful ... in maintaining,
practicing, and professing the faith that has
been handed on, there should be a remarkable
harmony between the bishops and the faithful.

—*General Catechetical Directory*

Henri Gheon's little book *The Secret of the Curé of Ars* (Sheed and Ward, 1929) is an eloquent reminder that if a priest is a saint he does not need to be a great anything else, evidence enough of how God confounds grand lords sometimes through simple peasants (see 1 Corinthians 1:27). John Vianney (canonized in 1925, and the first parish priest to be so elevated) was no Jacques Bossuet when it came to oratorical flourishes, and surely his seminary faculty doubted his talent to be a priest. His seeming bumbling ways and mumbling speech were too evident. Yet his later words, in the pulpit as well as in the confessional, did more to keep Christ alive in Napoleonic France than anything Bishop Bossuet accomplished for souls under Louis XIV. Somehow, oratory by itself is not the ultimate measure of a good parish priest. No seminary to my knowledge ever rejected a candidate for the priesthood because he was a poor preacher. Maybe because he stuttered, but never because he mumbled or was difficult to understand. Indeed, a well known pre-Vatican II book on "the good parish" makes no mention of preaching at all, while a recent book is entitled *Ordained to Preach*, demonstrating how inexact are the proclaimed sacerdotal priorities.

It is hard to understand why Catholic preaching is considered so bad in so many places, but it seemingly is. Saying the right thing is surely more important than saying it well, but there is little excuse for the dull preachers who allegedly plague more than Catholic pulpits. An Anglican divine of the nineteenth century once said that preaching was a byword for "a long and dull conversation," and that when people heard anything uninviting, they called it a sermon.

Preaching may not be the essence of the priesthood, which is why the Catholic pastorate is less an endangered species than its Protestant counterpart. Still, the word does mean "proclamation," and priests are called upon to proclaim the gospel: "... what you have whispered in hidden places will be proclaimed on the housetops" (Luke 12:3). If priests do this badly those listening will survive, of course, but the liturgy — the worship — will be less than the Church intends it to be. So, even if courses in the art of public speaking fail to produce eloquent preachers, it remains the parish priest's responsibility to make sure his people hear the Word of God regularly in some acceptable form.

Consider this responsibility under its several headings. One pastor says he does not ever permit a bad preacher to mount a pulpit in his church. Others of his peers let "Father Roarkes" walk out of the sacristy every Sunday morning, even though their congregations heave a heavy sigh, almost an "ugh," week after week, for the fifteen or twenty minutes of their Sunday Mass that will be spent in pain. Worship may entail boredom, at times, but is should not beget suffering.

Saint Paul, writing from Greece to Rome, once told an audience of new Christians: "Faith comes through what is preached, and what is preached comes from the word of Christ" (Romans 10:17). This is a fair expectation. Most churchgoers, facing the celebrant on any Sunday morning, are old-timers in the faith. What they need is enlightenment and reinforcement, not necessarily the kind of instruction that leads others to baptism. Deepening the faith is not the same as inspiring it, but hopefully still "the word of Christ," is heard with a good deal of content, even if the Pauline style is not replicated.

The Holy See speaks of two Tables of the Lord within the Church, "the Table of the Word of God," the other "the Table of the Bread of the Lord." We sense the special sacredness of the second table, and have been so trained in its holiness, because Christ himself laid hands upon it. To violate that altar is sacrilege. All churchgoers know that this is a confessional matter. The first table is shown no similar reverence, even though it prepares the way for Christ, and goes back to the Mosaic account of God's dramatic intervention in salvation history. It was materialized earliest in "the tablets" given to Moses himself, and when Moses announced *The Word*, his face was made radiant by God himself (see Genesis 24). The present pope calls our Liturgy of the Word an art form, and so it is (*Dominicae Cenae*, 1980). But, in his words, it is also a sacred witness for Christ in the Eucharist. Profanation of *The Word* may not, therefore, be a sacrilege in a canonical sense, as when the Table of the Bread is desecrated, but every priest is obligated to protect God's radiance in that Word whenever he mounts his pulpit.

Part of the Problem: Preparation

Once upon a time a newly ordained priest complained that he did not have enough to do. His pastor asked: "How much time did you spend last week on your Sunday sermon?" The youngster stood dumbfounded. The thought apparently never occurred to him. Novice preachers, even if they are gifted intellectually and have eloquence, do not have an easy time of it in the pulpit. They tend to think abstractly and to speak mostly out of their book learning. Time will cure that, of course; but one would have to be an extraordinary orator of wide experience to speak regularly without setting aside time for reading, thinking, and relating one's insights to the lives of those in an audience who must make sense of his remarks. Fulton Sheen was one such orator. Two weeks before he died in 1979 he sat on the side during the Centenary Mass of a church in a neighborhood where he was living, whose patron saint was Saint Monica. During the Communion hymn he inquired of the priest sitting beside him how the Church acquired its name, and learned to his surprise that the first pastor, on his way to take over the parish in 1879, was so disturbed by the roughnecks he saw on the unpaved streets that he named his new church after the patroness of wayward sons. Sheen remained seemingly deep in prayer for the rest of the Mass. But he must have sensed that the presiding Archbishop would call on him, and he did. When "Uncle Fultie" rose to the impromptu invitation, he proceeded to give the finest disquisition on Saint Augustine's relationship with his mother that the congregation ever heard. That was no off-the-cuff sermon; it was a lifetime speaking through a man's artistry. Not even Fulton Sheen spoke off-the-cuff.

Every priest ought to be aware week by week how the gospel and the Collect for the following week reads. Mulling over their sense throughout the week may bring to mind an occasional slant or insight that is worth developing. If a good theme or central thought does pop up, a little quiet time the night before Sunday Mass, perhaps with a *Catholic Encyclopedia* at hand (every church should have it in the rectory or parish library) or with a relevant book can turn out to be a boon for his people. One key concept is enough for one good sermon. However, the sifting ought to take place upstairs, at least the night before, not in the pulpit. Educated parishioners know when the preacher is unprepared, and when he has nothing to say worth hearing. A priest on the lookout during the week for a creative idea, perhaps while saying his Divine Office, is not wasting his time. He might notice — for example on August 27th and 28th — that the Church's new liturgy has united the feast days of Saint Monica with her son Augustine. The readings on those days tell the story of their relationship, of her death, of her happiness at seeing the son become a Catholic, and of her dying words to him: "One thing only I ask you, that you remember me at the altar of the Lord wherever you may be." This fifteen-hundred-year-old tale is the stuff out of which a sermon on motherhood, on priesthood, on the Eucharist, on purgatory, on salvation, comes alive.

Priests are destined to live with their personalities and their voices; all the coaching or preparation in the world may help only a little. Sometimes genes makes mediocrities of the best of us. A silk purse might be changed to look like a sow's ear, but the reverse process is not likely, especially for a preacher. If priests are serious about gaining an ear from people in the pews — or at least about looking less like an oaf or a bore — then preparing themselves for the appearance can accomplish at least what a beautician does for a less than handsome lady — hide their worst attributes. Jacques Bossuet was likely groomed to the hilt, and may have rehearsed before a mirror, for all we know. A famous Dominican preacher did that once before preaching in the presence of one of the Church's leading cardinals and, as a result of his effort, brought a nationally known Catholic politician back to the sacraments after a forty-year absence. When he asked the convert what words of his so stirred the man's soul, they turned out to be words he did not remember saying at that point of the sermon, for he had had a mental blackout of those well-rehearsed, but temporarily forgotten, lines. Count that one for God! Remember, however, it was the preacher's habit of preparation that readied him to extemporize significantly in a moment of crisis.

The Heart of the Matter: Content

The most beautifully crafted speech in the world, eloquently delivered, can still have little to say. Public speakers often do that, Will Rogers claimed. Politicians are often called "bags of wind." On the other hand, simple but prepared teachers often give pearls to the unwary, in the same manner of the Curé of Ars.

At an elementary school graduation years ago, while fiddling with the list of prizes to be awarded and pondering the unworthiness of the boy scheduled for the Excellence Medal, the aging pastor arose to address 100 fourteen-year-olds. Suddenly, something the old man was saying brought a hush to the audience. He was discussing his first automobile (a 1908 model), and the difficulties he had cranking it up in the icy winter of the very cold north country, where he was assigned. What a blessing, he said, when his later Model T Ford acquired a self-starter. As this solemn-looking, shaggy priestly gentleman compared these youngsters to his old car, the kids were transfixed. They had been cranked up for fourteen years, he told them, by a mother, a father, a nun, or a priest in order that they might eventually appear before the world clean, well-behaved, ready to learn more, and to practice their faith. But if by this moment of their graduation into life's real world, they were not self-starters — at fourteen — then God help them! The old man proceeded to develop the relationship between personal responsibility, character, and achievement, between religious habit and Catholic piety. Fifty years have passed, but many hearers, still alive, repeat that speech's content. That priest might have been a dull preacher, but he had a disciplined mind, and he spoke briefly. His words had a message. His delivery was hardly noticed.

A great deal of post-Vatican II chatter goes on about tying homilies into the liturgy of the day, a liturgist's pipe dream. Each Mass has its theme by design, one that is evident in the seasonal, solemnity, or sanctoral prayers. The living Church is not simply, nor precisely, the sum of what either the Collect prays for or the readings indicate. Since the Church has developed its creed and code from New Testament times, its present-day proclamation or theological discourse normally goes beyond what was simply declared to the Church's first converts. The deposit of faith contained in the primitive documents of the Church lives through the tradition of the Church fathers, and through today's *magisterium*. If a preacher ends up paraphrasing the gospel, he is likely to become a stale moralizer, inspiring some hearers to take the missalette home and do their own meditating.

Priests should own, or have immediate access to, an array of good catechisms, a few of which are the following:

- *Catechism of the Catholic Church* published by the Congregation for the Doctrine of the Faith (1994) is a must.
- The third edition of *The Teaching of Christ* by Bishop Donald W. Wuerl, Father Ronald Lawler, and Thomas Comerford Lawler, eds. (Our Sunday Visitor, Inc., 1991), is probably the most popular book of its kind in the English-speaking world, translated into twelve languages and with two million copies in circulation.
- *The Catholic Catechism* by Father John Hardon, S.J. (Doubleday 1980) is well known for its doctrinal precision.
- *The Church's Confession of Faith: A Catholic Catechism for Adults* (Ignatius Press, 1987), originally a creation of the German hierarchy, is good for its content and modern style, especially strong on dogmatic subjects, but weak in matters of moral theology.

- One might also include in this category *The Roman Catechism* by Father Robert Bradley, S.J., and Monsignor Eugene Kevane (Saint Paul Editions, 1985). It retranslates the Catechism of the Council of Trent, annotating its sections with Vatican II and Post-Conciliar documents, and with the new *Code of Canon Law*. Since many of the controversies today are repeats of what went on in the days of Martin Luther, this book provides a significant historical context for a modern preacher, especially since Trent defined so many Catholic doctrines.

There are other catechisms, oftentimes called Dutch, French, or American, but most of these are unsatisfactory because they explain away Catholic truth as often as they teach it.

But, when all is said and done, the nuts and bolts of the message involves more than generalities. Over ten years ago, on October 22, 1983, John Paul II told bishops in one of his *ad limina* addresses what it meant to be a preacher:[1]

1. Proclaim salvation in Jesus Christ through his dying and rising.
2. Preach all the truths that pertain to salvation.
3. Defend whatever compromises the purity and integrity of the Word of God.
4. Explain that there is only one Church *magisterium*, and it belongs to bishops, whose coworkers are pastors.
5. All others, including theologians and others, must respect that *magisterium*.

Whether the specific sermon deals with the "hot" issues of our time — the sexual (divorce, contraception, homosexuality, abortion) and the social (consumerism, human rights, women's issues) — these are the norms of gospel content.

The Homily or Sermon

The homily or sermon may serve any one of four purposes: (1) inspiration or exhortation; (2) catechetical or doctrinal instruction; (3) moral guidance for private individuals and public leaders; (4) introduction to the devout life.

The speaker may use the social sciences (history, politics, psychology, or socioeconomics) if he is comfortable with their findings; but above all he must be a preacher of God's Word, not a classroom teacher delving into abstract theories, even about the Church or the human condition.

Contemporary homilists sometimes talk like pop-psychologists worried about psyches, or act like political seers fretting over social revolution, in ways that neither solve human problems (for whose solution the Church claims no competence), nor advance the spiritual life of their hearers. Social science theories, which depend on what people think or say, or on statistical computations on their vital signs, or subjective opinions, are soft-science at best. They are not the basis, in a pulpit at least, for instructing pewholders on the nature of human life or its destiny, and certainly not about the truth or falsity of God's revealed word.

In spite of these cautions, modern preachers often sound more like Dr. Spock than Cardinal Newman, drawing more on articles in the *New Republic* or the *National Review* than on the Fathers of the Church. Descriptions of what people do or say are of little help in elucidating Mary's perpetual virginity or the wisdom of the Ten Commandments. Still, as the modern mind moved away from eternal verities to empirical hypotheses as a basis for belief or behavior, percentiles have assumed a misbegotten teaching role. If fifty-one percent says something is true or not true, this seems nowadays to settle, or dismantle, an established truth. As a result of social science influence, public opinion, or at least that of enlightened elites, has become the *magisterium* on religious matters, even for many priests. If the truth were known, however, social science theories are based on someone's assumptions about humankind's natural goodness, or his unilinear evolution, or the absolute value of the individual, or the way learning allegedly works, or the responsibility of environment or society for inadequacy or failure. All of these are, in truth, unprovable hypotheses which tend to move religious creeds and moral codes to the outer edges of acceptable teaching, because these latter defy empirical validation.

The Church — both in its theology and in its catechesis — has been negatively affected by the humanism, the individualism, and the process philosophy reigning in secular circles, the end result of which is that Christ, praised in his time for speaking as a man with authority, has a harder time getting a hearing today than he did from the scribes. So does John Paul II. So does the authentic Catholic parish priest. A preacher, therefore, who begins as an expert on the science of man (anthropology) may end up as a poor spokesman for the science of God (theology). The Catholic priest inevitably brings up those subjects the worldlings of any culture do not want to hear. If he is true to his calling, he must catechize as if he were back in the days of the Galatians and Thessalonians.

So the contemporary preacher must bring up subjects once thought settled for the Church, and catechize as if he is back in the early missionary years: Was Christ really the Son of God? Was he really born of a virgin? Did he establish a Church? Or a priesthood? Or the sacraments? Did he really talk about sex? And did he leave any commandments besides love? Is there really evil in the world? Or sin? What about heaven and hell? Does God really punish sinners, or are people just sick, more sinned against than sinning? The most unheard sermon today, for example, is about sin, the issue scripture says explains God's intervention in human affairs. Priests today are afraid of the subject, except in the most general terms, or within a political framework (e.g., sexism). How, during the Sacrifice of the Mass when offering "the blood shed for you and for all for the forgiveness of sins," can a priest say with his congregation, "*mea culpa*," without being reminded from time to time of the particular sins he and his hearers are obligated to acknowledge, to confess, and to repair through Christ? Or is the Mass that kind of a sacrifice anymore? Here is the stuff of important sermons, no longer commonplace in Catholic pulpits, but remaining still at the heart of the gospel.

The Soul of the Homily: Style

Make no mistake about it, good preachers sometimes die without credit for their influence on people's lives; others revel all life long in public acclaim for their "personality" or "stage presence," without deserving most of it. Still, whatever "it" is, it's a plus. Clara Bow had it, so did Will Rogers, F.D.R. certainly, strangely Groucho Marx. To be a good speaker one does not have to compose sentences like those in Newman's "Second Spring," or roll out "R's" like Democrats. But if the homilist is to be good, he is good only within the context of his personality, and within the expectations of his times. Cardinal Newman likely would not do as well today in Saint Patrick's Cathedral as Archbishop Sheen did. Will Rogers would hardly be the folk hero he is had he imitated the sentence structure, or the stutter, of Winston Churchill.

Intelligence is important. So is an idea. Learning to speak better, or willingness to practice, helps. Sincerity is also a great plus. But, whether one fumbles with words like Gary Cooper, or has the fluency of a Cardinal O'Connor, a speaker is heard only as he is seen.

An old pro has less need of props than the tyro, the rookie. "Canned" sermons may help, but many priests do not find much that is helpful in them, even when they are labelled "20th Sunday in Ordinary Time." They are not the fruit of personal meditation, nor do they reflect individual interests or styles. Those who cannot write for another are not comfortable speaking other people's words. If a priest does not think he was cut out to be a ghost writer, he is unlikely to speak well from handouts. The same may be said of written texts. Sometimes they are necessary, as when a speaker needs to be quoted accurately, or in formal lecture situations where the exact phraseology is demanded, or when the time limit is preset and impromptu additions by any one speaker become a menace to the program. Those who read a manuscript decently also find a text to be restrictive to relaxed presentation or improvisation. It is a matter of personality, no doubt, but even Herbert Hoover, good man that he was, might have left more of an impression on his nation, if he took his head out of a manuscript once in a while, if only to throw away an imaginative line.

Three kinds of priests customarily mount the pulpits of the nation every Sunday:

The flamboyant orator, whose challenge is to make his substance turn out as good as his appearance, and that he does not talk longer than it takes to say a Mass piously.

The good speaker, one who has the ability to relate Church teaching to the lives of the people before him. Beyond the occasional homily that aims to form public consciences or to contrast Catholic morals with secular mores, the Sunday-after-Sunday task is to reinforce the faithful's Catholic way of life, and to inspire some of them to the higher life, even toward a different vocation. Berating straw men, or causes, commonplace in some pulpits, conjures a stellar performance now and then but overdone histrionics is a homiletic bore. Good outside speakers are often used by pastors to uplift the lives of their Sunday churchgoers.

The poor preacher, the dull preacher, the no-ideas preacher is a burden to the Church. One pastor spoke for a curate every Sunday over a ten-year period, because the younger man was paralyzed before an audience. The pastor was one of the diocese's great preachers, and the curate had mercy on the parishioners by withdrawing from their weekly suffering.

However, a lot of poor speakers would do better, or at least less badly, if they spoke briefly on a short subject about which they have conviction, and avoided even the semblance of preaching. The parable of the Good Shepherd is about pastoring. Why would a very bad preacher, recognizing his limitations, not keep his homilies low key, chatty — and brief. If he is unable to handle Church mysteries (i.e., the Trinity), he should leave them alone. Explaining the meaning of faith or morals is easy enough, as long as he keeps the lesson simple. What demoralizes a congregation is the poor preacher who goes on and on and on and on.

Tricks of the Trade

Every priest undergoes at least one course on homiletics, perhaps two or three, prior to his ordination, and every professor knows that courses do not a preacher make. They may learn priorities, assemble a library of usable books, get a lot of practice in the presence of critics, and learn some of the tricks of the trade. If they are really interested in being more than chatterboxes, they will improve the performance over time. Certainly, by recognizing their mistakes, they will talk out of their own experience, and out of their own minds, however much they have been influenced by mentors. They will acquire a better sense of timing and the limits of patience in their audiences. (Why a preacher does not sense his hold — or lack of it — on the people before him simply by looking at them, is a mystery.) If he has any brains and eloquence at all, he can talk, almost without notice, for a half hour on any subject dear to his heart. But a five-minute talk, like a one-page article, takes a lot of preparation and honing to keep it brief.

The pulpit is like a stage. The most important moments are the coming and the going. If the entry is well thought out, and the exit too, the actor has some leeway in between to be less than the best. But the most powerful idea, brilliantly conceived, will come out of his mouth like a dud if the speaker fumbles his lead-in and then exits without clearly making the idea relevant to the lives of his audience. And, by introduction, the good speaker uses something beside jokes.

Humor has its place in the pulpit, but not jokes, particularly not one from a book. Nor should the exit line be a harangue. If he should not leave them laughing, he should not leave them upset. If the sermon calls for a little damning, do it in the middle. Allow parishioners to leave feeling good — or at least hopeful.

All kinds of authors on public speaking have all kinds of tricks of the trade. Any one or two of them may meet the public's taste. Years ago, an advertising gimmick was used by public relations firms to sell products, which proved effective. It was called "the AIDA Plan," not so classic as Bizet's opera, but its four steps are still useful for preachers who like to "plan" their presentation. The basic elements are (1) attention, (2) interest, (3) desire, and (4) action.

94

If, for example, the subject of the address is to be the Second Vatican Council, the speaker might gain ears (1) by telling the audience something that startles them, for example, how John XXIII, at one point, wanted to call the whole thing off. Or, how Paul VI and the Council Fathers engaged in a little fisticuffing over papal primacy, over marriage and the place of Our Lady in the economy of salvation. They might also remain reasonably attentive if (2) he interests them in earlier Councils, and how some of them ended well or badly. The intentions and the authentic accomplishments of Vatican II will surely (3) stimulate appreciation, and a desire to know more, for most people do not have the least idea of what actually went on in Rome thirty years ago. Urging them (4) to pick up or purchase a short account of the Council, available at the Church door, or to join some form of the lay apostolate energized by the Council, or to become a Eucharistic minister, would be a solid action step.

So much goes on these days in a parish, or a city, or the world, things that everyone knows via satellite, that an alert preacher has an easier time than his predecessors making his sermon relevant to parishioner's lives, if he knows how to do it. But he has to know his people and give some thought to driving his point home to them. People relate to what they love, know, or fear. A good preacher can start with a neighborhood event, a politician's gaffe, or a faraway human tragedy, then relate a Catholic doctrine and tie his teaching to the choices they have to make daily. Christ was good at that, for instance, in the parable of the Pharisee and the Publican. The priest is not a news commentator, since most of what anchor men have to say has little enduring value. Nor is he a therapist pouring out panaceas, whose curative power is iffy. But he sure can make them think. He can inspire them. He can make them mad. He can console them, strengthen their resolve, get them to do one Christian thing.

- Preaching is instruction if the priest is a good teacher.
- He is a success if he uplifts them.
- He does his work if he explains God's law.
- But he comes out a winner in the pulpit if his people visit the state of grace because of something he said.

An important question remains to be asked: Whatever happened to the doctrinal sermon? And to the courses of doctrinal sermons, once mandated in certain dioceses, as part of the regular pulpit instruction of the faithful? They may not have been the catechetical gems old-timers cracked them up to be, but their reason for being wasn't bad: systematic instruction of adult Catholics in the faith, morals, and discipline of the faith. For the past quarter-century they have been out of fashion, their place taken by recommended biblical and liturgical themes. The new generation of preaching experts, it is said, decided that old "canned" sermon series, like Callan and McHugh, were abstract, scholastic, and unrelated to particular Sunday liturgies; whereas today's suspicious-minded traditionalists complain that, following Vatican II, the reformers simply wanted to get away from doctrinal sermons, period.

Where the truth in that little dispute lies is no longer important, now that the *Catechism of the Catholic Church* has been published. Church authorities realize they are dealing with a new phenomenon, religious illiteracy among many young middle-age adults. How better, therefore, to cope with this new difficulty than in Sunday pulpits. It seems right and proper in these times that "the homily" (a Greek alternative to the Latin-based "sermon") can be more doctrinal without being unbiblical or unliturgical. After all, if the Eucharist is the food of the Christian soul, doctrine is the food of the Catholic mind.

As an example, take the Lenten readings with their recurring references to Adam, to Moses, to sin and the death of Christ, to the prodigal son, to the Apostles' behavior, to the Transfiguration. Here is an appropriate opportunity for preachers to deal, apologetically or theologically, with questions like original sin, the God of salvation history, fallen human nature, the promise of redemption, Christ the suffering Servant, his divinity, the mission of the Church, eternal life, and so forth. Every liturgical season of the year is susceptible to similar arrangements of sermon topics with a heavy doctrinal content, Sunday after Sunday.

Saint Gregory the Great (590-604), one of the Church's brilliant popes, called the preacher "a watchman" — he who stands on a hilltop, and by his foresight helps his people to see the truth. "Who am I to be a watchman?" the pope asked. And he answered: "Because I love God, and do not spare myself in speaking of Him." That's what preaching is all about.

Endnote

1. John Paul II, *To The U.S. Bishops at their Ad Limina Visit* (Boston, MA: Saint Paul Books and Media, 1984), pp. 71ff.

Chapter Six

Reverence
in Catholic Worship:
The Eucharist

There has been a shift in our Roman liturgical practice from a theocentric celebration of the sacraments to an anthropocentric focus. More than ever before we need to be reminded that "God is God and I am not." (Saint Augustine) And in our craving at times to satisfy the emotions of the worshipping people of God, we fail to worship the God Who formed the people. The principal way to recover the sacred in our worship is to remember the source and the summit of our worship — encounter with the divinity who deigned to join our humanity in Jesus Christ.

— Father Anthony D. Sorgie, Fellowship of Catholic Scholars (1989)

Once upon a time there was a pastor, wiser than his fifty years might indicate, who assumed command of a 1939 parish populated by post-World War I immigrants. Journalists would call it a slum parish, with eighty-five percent of parishioners on welfare. The church he inherited was as cold in feeling as it was in looks. Seemingly, and without careful thought (so it appeared), the new pastor dunned a friend in the art world to donate his talent, and his time, for turning his inherited barn into a worthy House of God. Lacking money, this cleric, himself an immigrant, proceeded to dig out of the neighborhood the least harmful corps of workmen he could find — a painter here, a few carpenters there, and the one electrician handy at fusing wires without burning the place down. All donated, of course, in exchange for an occasional homemade dinner on the pastor, and a carafe of Italian wine. Later, the pastor said they did it for the glory of God; the people remember doing it for the pastor, who also happened to be a con-man.

Voila, before the year was out, the town had a new liturgical jewel in its possession. The outer bricks had been washed, the wooden altar had received a baldachinum (canopy) plus a set of seasonal antependia (tapestry); the dirty statuary was repainted and given golden touches, the Stations of the Cross were tinted with coats of blending colors, and, above the main altar, a magnificent medieval crucifix looked down on everyone. The church was now the loveliest thing in town and, what with new homemade vestments cut to a fine Gothic taste, the parishioners began to find joy in their Mass. The pastor shortly had them praying with the priest, and singing, too, with a homemade choir. The grateful people were not simply responding to an eloquent priest; they had acquired a "feel" for worship a full generation before the Second Vatican Council.

Invited to tour the renovation, this newly-ordained tyro — rookie — was impressed, but dumb enough to ask: "Considering the slimy nature of the streets and bungalows, wouldn't it have been better to make your start as pastor by cleaning up the neighborhood?" With steel in his eyes the older man whirled as much in surprise as in scorn: "Look, Kelly, there's nothing much of God, let alone beauty, in these people's lives or in their hovels. I'm going to give them a little bit of both, beginning with the beauty of God's House. Once they appreciate that, they'll look a little more hopefully on a few other things, maybe even on their kids."

Fifty years later the appearance of this Church still suggests that the first call on a pastor's duty is the proper worship of God. One might say, his (and everyone else's) first commandment.

A priest who does not see the truth of this statement is unlikely to be persuaded by argument. Unquestionably, the pious worship of God has been betrayed down the centuries as much by mediocrity, as by sacrilege. Truly, we have a long list of great cathedrals, and cathedral-like churches built with the faith of peasants and their pennies; we have Gregorian chant and the monks of Solesmes, and great preachers, too, from the golden tongue of John Chrysostom to the rhetorical flourishes of Fulton Sheen; but in catacombs, concentration camps and gulags, in Irish cellars and Mexican undergrounds, on lonely prairies and bloody battlefields, we remember also the impromptu Masses with only bread, wine, and a priest (a saint maybe, more likely a sinner) with his words of consecration, but a Mass, the very stuff out of which God's eternal presence remains alive among his creatures, even in the hearts of those who curse him.

One of the great expectations of the Second Vatican Council, indeed the very first if you go by the approved documents, was a richer and more attractive Catholic worship. The liturgy surely is more meaningful because it is vernacular and participated, but there are fewer Catholics at Mass on Sunday who show more irreverence. Contrary to the mind of the Council fathers, some of the solemnity associated with Latin has been superseded, vernacular translations are often banal, and horizontal participation by pewholders (including hugging, clapping, or shaking hands, etc.) assumed greater place than reverence of the Almighty, and of the Eucharist itself. Christ may still rule in his heaven, but the "Other Christ" (namely the priest), once a chief actor in the drama of Calvary re-presented, was given the new title of presider.

As liturgical experts moved congregations in the direction of meaningfulness in worship, Sunday Mass, hitherto a distinguishing mark of Catholics and a canonical "must," became more voluntary. In the new catechesis, excusing reasons were less serious and sometimes read: "If you get nothing out of it, you don't have to go."

In the light of how common this unexpected scenario became, parish priests of today must determine how much re-catechesis their parish needs to invigorate the worshiping life of the local community. Older priests realize that Tridentine worship was, at times, too mechanical, too mysterious, too priestly. Still, the people knew that it was pointed toward Heaven, as their many Catholic churches indicated, that the Mass was a sacrifice for their sins, that Christ was really present, that the priest made it all possible, and that the state of grace was necessary to partake of the

Eucharist. The people had learned the right priorities, even if the instruments for raising people's hearts and minds to God were defective.

We cannot be sure any more how much correct information our younger generations have about the Church's sacramental system, or about the difference between a Mass and a prayer meeting. Catholics should go to Mass (even if they do not always think about it) to join with Christ, the Mediator, in offering their lives and sufferings to God with a view to bringing God's very life into their own. It was he who made that first offering by which mankind was bonded to their God, and created the relationship with God himself which is real and salvific. From that day forward, God's life was to come to mankind through the Church and, *a fortiori* through the Eucharist. Indeed, as Vatican II said so clearly, the Church derives its life from the Eucharist, and thrives on the Eucharist (*Lumen Gentium*, No. 26). When a church is dedicated, the bishop also dedicates the altar. How many Catholics know that the altar, the focal point of God's house, represents Christ, the reason why, liturgically speaking, there should only be one altar. In Catholic terms, therefore, the House of God is primarily a House of Sacrifice, and the reason why Catholics go to Mass.

All other motives — hearing God's word, enjoying fellowship with other believers, praying to God directly, finding rest from daily difficulties — flow out of that one central truth. The Church did not create the Eucharist to satisfy human needs. Christ instituted the Eucharist as the beginning and ending of the God-man relationship on earth.

Returning Solemnity to Liturgy

Almost every time the television industry chooses to depict a religious rite for the evening news, it turns a camera on the Catholic Mass. Somewhere. Not infrequently with John Paul II as star, or so it seems. Newscasters can feature clapping or singing congregations, and occasionally do; but more often it is the drama around an altar led by a mitered figure in golden robes which appears on the tube. Tom Brokaw-types are not interested in its otherworldly aspects, only in its religious look, knowing not what has made the Mass matter to Christians from the first breaking of bread.

In the Catholic tradition the Mass developed from a plain table to a majestic Gothic Cathedral. Christ offered the first Eucharist in humble surroundings, but as a result of "Do this in memory of me," the ritual became the awesome act of worship by the Church's universal family. Catholic liturgy unfolded as a public acknowledgment of our dependence on God, and of our salvation through Christ. It has also been a heartfelt work of the Catholic faithful together, not as a private enterprise enacted for private purposes, even though as a public act it confers private benefits. Local priests are free to explore these personal aspects of public liturgy, as long as they maintain the Church's emphasis.

Priests of my generation took the Roman Liturgy for granted. Indeed, many of us were involved in demystifying it, years before John XXIII appeared on our watch. We featured dialogue Masses, lay participation, popular missals, and the vernacular, every time we could use it legitimately, and left its mystery or its awe-inspiring aspects to the pope. We tried to humanize its seeming formality and stiffness, and much of what we did led to some of the important liturgical reforms that evolved out of the Vatican Council.

Most pastors are familiar with the controversies that have occurred over matters liturgical, and about the arguments between stand-patters and would-be reformers. Consequently, there is little need here to tarry over the moves which brought on the sudden collapse of the Latin discipline or to explain the pedestrian character of so many innovations. In spite of the good example presented in the Catholic cathedrals of our nation, the sacred aura of Catholic worship began to lose its glow in many parochial quarters after 1965. Some priests blame the strange language inserted in liturgical or biblical texts, like "feed box" for "manger," "no room for them in the place where travellers lodge," instead of "no room in the inn." Then, there are inadequate expressions to explain the Eucharist, like "spiritual food" and "spiritual drink" in today's Offertory Prayers.

More serious in the minds of some scholars are the mistranslations that diminish the sense of scripture or the force of the Latin sacramentary. Recently, important American bishops are expressing concern lest retranslations falsely revise Catholic ecclesiology, even doctrine. The efforts to remove the word "Father" as a reference to God, to diminish references to personal sins, to change the "Our Father," and weakening the Mariology customary in Catholic rituals, are examples of a process at work.

Many priests also have a few hang-ups of their own when they compare yesterday's Latin to modern English use in the liturgy. For example, "This is the Lamb of God" lacks the majesty of *Ecce Agnus Dei*," while

"Reign of God" is not quite the same as "*Regnum Dei.*" England's Queen Elizabeth may reign because she does not rule, but in the Christian dispensation Christ is Lord of the Universe, is called King by our liturgy, making "Kingdom of God" the suitable liturgical recognition of his governing role in the lives of believers. But this stress no longer is found in new translations. Thomas Day's book *Why Catholics Can't Sing* (Crossroads, 1991) offers only a partial explanation, historical and otherwise, of why Catholic liturgy has become more plebeian than sacred. His description of the move by post-Vatican II experts to introduce pop and folk music into the Mass was only one element of a wide thrust to enhance the people-side of worship. The drive for "multicultural" rites is another. What do churchgoers want anyway? Experts like to speak on their behalf, but they may not. Indeed, the poor people of the world are more likely to appreciate tradition and solemnity, and make far-ranging pilgrimages to seek them out. African-Americans or Hispanics are free to add their flavor to the Catholic liturgy, as Irish and Italians did earlier, but it is doubtful that the new rites, based on alleged subjective or ethnic needs, have necessarily made the Church more attractive to immigrant populations, even if that would be the purpose of liturgy. The Church has many different rites, all of them highly theocentric, based on an ancient linguistic tradition, congruent with the dominant Roman Rite, and pointing toward salvation in and through Jesus Christ.

But the Church also has had trouble with experimental "rites," notably the Chinese rites of Matteo Ricci and the Malabar rite of Roberto Di Nobili, both of which were the object of papal condemnation in the seventeenth century. (The Chinese rites went so far as to encourage the Confucian cult of ancestor worship.) The thrust in our time for multicultural meaning in liturgical practice often comes out of evangelistic Protestant sources and a weak doctrinal tradition, or out of a liberation theology which proposes salvation in the social order, not in the kingdom Christ preached. These movements reinforce the modern tendency toward individualism, subjectivism, and egalitarianism which desolemnizes worship by turning the accent from worship of God to emotional satisfaction for allegedly alienated or fragmented cultural groups. Contrariwise, the Church's liturgical content and form seeks to unify culturally different Christians, and to transcend the human condition, by "transporting" their attention to God.

A visit to Saint Peter's Basilica, on Low Sunday any year, can be an awe-inspiring event for any pilgrim. But in 1960 it was an experience I did not anticipate, largely because pomp and circumstance are not my strong suit. In our culture pomp signifies pomposity, the characteristic of royal houses from London to Bucharest, but hardly the custom in churches of the American poor.

Seated in the front row before the main altar, I was unprepared for the wave of applause surging from the rear, whose volume increased as John XXIII was carried high above the crowd down the middle aisle. My skin tingled as he came into view, and more so as he took his place on a chair five strides away. And then, just when my cup of emotion seemed already full, from a loge on the left came the orchestrated voices of one thousand male German choristers, on a pilgrimage to the Holy See. It was the most inspiring rendition of the Third Creed of Gregorian Chant that I have ever heard. *"Credo in Unum Deum"* resounded through the Basilica the moment the Pope's feet hit the ground, a testimony of community faith if there ever was one. I understood then what Peter, James, and John must have felt on the day when a voice from heaven announced: "This is my Son, the Beloved; he enjoys my favor. Listen to him" (Matthew 17:5).

That sense of divine, I submit, is what Church rituals contemplate, even when local groups use their freedom to make parishioners feel at home.

Staying with the Rubrics

"Written in blood" was an old expression used to explain why an agreement was sacred. "Rubrics" are the red lines in the Catholic missal which spell out how the prayers are to be read and the actions performed. Rubrics are the Church's way of protecting the solemnity of the Mass and the administration of the sacraments. Priests who are careless with the rubrics are hardly exemplars of good public praying.

Since the parish priest is responsible for the quality of Catholic worship, he is duty-bound to preserve its integrity and foster its beauty. In earlier days when observance of norms, even of rubrics, was taken for granted, a priest could be forgiven for a certain carelessness. The system seemed to take care of itself. We used to josh about Jesuits who never seemed to know rubrics, yet no one seemed to mind. However, today efforts to denigrate the priesthood, and the authority of the pastor particularly, are not matters of minor significance; there is enough unbelief and doubt out there about the Last Supper, about Christ's intentions, and the Sacrifice on the Cross, about the Mass, the Real Presence certainly, all of which tend to make the ordained priest less than the central liturgical figure of the parish, that the Church insists he is.

Strangely, when the new *General Instruction on the Roman Missal* was issued in 1970, the Holy See reminisced as follows about the Tridentine Missal of 1570, which the Vatican II book was replacing: "In those troubled days, Saint Pius V was unwilling to make any changes in the rites except minor ones: he was intent on preserving more recent tradition because, at that time [the Protestant Reformation], attacks were made on the doctrine that the Mass is a sacrifice, that its ministers are priests, and that Christ is really and abidingly present under the Eucharistic species."

In the '90s Catholic pastors must be aware that these attacks, made four hundred years ago, are quite commonplace today, and be reminded to take precautions against their infiltration on local congregations or bad affect on the celebration of their liturgies.

We all know that priests themselves have contributed in recent years to their own decline: saying Mass without vestments, playing loose with the approved translations of the Bible or the liturgical books, using invalid or illicit matter, violating norms in liturgy on the proper use of women, religious or laity, etc. Of course, complaints about vague guidelines from headquarters, and inconsistent enforcement of regulations within the same diocese, are not without merit. Some pastors with errant associates, and young priests living with freewheeling elders, find little support for rule enforcement in certain chancery circles. Still, other priests' abuses do not exculpate individual pastors from doing their duty.

A good *vade mecum* for guidance will be *The Pastoral Handbook* of the diocese which will specify the details of pastoral obligations. (If such a volume does not exist, the pastor will find authentic guidance in those produced by archdioceses like Denver or New York.) Not everything is governed by rules, of course, especially good sense or good taste, both of which are of critical importance to the good parish priest. Competent advisers are always helpful, especially in matters pertaining to the beauty of the Church and its liturgy.

One thing to keep in mind is that there is a certain genius in the Roman Rite, under which most English-speaking priests function. The Roman Rite did not prevail in the Church because it was mandated; it became well-nigh universal because of its clean lines, its attractive chant, and its relative brevity. Anyone who has attended a solemn Roman liturgy, as compared to its solemn Byzantine counterpart, realizes why Sunday Mass has always been better attended in the West than in the East, even in countries where Catholic piety was at a low ebb. There are times and places in the West when what some critics called "cheesecake" or "junk art" prevailed, and for long stretches of time. But the Basilica, the Romanesque and Gothic styles of art and ritual, with their emphasis on eternity and the cross, eventually prevailed over the sixteenth-century Baroque and Rococo, with their irreligious disregard of Christian beliefs and tradition. The modern mode takes a different direction, toward the non-ritualistic simplicity of the primitive church, dressed up in what the inventors consider relevant contemporary accouterments. A bathtub font in the floor of a church as a parallel to baptism in the Jordan river, simplified attire (or none) as preferable to medieval-type vestments, homilies by women as substitutes for priests, standing in Church, not kneeling, the clatter of hands and voices instead of solemn silence, are all deficiencies in the art of liturgical renewal that were not contemplated at Vatican II. Something of their kind can be faced by any incoming pastor, along with confrontations with traditionalists who want Saint Pius resurrected.

Parish priests have a lot of leeway within the present guidelines about the number of and training of ministers; the access of laity to pulpit, altar, or tabernacle; and the quality of the music. Pastors, particularly, are responsible for the conduct of their clergy, even for visitors, especially the Speedy Gonzales types, or the Father Turtles. There is no reason why people have to be regularly inflicted with either kind. If the parish is burdened with a priest (or priests) who speak English (or the native language) badly, it is his task to circumvent the problem, even if he is a pretty bad preacher himself.

One other aspect of worship requires the careful pastoral eye: the timing and frequency of administering other sacraments within the Mass. Since Vatican II, it is not uncommon for baptism, confirmation, matrimony, and the last anointing to take place then, sometimes only then. However, sound pastoral judgment is recommended. Many parishioners have come to resent baptism administered at their convenient Sunday Mass. If young children at home interferes with parents' attendance at another Mass, they can be further annoyed having to listen to baptismal sermons Sunday after Sunday. Such sacraments should be administered on Sunday outside the normal schedule, or on special occasions with well-promulgated advance announcement.

Returning to that *General Instruction on the Roman Missal* (1970), it is important for priests to study what it says about biblical readings, how they are to take place, about gestures and bodily postures, about the importance of singing, how altars are to be adorned, about sacred images in the Church, vestments and vessels, and Communion under both species. In 1980, the Vatican issued *Inestimabile Donum*, dealing mainly with abuses that had developed since the Council — laity sharing the recitation of the Eucharistic Prayer, laity giving homilies, distributing Communion "while priests refrain from doing so," abandonment of vestments by priests, the use of private texts, unapproved Eucharistic Prayers and manipulating the liturgy for sociopolitical ends. People deserved better, the Congregation said, so it behooves pastors to review these and other Roman documents available in *Vatican Two: The Conciliar and Post-Conciliar Documents* (Costello Publishing Co.). *Inestimabile Donum* concludes with a prayer of Paul VI: "In the name of tradition we ask all our sons and daughters, all the Catholic communities, to celebrate with dignity and fervor the renewed liturgy."

John Paul II on Worship

Many other things continue to be said today about the way our present liturgy is being conducted, frequently by those who think it is wonderful, and by those as well who think the reforms have been a disaster. For the purpose of this book, private opinions are irrelevant. We are only interested in the best worship the Church can offer. In such matters priests should follow the leadership of one who is recognized as a model of first-rate liturgical performance and an authoritative voice on the subject — John Paul II. The twenty-fifth anniversary of Vatican II's *Constitution on the Liturgy* (December 4, 1988) became the occasion for the present pontiff to draft "Guidelines for the Renewal of Liturgical Life" (see *Origins*, May 25, 1989, for the text). The following are his main directions:

1. "No other readings may supplant the biblical word." These words were intended to remind everyone, pastors especially, that they were not to substitute readings from *Time* magazine, or any other secular source, for the Word of God.

2. "It is not permitted to anyone, even the priest or any group, to add, subtract or change anything whatsoever." For example, omitting the Creed on Sunday, or retranslating the scripture, or tampering with the bread or wine, etc.

3. "Ministers … do that and only that which is proper to them." This monitum was directed against the use of laity, even of religious women, as homilists during Mass.

4. "Desired simplicity must not degenerate into an impoverishment of signs." Bread and wine, water and oil, incense and ashes, fire and flowers add to the beauty of the Liturgy, the pope said.

5. Postures or songs which are not conducive to the faith, abuses in the practice of general absolution, confusion about the ordained priesthood, composing private Eucharistic prayers, etc., are to be eliminated by bishops.

6. Popular devotions and pious exercises are to be encouraged, especially in our time when they may be treated with indifference, perhaps contempt.

Visits to the Blessed Sacrament

As the Second Vatican Council was drawing near its final session (July 1965) a world-famous German theologian made his first visit to New York City and to Saint Patrick's Cathedral. The hour was nine o'clock on a balmy summer evening. We entered from Madison Avenue through the back door, and by the time we reached the main altar all four priests were amazed by the size of the crowd, at least seven hundred people there in various degrees of piety. The theologian was impressed: "I would not see such piety in Germany," to which one of us rejoined jokingly: "We knew you were coming, so we arranged this just for you." Many visitors, of course, were moseying their way through a big city attraction, but that night, as we stood in the middle aisle, we saw much more than that. There, scattered all through the pews, were hundreds of worshipers in various stages of contemplation. Catholics, hushed in their silence, were alone with their God, some saying the Rosary, some making Stations of the Cross, but most just kneeling or simply sitting staring at the Tabernacle. Before the night was over, we visited another church nearby, an architectural beauty and much more polished. But empty.

The difference was the presence of the Blessed Sacrament. Believing Catholics know that difference. Indeed, a measure of the depth of the Catholic faith is the extent of devotion to Christ in the Eucharist. Most priests today are aware of the recent decline in this form of piety. This is the result, in part, of false theories propagated about the Eucharist, assumptions made by liturgical amateurs that the Council downgraded such pieties, or simply because parish priests, in metropolitan areas particularly, demonstrated a lack of creativity in keeping their churches open and safe at hours convenient for such prayer, particularly after work and in the early evening. One imaginative pastor arranged the electronic bells in his belfry to play each night "When You Come To The End of a Perfect Day" every fifteen minutes between 5:00 P.M. and 6:30 P.M. He was inviting his people to visit their Lord as they passed the Church on their walk from the local railroad station.

The *General Instruction on the Roman Missal* encourages Reservation of the Blessed Sacrament "in a preeminent place" so that "the faithful may easily, fruitfully, and constantly honor the Lord, present in the Sacrament, through personal worship." Simply because the Tabernacle is no longer present on the altar of worship (a proposal that makes sense) is no reason to "hide" the reserved Sacrament or to refer to it as "Eucharistic bread," as some mistaken innovators do. Few priests of long experience, or properly trained, have confined reservation to a niche or in a dark corner of the parish church. Yet, younger priests, cowed by a liturgical purist from a Church bureau, can be talked into a "hiding place" to preserve what they consider the primacy of public participation over passive reservation. Good sense and Christian tradition suggest, as worthy places for private adoration, a side chapel, a side altar, or beautifully carved tabernacle permanently affixed to a pedestal in the body of the church.

However, the *"situs"* becomes irrelevant if the parish priest does not provide ample opportunity for assemblies of the faithful which include Benediction of the Blessed Sacrament or which honor Christ on Corpus Christi Day, during Forty Hours' Devotion, and during periodic occasions of Nocturnal Adoration.

Special Considerations About the Eucharist

1. The obligation of assisting at Sunday Mass is a serious one and Catholics should be reminded of its gravity. Part of the decline in Mass attendance is due to the false view, circulated after the Council, that such worship was a matter of personal choice. Pastors ought to sieze every opportunity they can to reassert the obligation and the reasons why it is serious. Old-timers had that sense. Many years ago, an immigrant lady named Rosa went to her school hall for reorientation in the methodology of the new catechism, then being introduced for the religious education

of her children. She found out that the new message was to be positive, that God was to be seen as loving, who does not get mad at children if they lie, cheat, hit their brothers or sisters, or miss Sunday Mass. At an appropriate moment, Rosa, with her heavy Italian accent, stood up to tell the nuns: "Okay, God don't get mad at my kids if they do wrong, He don't get mad if they miss Mass. My kids miss Mass, I'll break their necks!" Rosa was surely not amused by the new catechesis.

2. Ordained married deacons may, of course, preach at a Sunday Mass, but the pastor must be sure of their qualifications for that role, particularly if the worshipers belong to a minority group. The same counsel applies to the choice of lectors and/or commentators. Lay persons and religious are forbidden to preach during Mass, except in liturgies for children when a competent catechist may be chosen at the discretion of the priest. Non-clerics may be called upon at special events (e.g., funerals, religious celebrations) to deliver a short address, preferably before Mass or after the post-Communion prayer. It is presumed that the person so chosen is recognized for the probity of his life.

3. Communion under both species is a fuller sign of Christ's real presence, commonplace today at ordinations, nuptial Masses, etc.; but this occurs at the discretion of the pastor who must estimate the difficulties of such Communions when the assembly is large.

4. Churchgoing Catholics should understand that for sufficient reason (e.g., public officials) they may attend Eastern Orthodox liturgical functions, even read lessons there, and fulfill their Sunday obligations, too; Eastern Orthodox may receive the Catholic sacraments of penance, the Eucharist and anointing, if they ask for them and have the right dispositions. Catholics may attend Protestant services occasionally for equally good reasons, but may not take Communion there. Protestants may not read the scripture in the Catholic liturgy, nor preach, nor be admitted to the Eucharist, since they are not in full Communion with the Catholic Church and, as a general rule, have not the Catholic sense of the Eucharist. Members of Reformation Church communities may read scripture or preach at services other than Mass. However, if a particular Protestant, in danger of death or in another grave necessity, manifests proper faith and is disposed, also separated from his own minister, and spontaneously requests penance, the Eucharist or the anointing, he or she may receive such. A Catholic, in similar circumstances, may not ask for sacraments from a Protestant minister. (Canonical authorities of the Orthodox Churches forbid non-Orthodox [e.g., Catholics] to receive sacraments during their liturgies.)

5. The worthy reception of the sacraments must be a matter of real concern to those parish priests in tune with the Church's faith, of which they are the guardians. Other Christians have demonstrated a noticeable interest in the Catholic Eucharist, and some priests have taken a tolerant view of its reception by those who do not believe in the Real Presence, sometimes by unbelievers. Less serious, but fraught with dangers to Catholic realism in its sacramental worship, is the practice encouraged by some pastors who have ushers line laity up for Communion row by row, equivalently taking free choice out of the hands of parishioners or visitors. It is a practice once banned by the Holy See for convents and monasteries. The Catholic discipline leaves "taking Communion" a move of laity, even if the lack of tidiness disturbs martinets. Catholics with a conscientious sense of their own unworthiness ought not be "forced" to follow a crowd on such a sacred matter. Such orderliness is less necessary than ever in the era of Eucharistic ministers. Doctrine prevails over order.

Chapter Seven

Matrimony: A Sacrament for Family Life

Let us reverence the Lord Jesus, whose blood was shed for us.

Let us respect those in authority. Let us honor the presbyters.

Let us train the young in fear of God. Let us lead our wives toward all that is good, Let them show by their conduct that they are lovers of chastity;

By their gentleness let them reveal a pure and sincere disposition;

By their silence let them manifest the control they have over their tongues;

Let them bestow an equal charity, without respect for persons, on all who have a holy fear of God.

Your children must share in the way of discipleship in Christ.

— Saint Clement, Third Pope after Saint Peter

Good parish priests have a larger family than anyone else in the neighborhood — without benefit of marriage. "To be a member of each family yet belonging to none" was not just Lacordaire's classic prayer, it explains the satisfaction of the happy priest. Except for the joys accruing from his priestly companions, it is through families, even the broken ones, that he finds fulfillment and, as he grows older, his best memories.

My most memorable day perhaps was the Second Sunday of January, 1960 (Feast of the Holy Family), when seven hundred fifty couples assembled in New York's Saint Patrick's Cathedral to celebrate their fiftieth wedding anniversaries with Cardinal Francis Spellman. Mostly aged Italian couples, they left the old country at the turn of the century, changed one kind of poverty for another, yet stayed together to become parents of large families. This particular Sunday, which henceforth would be known as Catholic Family Day, brought several score relatives with each jubilee pair, so that more than ten thousand Italian-Americans congregated all over the aisles of the Cathedral and the streets all around. The police could hardly restrain the crowds, and some jubilarians never received their parchment from the Cardinal (that day at least), because they could not manage passage through the barricades. The service was a sight to behold — one couple after another coming to the altar, looking like a million dollars, those onetime barbers, shoemakers, street cleaners, grocers, and their overtaxed wives of unusual culinary skill, who made it out of the ghetto, and still turned their children into practicing Catholics. Their respect and reverence, as some strove to get down on their knees, touched every onlooker. The year was notable, too, because the Church's family life apostolate across the United States was never better, and for many young Catholics in that Cathedral, marriage itself was looked upon as a religious adventure.

That Catholic Family Day also had its funny side. For example, there was the Italian gentleman who called so often to secure his seats, that he was asked a question: How come so many Italians and so few Irish were to attend? His answer was as good as his accent: "You see, it's this way. Irish papas and Italian papas left the old country about the same time, and spent their young years fighting some boss all day just to make a living. But, then the Irish papa had to go home to fight the wife all night, and he dies at sixty. But in my house I'm the boss, and I'm still here!"

The two sacraments, ordained *per se* for the stability and well-being of the Church, are those that create the office of the priesthood and the office of motherhood (the literal meaning of the word "matrimony"). The priesthood provides the hierarchy, matrimony provides the people. One is closely associated with the "big Church" because its membership are the shepherds, those who teach, rule, and sanctify the flock; the other is the flock itself, what popes have called "the little Church." The well-being of both Churches is deeply interrelated for the good of all, especially when cultural conditions are ill. Both Churches are in serious trouble when the hirelings among the shepherds abandon their people to the wolves of the world. Both Churches are also debilitated when married couples pay little or no attention to the Vicar of Christ, or to a local Curé of Ars: by diminishing or denigrating motherhood, by walking away from each other in favor of other sexual partners; by infidelity while married; by cohabiting, as if married, without benefit of sacramental blessing; by neglect of the worship of God to whom they allege faith; by rearing children in a totally ungodly atmosphere; by killing in the womb a child given them by God as the fruit of their sacramental love and a gift of his providence; by indifference to or disrespect for the preachments of the Church which pertain to their eternal salvation and their well-being; and that of society itself.

Mother Church, to say nothing of secular society at any time, has through centuries worked hard at promoting or stabilizing the office of motherhood. The attraction of fleshy pleasures, of riches and the devil's temptations to status, power, and self-aggrandizement often end up as anti-motherhood forces. The Church in the United States early on experienced difficulty getting its immigrant Catholics to marry properly. The first Catholic foundling hospitals and child-caring agencies, were evidence enough of the shaky family situation of those days. But by World War II, the Church had succeeded in tipping the public scale in favor of the Christian way of life. The overwhelming majority of Catholics were married by the priest, remained married, on the average had four children who were fully educated Catholic, worshiped God regularly, demonstrated remarkable piety, and built the most remarkable network of Catholic institutions in the history of Christendom, staffed by their children (those who became priests and nuns).

In those years parish priests did find youngsters living together without benefit of marriage, a girl here or there confessing to an abortion; they found broken homes, drunken fathers, neglectful mothers, non-churchgoers, and a share of outrageous teenagers. But these were contrasts to everyday stability, evidence only of our moral weakness, about which even the sinners were not boastful. Parish priests carried such people on their backs, as they gave support to the vast majority trying to measure up to the norms of the Church, assistance considered necessary for those who carried the daily burden of motherhood. Indeed, motherhood was as important to the Church as it was to the family, an office without which fathers of the "little" or "big" Church faded into minor significance.

The Present State of the World

It is hard to believe that the day would come when priests and nuns might tell Catholics they were not sinning by violating Catholic sacramental and moral norms, or inculcate an attitude among the young, often in Catholic classrooms, that these norms were irrelevant to the choices they made in life, especially about marriage. Few priests then ever expected to see so many young Catholics living together unmarried; or married without a priest; divorcing without concern for the sacramental consequences; so many small-sized families, so many Catholics favoring abortion; many regularly absent from Sunday Mass; others approaching the altar for Holy Communion without the sacramental absolution demanded by their way of life.

These considerations are important to mention so as to the scope of the contemporary pastor's marital and premarital problems in many parishes today, and to encourage priests to make the family a primary object of their apostolate.

These matters must be placed in context, however. Being a good Catholic Christian in any culture is never easy, whether he or she lives in a prosperous country or a poor one. Christ warned about the dangers of being well-to-do and told the rich to uplift the poor. He told his followers, including the poor, to bear the crosses of life, but didn't demand that they go out looking for pain or become masochists. Not surprisingly, Catholic countries are usually considered fun-loving, their people partygoers, as readily as any hedonists. On the other hand, the party-going courtesans of Henry and Louis XIV were no great shakes as Catholics, even though they usually carried their religion on their sleeves. Today those Hanover or Bourbon kings would be bedazzled by the prosperity enjoyed by modernity's pious Catholics who enjoy freedom, as well as comfort, of which old royalty never dreamed. Enjoy, that is, as long as they keep the scales of Christian life tipped in the right direction (holiness here, salvation later), and as long as the world, or the flesh, or the devil, do not become their gods.

It is the responsibility of parish priests to remind parishioners of these Christian priorities, to support those who earnestly struggle to maintain faith and virtue, and to uplift those who fall from grace and faith, particularly the ones seemingly overburdened. Amidst a Protestant culture, Catholic pastors had a difficult time protecting their poor, and poorly instructed flock, although the culture, dour as it was, was reasonably Christian. The secularist culture is far more dangerous because it is anti-Christian as well as anti-Catholic, and appeals to the senses with unshamed abandon. Because motherhood of itself is a painful process, the whole idea of matrimony has become a special stumbling block to those who walk under the Enlightenment banner — less and less understood as a holy institution of God, hardly as a lifelong vocation whose purpose includes bearing children and rearing them to become saints. The anti-child mentality, endemic to hedonism, is firmly anti-motherhood, and eventually anti-life. The secular state now has acquired the function of socializing its citizens to be pro-choice about love, about spouses, and sexuality, and to quarantine any church which dares preach otherwise.

The Work of the Church

The Second Vatican Council eased certain restrictions on who can be married and how, but nothing in its declarations has altered in any substantial way what Christ had to say about marriage, sex, and family life. The Decree which set up the New Rite of Marriage (July 1, 1969) goes out of its way to say:

"By their very nature, the institution of matrimony and wedded love are ordained for the procreation and education of children and find in them their ultimate crown. Therefore, married Christians, while not considering the other purposes of marriage of less account, should be steadfast and ready to cooperate with the love of the Creator and Savior, who through them will constantly enrich and enlarge His own family."

The Decree goes on to say that matrimony presupposes and demands faith, and priests are told to tailor their instructions accordingly.

The Church's new *Code of Canon Law* (cns. 1063-1165) restates what is required of parish priests (and bishops) to see that those who enter the state of matrimony are free to marry, that they have the right intentions, that they exchange consent without coercion, in the presence of the proper minister, and that the marriage, so entered, is sacramental and indissoluble. Pastors are called upon then to lend support to couples' efforts to sustain their love, to accept parenthood lovingly, to grow in holiness and to give service to the outer community, the Church included.

The parish priest's first duty, therefore, is to investigate the couple's freedom, and state of mind, prior to the arrangements for a wedding. Formal investigations of this kind began a few years before World War II because the informal practices of an earlier period appeared to be unrealistic. Even a half-century ago, Catholics were known to approach the sacrament of matrimony with less than full Catholic conviction on marital unity, indissolubility, and parenthood. But, because the problems were minuscule then, the premarital investigations were routine, almost informal in comparison to the more thorough investigations expected today. Priests are understandably embarrassed by prying, and there are few "bully-boys" in the priesthood, but modern youth are accustomed to being investigated, so wide is the distrust by corporate and government leaders of people's veracity. Critics of clergy try to insist that celibates are incompetent for this task, but those who say this are often in a second marriage which some priest originally opposed, or are those who no longer care for any direction from the Church on how to be married. Practicing Catholics, on the contrary, having little to hide, would normally take a priest's inquiry in stride. The alienated and those with things to hide, however, can be counted on to give priests a hard time and to build within themselves additional resentments against the Church. Still the process must be carried forward because the validity and sacredness of the common life are at stake. A given pastor, of course, may have his parish difficulties compounded by a confrere in the next parish, or even in the chancery office, who is slipshod in their methods or because their faith in Church teaching or its policies is less than firm.

The parish priest, true to his calling, should expect no better treatment than what Christ received from his disciples when he spoke on marriage. It was Christ, after all, another celibate, who spoke as from God, about "two in one flesh, about monogamy, about indissolubility, of the adultery involved in marrying another man's wife, of lusting in the heart (another form of adultery), of the sinfulness of evil thoughts" (see Matthew 5). Where did Saint Paul obtain the idea but *from Christ* that fornication and homosexual activities were foreign to the demands of

Christ's Kingdom? Why did the early Church (long before there was a Vatican) demand public penance, lasting a lifetime, for sins against marriage, including abortion, if these were not grave offenses against Christ's own moral norms? So, when the priest speaks on marriage or pursues Church protective policies in its behalf, he is not transmitting human traditions created by *ignoranti*, but God's word revealed through the prophets of the Old Testament, through Christ, and today through those bishops in union with the pope.

The second concern of the parish priest is to see that Church procedures for contracting a valid and licit marriage become the norm of parish behavior.

Once upon a time every priest presumptively knew what was required for the validity and licitly of a marriage, and that the Catholic school system had effectively provided young laity with the ABC's of marriage readiness. Recently, however, the varieties of sacramental practice from parish to parish, and the fact that most Catholics are educated in public schools, make assumptions questionable. Marital procedures, therefore, take on new importance. They represent the Church's caution about a sacred rite, and about the most fundamental human experience vital to the well-being of family and nation. Young people occasionally think that they can walk into a rectory and be married simply for the asking. They could not buy an automobile with such ease. Still, unspoken reasons may explain their haste, not the least of which is the trivialization of marriage itself, which they have imbibed from their surroundings. With no-fault divorce so common, "until death do us part" has become something of a joke to many Americans, including certain young Catholics.

In the Catholic scheme of things, therefore, the norms are still as firm as the professed faith: marriage ordinarily must take place in a church, never in a secular setting, rarely at home, and in a college chapel only for a student; the priest (occasionally a non-Catholic minister) must have the proper faculties, and he must have in his possession the proper documents (new baptismal record, first Communion and confirmation papers, death certificate [if necessary], etc.); all regulations for mixed marriages (which now take place in church) must be observed, especially the need for a bishop's dispensation from canonical impediments or from the Catholic form of marriage. Hardly anyone, especially a priest, is ignorant of the civil requirements, including the need for a marriage license.

Most dioceses also have special norms for celebrating teenage marriages, in large part because at least half of such marriages end in divorce, at a higher rate when the girl is pregnant. Smaller dioceses have evaluation programs for these situations, but metropolitan dioceses, because of the sheer variety of their dense populations, place the burden of deciding whether to proceed with such a wedding on parish priests. In these cases parental consent may be necessary but, even with that in hand, parish priests are sometimes advised by the bishop to refuse marriage where they judge the couple to be immature or otherwise incompetent, emotionally or socially. In a few cases permission to marry must be sought from the bishop, who may insist that a diocesan counselor interview the couple in advance of any decision on his part.

Few observers are confident that anyone far from the scene can make a judgment better than the interested and competent parish priest, unless the case involves a psychopath or a sociopath. In normal situations not even a psychotherapist can make a certain or credible judgment about the stability of a new marriage. So, the buck usually stops with the priest involved, especially if he clears with the pastor any decision he has in mind. The presumption is, of course, that the priest has done his "homework" by an in-depth investigation, a term advisedly chosen to suggest something more than a single interview.

Experienced priests often have their judgments against Catholic marriage vindicated by the breakup of a subsequent civil marriage; the ability of one party to a risky mating to make an impossible dream work demonstrates on occasion that even the best priest is not infallible. In a big city, couples are free to go shopping until they find a "compassionate" priest, one who may believe that saying "yes" to people is what the word "Christian" means. Sometimes, these interloping clerics, no more prophetic than the proper pastor, do more harm than good by administering a sacrament, like marriage, to very doubtful candidates. As long as the priest saying "no" is warm, tactful, and intelligent in his reasoning, he leaves the candidates themselves with the option of making their own mistakes and to recover in time, if that is what destiny has in store for them. But the priest should not be — and he should tell them so — a party to almost certain disaster, when all the extant evidence indicates a further testing period is necessary before a prudent Catholic marriage can be undertaken. Naturally, one presumes that pastors in a common neighborhood agree that "poaching" on other parishes' parishioners is the wrong, and improper, thing to do. This danger exists especially when national and territorial parishes intersect.

Two extremes of priestly behavior are to be avoided. One is carelessness, an old failing of a minority of priests in bygone days, men who handled marriages like they said Mass: in fifteen minutes, no more, no less. But younger priests can be careless, too, by overestimating the value of dialogue in reaching tough decisions. A young fiancé with a substantial jail record, a teenage girl with a drug habit, an average candidate for marriage who cannot produce a baptismal certificate (the church burned down, he says), strong opposition from one or both parents to a teenage marriage, alleged anti-Catholicism in a non-Catholic, firm positions favoring contraception and/or divorce — these are formidable objections to any putative Christian marriage. Patient listening over many hours may put everyone at ease, and the couple may feel good about their treatment by the priest, but long chatter does not change anyone's character, nor convert chronic liars, nor alter facts. The priest is the guardian of a holy thing, and he must be choosy, if sacramental reality is to be preserved. One of the dangers in our culture is that subjective feelings, or seeming good will, or agreeability, triumph over truth and right. In the last analysis, young moderns have been well-taught that they are their own gods.

At all times, however, the priest must remember that couples of marriageable age, however silly, foolish, uneducated, weak, or impious, have a natural right to marry, whose legitimate requests may be denied or delayed only for the gravest reasons, by reason of incontrovertible negative evidence, supported by witnesses, if that is necessary. Only in these latter cases may a priest substitute his judgment for theirs and, then, he must have the courage to make it.

Thirdly, primary responsibility for preparing an engaged couple for the Catholic married state devolves on the pastor, or on his associate, or on a priest whom either may delegate, or on all three, as the case may be.

This responsibility cannot be passed on to a committee, to a conference, not even to the diocese. A responsible priest must give the couple his time, his counsel, and his judgment. This does not mean that instruction classes, pre-Cana conferences, and their like, are not helpful. Fiancés should be encouraged to attend them, all circumstances making this a reasonable request on the part of the priest. This proviso is necessary only because failure to attend class is not an impediment to Catholic marriage. Some priests would make it seem so. But, however strong the priest's insistence on class instruction may be, especially for the truly ignorant or the badly catechized, he must remember that one or the other parties may have a work schedule (e.g., police, firefighters, etc.) that makes attendance all but impossible. Also, there are fully educated and practicing Catholics, some even with appropriate theological degrees, who should be dispensed or excused, if they insist, from lectures intended for the less enlightened. The priest has a touchier problem when he makes himself available for personal instruction at their convenience, and they still resist instruction. Such refusal may indicate irreversible bad will toward reasonable marriage preparation.

There are other things good parish priests must also keep in mind, such as the parochial support priests give couples after the wedding.

Present-Day Dangers in Catechesis

Historically, the Church has had trouble protecting its Catholic couples from the world around them. Contemporary parish priests, however, must also identify the places within his diocese where solid teaching goes on. Some Catholic programs are high on psychology, but low on doctrine; long on techniques of communication and personal encounter, but short on conviction about sacramental unity, indissolubility, fruitfulness. When "hot" subjects come up for discussion in these centers — babies, contraception, working mothers, marital roles — they may be treated, but once over lightly at best. Respect for Church teaching may be recommended, but maturity and conscientiousness in decision-making may also be stressed, even when such judgments patently contravene Catholic teaching on matters essential for a valid marriage. In more than a few Catholic circles conscience is offered as the final arbiter of faith and morals. Sins against marriage, or the need to avoid such sins because when freely chosen they are almost always mortal (or disqualify the couple from the reception of the Eucharist), are scarcely mentioned in some conferences.

It is also well established that many diocesan teachers of the young are themselves contraceptive users, or already have been sterilized, and thereby are incapable of reflecting in their lives Catholic teaching on chastity.

When these reminders of the contemporary status quo come to ecclesial attention, parish priests not infrequently face denials of facts from their peers or superiors. But poll after poll does show that Catholics, especially the younger generation, do not "think with the Church" on sexual and marital morality. Our people seem to have given up saying

121

"no, no" to the contemporary culture's passion for passion. We hear little in our conferences about the dangers inherent to couples living as if married, though single; of the difficulty in sterility or of small families; little about complementary roles for husbands of wives in family life; or about the intrinsic relationship of contraception to abortion and divorce; or about the virtues of homemaking, of the large family, of asceticism. These are the integral elements in any Catholic package called "marriage preparation."

Last, but not least, is the parish priest's responsibility for the proper celebration of the nuptial liturgy.

"Proper celebration" means "sacred celebration." In former days the quintessence of secularity meant a red rug down the middle aisle, with the hymn of the day from someone imitating Perry Como singing "Because." The present ritual calls upon priests to nourish the couple's faith *first*. And he can do this, in part at the rehearsal, when he explains the symbols and the elements in the ceremony from the first "giveaway" by Dad to Father's final blessing. The adornment of the church, the tastefulness of the appointments, the demeanor of the celebrant, and the homily also reinforce the Catholic marriage, when each is fittingly addressed. The importance of the state of grace and the availability of confession, perhaps at rehearsal time, is stressed. (Some priests are careless about this — not mentioning the subject at all or dispensing general absolution after rehearsal, as if it were his personal gift to the couple.) While the liturgy is drama, it is not theater. Therefore music or conduct suitable for a nightclub or jazz concert is proscribed, regardless of requests to the contrary. During the homily, the priest might keep in mind the specific questions raised by the Church in the nuptial rite — about love, honor and respect, about indissolubility and children, about right intention, patience, fortitude, and piety. Love in marriage is not the end of marriage, but hopefully will remain its driving force, especially if it includes the will to honor the purposes God has in mind when he called this groom and this bride to be of one flesh.

The Parish Family Apostolate

Young Catholics cannot be expected to go the Church's way on family life without support and reinforcement from the parish. "Everyone does it" is a powerful social force of hurricane proportions. So the witness of a "couple apostolate" is critical, the kind of leadership and

122

example once given by those who were affectionately called "Cana couples." If social activism is the specific witness of laity, energized by Vatican II, the family apostolate holds primacy of place. (More on this later.)

Five years after the first Catholic Family Day in many dioceses, a bishop prayed over people shortly to appear before God in judgment:

"You, our golden jubilarians here today, witness in your own lives the truth that marriage best fulfills itself when it is lived under God and for God. It was by harmonizing your will and God's will that you achieved the contentment and the joy that today are yours."

Amen.

Chapter Eight

The Parish Priest and *Humanae Vitae*

Since, therefore, openly departing from the uninterrupted tradition some recently have judged it possible solemnly to declare another doctrine regarding this question, the Catholic Church to whom God has entrusted the defense of the integrity and purity of morals, standing erect in the midst of moral ruin which surrounds her, in order that she may preserve the chastity of the nuptial union from being defiled by this foul stain, raises her voice in token of the divine ambassadorship and through Our mouth proclaims anew: any use whatsoever of matrimony exercised in such a way that the act is deliberately frustrated in its natural power to generate life is an offense against the law of God and of nature, and those who indulge in such are branded with the guilt of a grave sin.

— Pius XI, *Casti Connubii*

From time immemorial, going back to the earliest days of Christianity, the Church has condemned as sinful all contraceptive practices, in and out of marriage. Paul VI in 1968 only reiterated the doctrine stated earlier by Pius XI, who in strong language affirmed the constant teachings of all Christian churches up to 1930.

Indeed, rejection of contraception as immoral goes back to Old Testament times, and far beyond the example of Onan (see Deuteronomy 25:5-10), which revisionist historians today tend to discount. In 1964, when the contraception controversy within Catholic circles was at its height, the American Broadcasting Corporation (ABC) was interested in a panel discussion of the subject by three representatives of the Judeo-Christian tradition. The rabbinical scholar refused to participate with a Greek Orthodox priest and his Catholic counterpart, because he was persuaded that the Catholic Church was about to abandon that rejection.

The rabbi was wrong, of course, but contemporary Catholic priests well know today that universal acceptance of that teaching, even by priests, no longer exists.

To cite one example: a pastor in upstate New York, one who was ordained after Vatican II but before *Humanae Vitae*, in 1992 used his column in the weekly parish bulletin to provide his people with moral guidance on birth control. This is what he wrote:

"The Church looks with disfavor on artificial methods of birth control (contraception) because these methods interfere with a natural process, and may be injurious to the health of a woman. Ideally, Catholics ought to be able to use Natural Family Planning to determine the size of their family. In my opinion, so long as a couple are willing to discuss these factors honestly and prayerfully and come to a mutually agreeable decision, they may make a morally acceptable choice, even if that choice involves contraception. Of course, should circumstances change, the discussion must be renewed, and the decision reviewed.

"In short, I believe it is possible for a couple to practice contraception and continue to receive Holy Communion, without any sin being involved, as long as their lines of communication with God and each other remain open."

The Church Fathers, like the rabbis before them, wrestled from the earliest days with contraception within marriage. Examine closely what is being said on this subject by priests in many places, and relate their counsel, from the Church's viewpoint, to other moral issues:

For the words "married couple" in the parish bulletin substitute "Christian," and replace the word "contraception" by any of the following expressions:

- Abortion by a pregnant woman
- Funding abortions by a Catholic governor
- Taking graft by a politician
- Doing violence on a picket line
- Dropping an A-Bomb on Baghdad
- Withholding food and water from a dying parent
- And so forth.

Using this priest's rationale, anyone's subjective evaluation of his or her own circumstances, following his private consultation with God, renders licit whatever decision he or she reaches in the process. Under this rationale no law of God binds everyone under all circumstance. The Church, too, becomes irrelevant to the conscience formation process.

Paul VI on Contraception

Sections 11 and 12 of *Humanae Vitae* contain the teaching of the Church on birth regulation: "The Church calling men back to the observance of the norms of the natural law, as interpreted by their constant doctrine, teaches that each and every act must remain open to the transmission of life. The teaching, often set forth by the Magisterium, is founded upon the inseparable connection, willed by God and unable to be broken by man on his own initiative, between the two meanings of the conjugal act: the unitive meaning and the procreative meaning." Paul VI went on to predict the harmful personal and social effects of contraceptive practice — lower moral standards, lower status for women, abortion, government interference in family life, and so forth. Time has proven him right. His explication of what may be called "the mind of a Christian" must be understood and accepted by parish priests. The evil of contraception must be seen within the entire context of Christian love of God for his creatures. There are five special considerations to keep in mind.

1. The sanctity of human life. *Humanae Vitae* reminds us all that human life is unique. Every human being is a person whom the world has never seen before and will never see again, one whom God himself wants to live with him for all eternity, an individual empowered by his special nature to build new worlds and transform the one into which he was born. Because of who they are in God's sight, the act that brings

them into existence involves cooperation by a man and a woman with God and his creative power, he who alone can vivify an immortal person. Thereby this act of procreation acquires a sacredness that may never be denied.

Why does one think the Church, from her Semitic and Roman days, has been preoccupied with abortion and euthanasia? Why has she taken care of infants born so malformed that they never reach mental maturity in this life? Why has her social doctrine been so concerned with helping people live in the conditions worthy of their Godlike dignity? Why is she so preoccupied with the terrorizing weapons of war that obliterate millions of citizens by a single act?

Humanae Vitae is the Church's recall of humankind to the Christian sense of Godlike dignity in every human being and in the act of married love by which God brings him into existence.

2. The sacredness of sex. *Humanae Vitae* reminds the world that sexual behavior may not be cut off from its relationship to the origin of human life. Sex has more than one role in the life of men and women — as something joyful, as an experience of marital unity, as a celebration of God's love of the family, and of Christ's love of the Church. Once separated from its profound procreative meaning (the relationship it has to human life's very beginnings) it becomes an end in itself, something God did not have in mind. What would be wrong, then, with single people enjoying its pleasures as a matter of right? Wrong with commercializing it on stage and in films so that the world, any world, might savor its delight? Wrong with pornography? With homosexuality? With abortion? *Humanae Vitae* recalls mankind to the intrinsic reason for sexuality — to procreate with God new human beings — his choice, as much as that of the couple.

3. God's "Thou shalt nots." *Humanae Vitae* reminds humankind that, in a world known for its shifting values, certain moral norms hold true, now as in the past, in all places and circumstances, and will still hold true on Judgment Day. Many things once considered worthwhile are no longer held in high esteem. The modern urge for the good life, for ease, comfort, pleasure, or self-fulfillment, has fractured old ways of doing things. Although worn-out customs may go, and sometimes should, truth and right always remain what they are — the basis of human life, written into human nature by God. Some of these have been proclaimed by prophets of old like Moses, some by Christ in the new dispensation, and after him by Peter and Paul, by the Fathers of the Church, and popes

from Pentecost onward. The easy life is nice to have, but it also leads men to give up what they believe in, and to forget their moral responsibilities — at a price. The old saying is that God always forgives, nature never, has the ring of truth for those who tamper with its laws.

Humanae Vitae reminds men and women that God wants his laws obeyed, that what seems easiest is not always best, that God's grace enables us to live up to his norms, even when it requires great effort. Impartial observers, with the faith of the Church still present, recognize how easily sex becomes safe sex, and later unsafe sex — for the young, for couples themselves, for the unborn, and for American society, now that it is awash with unrestrained violence often-times rooted in unrestrained sex.

4. God's very life. *Humanae Vitae* reminds us that the Holy Spirit dwells in the lives of those who accept his presence. This we call "the state of grace." It is real; it is also a supernatural power. Do we really believe this? Paul VI appealed to Christ's promises of the Spirit, once made to Peter and the apostles, as energizing still the faith and conduct of modern believers. The pope knew that Catholics, whose lives are built on faith in things not fully seen by everyone, sensed God's presence, even when the world had something more superficially attractive to offer, or provided a simpler but wrong solution to a human problem. The outsider, looking at a consecrated host without the eyes of faith, misses the true reality that is there; someone speaking to Jesus in Jerusalem never, on his own, saw him as God's beloved son; a skeptic at a baptismal font with a babe in her arms does not visualize the child's newly acquired grace; the trapped thief could not believe Christ had the power to save him at that last minute. Yet the knowledge that comes with faith brings gifts of hope in and love of God, who loves us more than we love him, even when he asks us to share a cross with Christ. His assurance that God's ways are the best ways, in this as in all other things, is enough.

Humanae Vitae looks beyond the surface view of things to the divine truth beneath the daily tasks of those who live in this no-abiding time.

5. The love of neighbor. *Humanae Vitae* is a sharp reminder that every Christian must be concerned about every other human being. People may have problems, and the teaching of the encyclical does make hard demands on some of them. It is not enough for pastors, or anybody, to consider only fruitful marriage a problem, or to ignore the marital and social difficulties to ensue from a widespread contraceptive mentality. If

Catholics can eliminate or relieve undue burdens on their neighbors with better information, economic assistance, spiritual guidance, support of the sacraments, or with sympathy or concern where there is no simple answer, they are so bound.

Humanae Vitae is the Church's call for believers to walk through life with faith in their creator, hope in their Redeemer, and in the love expressed by the Spirit with those less fortunate, and the practical steps to uplift the needy in marriage.

Chastity Is Charity

Chastity received an ugly meaning from warped Christians who, believing that mankind's original sin was sexual, looked down upon all sexual pleasure; charity's bad name came in the nineteenth century to describe people as "bleeding hearts," who gave their money to idlers, fakers, and others of the world's unworthies. In reality, *castitas* and *caritas* are solid Christian virtues, positive assets to the good life, and closely interrelated in meaning. *Caritas* is another word for "unselfish love" and *castitas* is the equivalent of "pure love." Both terms are two aspects of the same virtue. "See these Christians how they have love for one another," was an accolade from a heathen source, remarking on the uniqueness of their alms-giving, and also of the lifestyle of New Testament virgins and widows, husbands and wives, deacons and presbyters, a way of living far removed from the licentiousness of their pagan surroundings. Early on in his ministry, Jesus Christ, challenged to name the greatest commandment, said love of God, first, and the second, "You must love your neighbor as yourself" (Matthew 22:36-40). This response to the Sadducees was pure Old Testament (see Deuteronomy 6:5) — love of self the norm for love of neighbor. But his admonition to the apostles the night before He died was different: "This is my commandment: Love one another, as I have loved you" (John 15:12). To the point of self-sacrifice, obviously, even to the point of death, if need be. "Anyone who finds his life will lose it; anyone who loses his life for my sake will find it" (Matthew 10:39). Do we believe the truth of that command, especially we who are the pastors of souls? That's a question Christ asked of his apostles in the Upper Room (see John 16:31).

Why should Christian charity mean anything other than devoting one's powers, one's energy, one's talents, one's money — one's sexual abilities in marriage — to the well-being of a beloved? If the object of love is need of the beloved, then need of self takes second place. Loving sexually is Christian love if directed to the right person, for his or her well-being and in the proper manner. Otherwise, giving becomes taking, is more passion than loving, is pleasure of self (or of selves) over love of goodness, love of God. Similar disorders are present in areas other than sex, as when husbands (or wives) devote their time, and themselves, to others (even to good causes), while neglecting their spouses and children.

What Christian charity calls for is the right use of all faculties in the interests of a beloved. Human appetites directed to self-satisfaction, at the expense of others, are misdirected, and mismanaged. People use brute strength to serve anger, hunger to feed gluttony, speech to enhance pride and envy, sexuality for purposes of lust. But, if married love is "pure love" then the connection between *caritas* and *castitas* is clear, a response to life's differing situations that is sometimes "yes," sometimes "no." It is always easier to say "yes" to demands, but not necessarily always charity, or chastity, both of which may call for "no."

When one speaks of sin, therefore, we speak of actions against the virtues. Uncharity and unchastity are aberrations. The claim that the human drive to lust is more powerful than the drive to power (pride), to selfishness (covetousness), to violence (anger), to pleasure (gluttony), to hatred (envy), to ease (sloth), thus suggesting that sexual virtue is virtually impossible, is not recognized in authentic Christian circles. Sins of lust, even in marriage, may not be the worst sins (blasphemy would be worse, so would murder), but they are sins still against chastity and charity.

Natural Family Planning (NFP)

Many friends of the cause do not like the term, in part because the presumption is that it is a new phenomenon, when in fact it's as old as human beings, once they discovered they were "lords of the earth" as God commanded them to be in Genesis 1:28; in part because, as a non-contraceptive methodology, it has received a bad rap from pill-pushers and propagandists, who would make no profit if people learned to achieve child spacing freely and naturally. Our culture is awash with myths that NFP is too much trouble, and that it doesn't work anyway. Our people, too, thanks to our own ineptitude and to the contraceptionists in the Church, have been indoctrinated to trust Planned Parenthood or the drugstore more than their own intelligence, determination, Church support or the grace of God. Furthermore, we live at a time when more medicinal regimens than ever are recommended for pregnant women, heart patients, diabetics, athletes, senior citizens, and for birth control (except sex); when interested parties take all kinds of trouble to measure and dispense contraceptive pills and insert and check devices for safety; when one-third of the users are eventually sterilized, because the devices did not prove so safe as advertised; and when an estimated 1,500,000 and more induced abortions annually, are the *prima facie* evidence that not all is well in birth control land.

Thus far, the Church has failed to counteract effectively the contraceptive culture. Cardinal Patrick O'Boyle tried in 1969 when he persuaded the American bishops to allocate $800,000 for a newly created Human Life Foundation, but the effort came to naught. Large ecclesial bureaucracies are not good at "trickle down" programming, when there is so much divided opinion at high levels, even among NFP leaders. So, until the Church gets its national act together, hope must spring eternal for what local pastors can do, alone or in concert, if they truly believe that what the Church teaches is intrinsic to the salvation history of those they serve.

This book is not designed to be an NFP handbook but parish priests, if they remember the gospel story, ought not think the cause hopeless, as long as they themselves are not victims of half-belief of contraceptionist propaganda. For centuries full-time, thorough breast feeding helped space conceptions, explaining why children were not born every year, and why those who were born enjoyed good psychological care, as well as good nutrition. Such breast feeding, properly understood and implemented (not part-time or occasional breast feeding) is still a factor, but not likely in our culture to be an important element in Natural Family Planning. Neither is the old "rhythm" (or "calendar") method much help anymore, although it was serviceable to many couples when it came into use more than sixty years ago. Originally called the Ogino-Knaus method after the two scientists who developed it, rhythm was based on knowledge (going back to 1840) that there were fertile and infertile periods in a woman's monthly cycle. Since ovulation normally occurred fifteen days before the next menstruation, many women found it possible to plot the fertile and infertile periods in the given month when pregnancy was or was not likely. Women who were regular found the calendar helpful, but there were also many reasons for women to be irregular, and so to make the

131

"calendar" unreliable for many. The "rhythm method" is now outdated and is no longer recommended.

We have come a long way with Natural Family Planning since World War II. Today the sympto-thermal method (STM) has demonstrated a remarkable effectiveness for two purposes — conceiving babies or avoiding pregnancy. "Sympto" refers to the cervical mucus which is thick during sterile days, watery at time of fertility, disappears after ovulation; the cervix closes and opens to provide easy or difficult access to the transit of spermatozoa. Such is nature's way of facilitating or frustrating conception, and women, properly instructed, come to recognize the bodily signs. "Thermal" means the rise in temperature which occurs shortly after ovulation. A sustained elevated temperature is a positive indication of infertility. Women come to recognize the sign, once they know what to look for.

With the Natural Family Planning regimen women develop a keen sense of their own fertility patterns. Is the method "safe"? Those who use STM assert its effectiveness. John Kippley, founder of The Couple to Couple League, says its user-effectiveness ranges from "85 to 99 percent" and "when it is used by couples of serious motivation it is in the same effectiveness ballpark with anything else." Of course, it is "open" to procreation, if that be God's will, a state of mind one would think good pastors would hope to inculcate in the thinking of those in their flock who call themselves believers.

In *Familiaris Consortio* (No. 32) John Paul II, speaking of NFP, said the following: "The couple respect the inseparable connection between the unitive and procreative meanings of human sexuality, they are acting as 'ministers' of God's plan ... the couple comes to experience how conjugal Communion is enriched with those values of tenderness and affection which constitute the inner soul of human sexuality."

Hence, if the objective is "God's plan" and Christian love, not simply pleasure or pure self-interest, then parish priests must make this an essential element in the Church's ministry. And there are enough couples around, when the pastors go looking for them, who know how to instruct young Catholics before they enter what they, ignorant of nature, may come to perceive as a crisis in their life.

Paul VI the Prophet

Paul VI wrote *Humanae Vitae* merely to clarify constant Catholic teaching on marriage and child-bearing. But, tucked away in a corner of that encyclical are a few prophecies which Catholic contraceptive users, who seem to have acquired majority status in the Church, might ponder. Four, especially, are relevant for parish priests engaged in supporting Catholic family life.

1. Contraception, widely used, leads to conjugal infidelity and a general lowering of morality. Need we remind priests of the leaps within a generation in divorces, abortions, illegitimacy, and venereal disease?

2. Husbands would lose respect for wives, consider them mere instruments of pleasure, no longer respected and beloved companions, nor responsible for their physical and psychological well-being. Can anyone doubt that women complain more about men today than ever, that family violence is on the increase, that the ones liberated by the contraceptive marriage are men, not necessarily women?

3. Widespread contraception places a dangerous weapon in the hands of public authorities. Are we surprised that government is a major funder now of family planning programs, including abortion, interferes with the family culture of its own people as well as that of other nations, and is leading nations toward a generalized anti-child animus, one that will be difficult to eradicate?

4. Contraception leads humankind to believe its power over human nature is limitless. Can we not see this in test-tube babies, surrogate motherhood, homosexuality, even euthanasia?

The special quality in human beings that Catholic doctrine considers vital to happiness on earth, apart from salvation, is the self-discipline associated with virtue. And inculcating virtue is what the Church is about, and is what, more than anything else, a secularized people need. It is not easily acquired without religious faith, frequent use of worship and of the sacraments.

Those priests interested in the full coverage of this issue, critical to their ministry, are advised to consult Janet Smith, *Humanae Vitae: A Generation Later* (Catholic University of America Press, 1991).

Chapter Nine

Five Other Ways to Christ: Baptism, Penance, Confirmation, Orders, Anointing

The purpose of the sacraments is to sanctify men, to build up the Body of Christ, and finally to give worship to God. Because they are signs they also instruct. They not only presuppose faith, but by words and objects they also nourish, strengthen, and express it. That is why they are called the "sacraments of faith." They do, indeed, confer grace, but, in addition, the very act of celebrating them most effectively disposes the faithful to receive this grace to their profit, to worship God only, and to practice charity.

— Vatican II, *Sacrosanctum Concilium*

T*he Rites of the Catholic Church*, revised after Vatican II, call baptism "the door to life and to the Kingdom of God." It is also the door to the parish for many parents, which explains why the priest should interview them beforehand, and join the "baptismal party" at home later, if he has the time. It is an occasion for inspiration and renewal of faith, as well as God's favor. Therefore a special duty falls upon the pastor to see that the administration of this sacrament is well done, that is, by fine appointments in and around the baptistry, and by careful celebration in conformity with the rubrics.

The Sacrament of Baptism

The reason for special caution here is explained by the pervasive nature of our secular culture, and the nature of infant baptism particularly. Half-believing adults may postpone receiving other sacraments, but feel compelled, almost as a superstitious act, to have their baby baptized. The priest's introductory remarks are important, if only to complement any earlier instruction the participants may have received. Care must also be given in a community celebration to insure relative calm within the church, lest the sense of the ritual be lost by restlessness in the pews or by activity in the aisles.

The community celebration of baptism, either of children or of adults, is not an invention of Vatican II. Many American parishes regularly did this during the World War II period, even with Latin, and in "dialogue fashion." The Council institutionalized the practice worldwide. However, the Council did not outlaw private baptism, even without Mass, or exclude outside priests from such parish rituals, or otherwise restrain the priest's generous concern for the wishes of parents and the needs of infants.

Many extreme claims, sometimes made in the name of Vatican II, are baseless and neither serve God's purpose nor those of his people. For example, the suggestion, or the occasional demand, that parents must be perfectly honed into parish life, or especially instructed, before they can have their baby baptized, is a *desideratum*, but not a Church requirement; and it is not a new difficulty. In former days the parish community was so strong, with pious Catholics living in the same town or nearby, or up the street, or around the corner, but not far away, that backsliding parents were inevitably caught up in what other parents were doing to rear decent Catholics themselves. The "backsliders" of the time had at least a subdued belief in the meaning of baptism — if only to know that it removed original sin — entitling them to the benefit of the doubt. One priest in the parish usually knew enough about those parishioners to make a judgment in favor of a child's baptism.

Poor catechesis, the withering away of the parochial school system, and the shortage of priests/religious, perhaps the way younger priests have been trained, may explain why born-Catholic parishioners today are sometimes asked to provide advance evidence of their faith commitment before their baby will be admitted to the font. A set of three, four, or six instruction sessions may be prescribed as a litmus test of parental worthiness. Occasionally, the baptism may be delayed or even denied, unless there is a favorable response to the priest's request. And, although the child (or children) is exorcised early during the rite ("set him/her free from original sin"), some priests, following selected academic theories (and in spite of John Paul II's urgings) look upon the need for infant baptism as less than urgent, and so have no qualms about delaying the rite.

Throughout history, in the fourth century and particularly during the Protestant Reformation (which laid such stress on personal faith as the source of justification) attempts were made to do away with infant baptism. This has never been a Catholic belief or practice. The teaching of the Church is clear, deriving from Apostolic tradition and the witness of the Fathers. It cannot be argued that Christ, who went out of his way to embrace and bless children (see Matthew 19:14 and Mark 10:16), would withhold from them the baptism he held essential for salvation. Saint Paul baptized whole families (see 1 Corinthians 1:16) and Vatican II called for a special rite of infant baptism. To deal with recent resistance, the Congregation for the Doctrine of the Faith (October 20, 1980) drew up a specific "Instruction on Infant Baptism." Of course, part of the problem for a modern priest is the theory of some theologians that original sin, if anything at all can be called that, is not the personal sin of a mythological Adam, but a social condition of the universe, and so is not "inherited" in the traditional sense, but is merely a fact of life. The Church rejects these theories, citing Saint Paul (see 1 Corinthians 15:40) that when Adam sinned, we all became members of a fallen race, redeemed by the Second Adam. It is *de fide* that baptism, even of children, is necessary for salvation.

Perhaps very early baptism (three days old) in Catholic countries was overdone, but the Catholic norm is still early rather than late. Canon

867 obliges parents to see that the child is baptized "within the first few weeks after birth." To reject a parental request, therefore, even to delay baptism unduly, calls for solid justification and discreet handling. Resistance to, or even rejection of, formal lectures or counseling is by itself not sufficient justification for delay when one or both parents have a full Catholic education, and especially if the "instruction" is conducted in someone's home by a person or a couple with no better academic qualifications. Furthermore, many parents are employed at impossible hours, while parish classes are usually scheduled for the convenience of the teachers. Additionally, nothing prevents the priest, on whom the responsibility chiefly rests, from giving private instruction, especially to parents who, though not well-educated Catholic-wise, are pious practicing Catholics. When all the options are considered, negative decisions may still be made, but as a rule they should be comparatively few.

Presuming that the essential meaning of the baptismal rite is clearly understood, the Church expects that pious reinforcements of Catholic doctrine, developed over centuries by the Church, also receive proper attention. One requirement is the insistence on qualified godparents, another is the conferral of a Christian name on the infant. Godparents go back to the days of epidemics and plagues which wiped out young parents in wholesale fashion, and during periods when maternal mortality was high and life expectancy low. They were the Church's insurance policy for the ongoing catechesis of infants. In modern times godparents tend to be superfluous, often choices made on the basis of criteria other than piety. They became even more marginal after Vatican II when the ritual shifted center stage to the parents. The insistence on at least one godparent indicates, nonetheless, the Church's ongoing concern about the effects of life's tragedies on the Catholic formation of the young. Parochial scrutiny of the qualifications of parental alternates should not, therefore, be haphazard, especially when the mother or father is less than an exemplary Catholic. A member of the family, like an aunt or uncle, is a better choice than a friend, because of the likelihood that family contact will more likely perdure through the preschool years. Bridesmaids and best men, though often chosen, are less suitable because they represent the past, not the future. In any event, pastors should not let the occasion elude them to use godparents as an opportunity to reinforce the religious significance of the baptismal commitment — faith in Jesus Christ, personal holiness, and membership in his Church.

The adoption of a Christian name (or names) is a long-standing Catholic tradition. Indeed, the old *Code of Canon Law* told a pastor to provide such a name himself, if the parents did not, and record both in the parish record book. Apart from a reputable custom of transmitting family names from one generation to another, usually Christian, the ancient practice included giving a name of a saint as the child's patron in heaven, and a model for life.

In post-Christian times few infants are named for reasons the Church deems acceptable. More likely they receive the name of a media star, a popular surname, or a hybrid creation of no religious significance. Parish priests have acquiesced in this trend by remaining silent on the subject. Rarely does one hear a homily on baptismal names, or objections raised in private conversations to the modern practice. It is difficult, of course, to intervene at the last minute when minds have already been set, and the name publicized within the family circle. However, a priest may create a suitable mood for saint's names, if he catechizes his parish in timely fashion.

The Christmas season, when the feasts of great saints occur, or when the patronal feast of the parish occurs, are opportunities to reestablish the Christian link between birth and eternal life. Use of the pulpit is only one way to raise consciousness. Parish interviews, the parochial bulletin, and the diocesan newspaper can also be helpful. Even if modern parents are looking for distinctive names, the varieties of Marys, Elizabeths, Charles, etc., are legion, especially if those open to the suggestion explore the varieties that come out of national traditions. Books like *Butler's Lives of the Saints* provide the biographies of well-established Christian heroes, even if parents will need additional help in learning the varieties: Molly for Mary, Isolde for Elizabeth, Carol for Charles, and so forth.[1]

It would not be remiss, as a final note, to mention somewhere that, while the bishop or the priest is the ordinary minister of baptism, any person intending to do what the Church does may baptize an infant in danger of death (or any adult so disposed) by pouring plain water on the forehead with the words "I baptize you in the name of the Father, the Son and the Holy Spirit." This obligation has been reaffirmed in the Holy See's "Introduction to the Rite of Infant Baptism" in 1980, where the history of infant baptism is treated in some detail.

The Sacrament of Penance

There are five things about the Church's penitential discipline, from its earliest days in apostolic times to the present post-Vatican II period:

1. From the very beginning the forgiveness of sin has been an institutional process of the Church, administered by bishops, and the ordinary means by which serious sinners have been reconciled, not only to God but to the Church.

2. The exact details of how the penitential discipline should work out in practice have been left to the determination of the Church itself.

3. The power of binding and the power of loosing have been used unequally during the history of the Church, even though neither power of itself guarantees the results expected from its exercise.

4. Each element in the sacramental process — satisfaction, sorrow, confession — has had its day of preeminence in the history of the penitential discipline, and after the reforms of Pius X so have "confessions of devotion."

5. As a matter of public record sexual sins were always major objects of the Church's penitential discipline.

The sacrament of penance was widely used by Catholics in the United States during most of the twentieth century. However, the second dysfunction of the Second Vatican Council — dysfunction being a fancy word for what happens bad when only good is intended — was the virtual wipeout of "confession" for the body of practicing American Catholics. The first surprising disorder was the falloff in Mass attendance.

The late Council actually said: "Those who approach the Sacrament of Penance obtain pardon from God's mercy for the offense committed against Him, and are at the same time reconciled with the Church they have wounded by their sins." (*Lumen Gentium*, No. 11). The new *Code of Canon Law* (cns. 959ff.) prescribe "individual and integral confession" as the ordinary way of reconciliation with God and the Church. All serious sins are to be confessed as a matter of obligation, venial sins by recommendation. Holy Communion may not ordinarily be received worthily by anyone conscious of having committed mortal sin, and all Catholics are still seriously bound to receive Holy Communion once a year, preferably during the Easter Season. (This means reception of the sacrament of penance, if that is necessary.)

Vatican II, therefore, merely reaffirmed the substance of the Church's penitential discipline. To increase its attractiveness, the mode and style of administering and receiving the sacrament were given a modern look, especially for those habituated in a life of mortal sin, and also to reduce superstitious use or overuse by the scrupulous.

Surprisingly, renewal became disestablishment. Hardly any Catholics go to confession any more, especially the younger generation. A good deal of talk goes on about "bringing them back," but at this time the possibilities are slim without a major effort organized by a unified hierarchy.

It serves no purpose to rehash in boring detail the decline and fall of penance, its causes or prospects, especially for Catholics who were always relieved after a good confession.

The scope of the problem every good parish priest must face in today's climate is wide neglect. Many Catholics no longer believe they need to confess to a priest. Others do not think of sin at all, if it is a case of their conscience versus the pope's. Having also heard about "general absolution," they are sure that the Church's old teaching on the subject has been quietly reversed.

They are wrong, of course, in good conscience likely, many of them because they are victims of bad teaching or bad example. A wide body of theological thought exists within the Church which doubts, or denies, that Christ ever instituted sacraments beyond baptism and the Eucharist. The other so-called instruments of grace are really institutions of the Church, guided by the Holy Spirit, and have spiritual effect as much a result of the recipient's faith (i.e., *ex opere operantis*) as from anything the priest does. As stated, this is a Protestant view of sacramentology against which the Canons of Trent pronounced anathema. The Second Vatican Council reaffirmed the ancient teaching (*Lumen Gentium*, No. 11). Still, historians continue to insist that it was Irish monks of the sixth century, during the so-called Dark Ages, who imposed the sacrament, as we know it, on the mission Churches in Europe, and, through Trent, on the Catholic world. If those theories are insufficient to degrade "penance" to what critics think was its primitive size, then social science discoveries have been alleged to deny that it is possible to indict anyone for sin, especially mortal sin (this in spite of John 5:14-17). Following the Council, the Tridentine system was depicted as cruel, unwarranted, and unacceptable to moderns who need uplift instead of penalty. During the 1970s the heated discussions over the confession of children also contributed to short lines of adults on Saturday. A short review of penitential history may not be without avail.

Few people today understand what damage the rebellion against the discipline of children's confession, which occurred almost overnight by religious educators, did to penitential habits of Catholic adults. The first was the habit of disobedience to legitimate authority inculcated in the Church by erring bishops, priests, and religious. Secondly, as a consequence, the attitude developed that sinfulness itself was not as deadly to faith and holiness as Tridentine divines made it out to be, that (in spite of what scripture says) mortal sins are rare, that the older discipline was bad because it filled people with guilt, that children are incapable of sin anyway, while Christian adults ought to be mature enough to make their own decisions about their worthiness for Holy Communion. This kind of mind-set — the loss of "a sense of sin" — drew the fire of Pius XII long before his tiara was placed on the head of John XXIII.

Because this controversy was pervasive in the Church and was a paradigm of how Catholic order can be dissolved *de facto*, if not *de jure*, it is worth extended comment here, in order that priests, who never experienced its trial and its consequences, might gain understanding. The revolutionary thrust derived from a simple proposition: Change the practice, and Rome will eventually change the theory. Yet, the Church's ancient practice was based on doctrine, not theory.

Consider first of all the notion of discipline itself. Discipleship is a normal requisite of citizenship in any civilized society. Discipline simply means a developed pattern of suitable behavior which reflects socially approved norms consistent with the aims of a given society. Such cultivated styles of approved speech, behavior, toiletry, neighborliness, patriotism, and piety are taught by parents everywhere, and reinforced throughout life as a matter of orderly living by the larger society. (Saintly groups have such codes, as do gangs.) Discipleship is never easy for the congenital rebel or the social misfit, but discipline does make life easier for most people when they live properly, sometimes under enforced public law, but mostly under whatever the "Marquis of Queensbury" rules suggest as sanity.

In the case at hand, the objective of the Church is that Catholics receive the Body and Blood of Christ as often as is proper and worthy. Should they be serious sinners and are ready to clear their consciences for Holy Communion, usually through the sacrament of penance, the "penitential discipline of the Church" developed in Apostolic times precisely to accomplish these purposes.

In the early Church, Communion was given to babies at baptism, even under the species of wine (because of its convenient administration); the sacrament of penance was often public then, or at least the works of penance required of adulterers, blasphemers, and abortionists. By the Middle Ages, Church law made the reception of both sacraments a matter of right for anyone reaching the "age of discretion" (age of reason). The obligation of Easter Duty took effect at the Fourth Council of the Lateran in 1215, later to be reinforced by the Council of Trent in the sixteenth century. But, with few exceptions, the frequent reception of either sacrament by masses of Catholics remained uncommon. In the late nineteenth century, though, youngsters of seven or eight were considered ready for confession (though some priests would not give them absolution, on the premise they were sinless). Holy Communion was administered for the first time only to thirteen- and fourteen-year-olds. By then, and then only, was it assumed that youngsters were mature enough to appreciate the Body of Christ. When Pius X ascended the throne of Peter in 1903, both sacraments were lightly used and, to the new pope at least, this was unacceptable Eucharistic piety. If the Church believed that a person was ready for confession when he or she knew right from wrong, and for the Eucharist when they knew the difference between ordinary bread and Communion, then there was reason to change the Church's discipline to reflect that understanding.

So, on December 26, 1905, Pius X, by decree, declared that access to Holy Communion was free to all, old and young alike, the sole condition being that people be in the state of grace and be determined to avoid sin. On July 15, 1910, in the well-known document *Quam Singulari*, Pius X further decreed that "the custom of not admitting children to Confession or of never giving them absolution, when they have arrived at the use of reason, must be wholly condemned." And thus began the discipline of frequent first confession, first Communion. As far as the Church in the United States is concerned, the new piety worked, producing a unique body of devoted Catholics who used both sacraments diligently throughout life. The present law of the Church — Canon 914 of the 1983 *Code* — insists on Pius X's requirements. Regrettably the frequent reception of penance is today no longer the rule of life for young or for old in the American Church, although it can hardly be asserted that the present generation of Catholics are less in need of this sacrament than their immediate forbears. And the reason for the default (if it is necessary to single out one explanation) is the assault that was carried on against children's confession after 1965 by religious educators with the approval of many bishops. The rationalization for the proposed change (Communion first, confession later) was "experimentation." But there was no experimentation at all. The practice of postponing confession was imposed on parents and priests by religious educators, in spite of Rome's efforts in the *General Catechetical Directory* (1972) to stem the abuse. (The return to the discipline of Pius X is presently in process, but repairing the damage to the penitential discipline will take decades, if it can be done at all.)

During the 1960s and 1970s people in the pews did not know at first what new theologians were saying, but they learned quickly from what their children were being taught. The arguments used to liberate eight-year-olds from the penitential discipline were liberating also for a majority of adult Catholics. Revisionists were so hostile to "confession" (called a "guilt machine" by some) that they set about to alter its character in the name of mental health. And they compiled their complaints with care. Every institution, including confession, has its downside for certain people, but the alleged evils of those long pre-Vatican II confessional lines lay in a direction quite different from ones advanced against them. Most American Catholics in 1962 formed their consciences properly, and were far from guilt-ridden. However, penitent crowds were rarely given the spiritual counsel or uplift that should accompany absolution. If they were absent for a long time, for instance, because of a serious immoral habit, they likely received a priest's close attention, and perhaps a long lecture. But the time spent on the "big" sinner meant that the rest of the line received little more than "Three Hail Mary's," and a wave of the hand. It was this routine in pre-Vatican days that dulled the full impact of the penitential rite, although it left a Catholic sense of sin intact.

The recent effort to turn the sacrament from penance to reconciliation can hardly be called an improvement, at least one consistent with the Church's mission, if Catholics stopped receiving it. A psychological boost to a penitent through counseling has always been an integral part of the rite, not always used to advantage, to be sure; but this is not the heart of the sacrament, which remains: confession, contrition, absolution, and works of penance. Every priest worth his salt knows the advantage of using a soothing voice in the confessional, whenever he is dealing with an upset penitent, or with a hard-nosed sinner unsure about why he or she is there. But he is also the judge, not as God is Judge, but a judge who must decide whether the petitioner is properly disposed. Whatever Christ's gospel is, it deals with the reality of real sin, with admission of sin and true sorrow, with valid absolution and specific reparation.

We come, therefore, to the heart of the penitential matter.

God and Sins Against God

Cardinal John O'Connor stated the Church's contemporary problem well: "Much of the world laughs at the whole idea of sin. We live in a society where anything goes. That is especially true in the area of 'sexual morality.'... If much of what the world takes for granted is not sinful, then there is little need for confession or sorrow or penance or reconciliation. But the world is wrong — dead wrong. Sin is still sin. For serious sin we can go to hell, and that is not a joke."

So, before we can expect Catholics to go to confession again in any serious way, we must convince them all over again that Christ instituted this sacrament for the forgiveness of mortal sin, and that it helps them become better Christians. Should perchance they be such serious sinners, it is their opportunity to reclaim good standing with God and with the Church, especially for receiving the Eucharist or the sacrament of matrimony worthily. Once more, priests must become preachers of the Word — about virtue and vice, of religion and irreligion, of reverence and irreverence , of obedience and disobedience, of friendship and enmity, of anger and meanness, of the sanctity of life, of violence and death, of chastity, of lust and fornication, of openness to life and of contraception, of hard work and honesty, of greed, theft, or laziness, of good thoughts and bad thoughts. The Church canonizes freedom, as does the world, but the Church directs that freedom towards virtue, not toward vice. In our day, priests have acted more like therapists than as preachers, as if their premier teacher was Freud, not Christ, acting as if evildoers were sick rather than sinners. Those old parish missions, even if they contained a measure of "blood and thunder," sought conversion. Today's Catholics have the same need to do penance, not babying by priests who would only "salve" their consciences.

Saint Augustine said it well: "God sent His Son to die not for good men but for bad ones, not for the just but for the wicked." Willful sinners need redemption more than the sick-minded. But they must be reminded how they sin. Vatican II was not long over (January 1st, 1967) when Paul VI (in his *Apostolic Constitution on Indulgences*) made the following statement:

"The truth has been divinely revealed that sins are followed by punishment. God's holiness and justice inflict them. Sins must be expiated. This may be done on this earth through the sorrows, miseries, and trials of this life, and, above all, through death. Otherwise, the expiation must be made in the next life through fire and torments of purifying punishment. That is why the faithful have always been convinced that the paths of evil are strewn with many stumbling blocks. They bring to those who follow them adversities, bitterness and harm."

How many parishioners these days hear such strong words, even from the good pastor? Whatever the renewed rite of penance is intended to mean, it certainly is aimed at perfecting the good sheep and bringing back the lost. The new rite specifically says that "every sin is an offense against God ... and penance always entails reconciliation with brothers and sisters who are always harmed by [sins]." Sin is personal, because it turns a person away from God, and communal because it does injury to our human and institutional relationships. There is no such thing as "victimless sin." The new rite tries to remedy both aspects of sinful behavior.

The New Rite

Three elements in the "new rite" deserve special mention: (1) confessions are to be heard; (2) in a quasi-chapel room, not in a closet or sacristy; (3) and in any one of three forms.

Hearing Confessions

In the Council document, *Christus Dominus* (October 28, 1965, No. 30, on "The Pastoral Office of Bishops"), parish priests are advised to "be readily available for the hearing of confessions" and "if necessary to call on other priests." At the 1988 meeting of the NCCB, when confession was under discussion, one Western bishop opined that the reason for short confessional lines was the inability to find available priests. And the absence of clear-cut confession schedules has, in the eyes of busy laity, also become a problem. One hour around noon on Saturday, involving one priest, is hardly "ready availability." Where more than one priest is assigned to a parish, there is no reason why all priests are not available, even if they have to do little more than wait, or pray, or study. Parishioners still have a right to choice, where it is possible, and to have their convenience served, not the priest's, if a return to sacramental penance is ever to occur. Also, confessions before and after Mass, which were once commonplace in missionary dioceses, where there were few priests and large distances, are also being used today by apostolic-minded pastors as mechanisms of reconciliation and spiritual development for those out of practice with regular confession.

In a Quasi-Chapel

The administration of the Eucharist or the reservation of the Blessed Sacrament are quite different from "hearing confessions" or "reconciling sinners." The former calls for chapel-like settings, the latter simply for a proper sacred environment. We all know about chaplains in wartime absolving a soldier in a trench or a troop *en masse*. Priests have heard an occasional confession on a public street, or in a barn, or on a subway. All the new regulations do is demand that, as a rule, a fitting atmosphere be created for sinners to sit or kneel before the priest, as if before God, and tell him what nasty persons they are, or how they are adulterers, or thieves. For older Catholics this is usually a commonplace act, hardly given a second thought; for some it may be a terrifying moment; but in either case it is always serious and solemn. This is God's forgiveness they want to experience, the Church's, too, and it is more than a human gesture. So the setting must be appropriate.

We must remember also that the stark confessionals of pre-Vatican II days — the "black marias," as someone called them — were not created out of someone's sadomasochistic mentality, but as a reaction to abuses, of which Protestant reformers and anti-Catholic bigots spoke ceaselessly. The grille, the stern enclosure, the darkness, were timed at protecting the priest and the penitent from over-familiarity, especially when the petitioners were women, religious or otherwise. All those canons against solicitation and absolution of accomplices would not have crept into the Church's codes had they not been necessary, if only by reason of the sacredness of the sacrament itself.

This may be the place also to add something about face-to-face confession, as distinct from telling sins kneeling down before a grille. The new rite gives the penitent the absolute option, and pastors are obligated to see that it is a real one. Most priests have had personal experience in their lives, long before Vatican II, with face-to-face confession, sometimes embarrassingly so. Face-to-face confession is easy when there are only peccadillos to confess. Some of us have had criminals almost boast of their daring-dos while sitting in the parish office. With sorrow, of course, and requesting absolution right on the spot, as if they were afraid of crossing the Church door. Some people have few inhibitions and just like to talk anywhere. Children (though not all) if they are initiated to the practice, find face-to-face confession to be normal, maybe even pleasurable. (Older priests never bought the idea that eight-year-olds were afraid of the "black box" either, unless someone made them so.)

However, a strange thing happened after John XXIII's Council. Many religious educators (like liturgists with the vernacular) unilaterally declared open confession to be more suited to the modern mind. Confessional boxes were out (like Latin) and reconciliation rooms sprung up everywhere. In many places these were all the young ever saw, and older people were induced to go with the Vatican II reform, as if the jolly pope invented the new device personally.

As time went on, however, questions began to raise whether some reformers really believed in the sacramental institution itself. They seemed too anxious to turn the priest into a counselor, rather than a judge or absolver, even though many priests do poorly at the new role. In due course, the pious priest or the brand new priest, fashioned by up-to-date seminars or seminary techniques, treated everyone who confessed as if he or she were a Mary Magdalene. In some cases the long time spent with each person began to test the waiting patience of those who simply came to confess and be absolved.

Pastors must deal with the reality that face-to-face confession is an option for Catholics — a preference, not a fetish. If traditional experience is the guide, it is a minority preference among adults, at a time when majority use of the sacrament is the pastoral goal. This means anonymous confessions as the rule.

Three Forms

By now all priests, and most laity, know what these forms are: private confession with private absolution; public penitential service (including biblical readings, homily, publicly expressed sorrow) with private confession/private absolution; and a public penitential service which, because of unexpected crowds or some emergency, involves general public confession and general absolution, with the understanding that each participant will seek private confession before the next Eucharist, or in a reasonable time, approximately within a month.

For the second form to be effective extra confessors are necessary. At devotions such as Forty Hours the rite can be impressive, and can serve to indoctrinate Catholics with the public nature of their sinfulness. However, in some situations it is impractical because priests in adequate numbers are unavailable. There are times, however — for example, during a parish mission — when one evening is given over to a penitential service, with the understanding that on the morrow, before and after the final assembly, priests will be available for private confessions. Many years ago in Harlem, when pastors had convert classes running into the hundreds, public services, public baptisms, and private confessions followed with scores of outside confessors on tap.

It is the third form — general absolution — that has been most abused, causing Rome and many bishops to outlaw its use, unless specific permission is given in advance by higher authority. The idea itself is simple and meritorious. In an emergency, very often an impending spiri-

tual crisis or death for a multitude, a priest asks the congregation to acknowledge their sins before God, and express their sorrow as he bestows
his blessing and God's forgiveness for their sins. Images are vivid yet of
a Father Frank Duffy at the Battle of the Marne in World War I, or a
Father Joseph N. Moody on a cruiser which was about to shell the coast
of Africa in World War II, raising their hands over kneeling, and grateful,
soldiers and sailors, many of whom would go to God before their wives
and mothers would have a final look at them. To the men it was a simple,
beautiful, and Catholic sacramental ritual. Not one of those who survived ever entertained the notion that he was exempt from confessing his
sins privately, the same sins Father Duffy and Father Moody, at a critical
moment, said God had forgiven.

Missionary or rural bishops, too, visiting large congregations in
places where a priest's regular presence is negligible, legitimately avail
themselves of general absolution from time to time.

Different is the case, however, of pastors who use the excuse of
"crowds," sometimes manipulating a situation to create an emergency, to
grant general absolution, leaving the impression, if only by silence, that
this rite was now another acceptable form of confession and absolution.
People in the pews, especially those who are no longer or often there,
hear what, to them, is a new message. Even though some of them live in
bad marriages, or use contraceptives, or are otherwise and habitually involved in serious sin, they now see themselves reconciled to the Church
through general absolution, and worthy of regular Communion, if they
so desire. As the practice spread, sometimes on the initiative of a bishop,
some priests and some prelates justified its use as a means of bringing
sinners back to the use of private confession. Rome and many other bishops saw, instead, only simulation, nominalism, hypocrisy, and the use of
a sacred ritual as pretense of reconciliation when, in truth, the veneer of
authenticity was bestowed on false consciences.

The overall effect of such abuses, and the general mood of the times
to place private conscience, even of priests, over Church regulations or
the Word of God, has surely led to laxity among laity in examining their
consciences, in offering an honest and integral confession of serious faults,
and in the scrutiny by priests of what they might sense were unworthy
confessions. How often does a penitent hear in confession today, "Tut,
tut, don't be upset, God loves you," or "You are still a good person," or
"Don't try the impossible," or "Do the best you can," without, in necessary cases, unraveling a long-standing habit of sin. Those expressions

have their place, always have had their place, in situations where persons on the other side of the grille were profoundly upset over their sinfulness. But rarely does correction occur today, especially about the habits of sexual sins.

It is almost as if the newer priests are afraid to probe consciences in confession, when that is likely to upset the penitent. Christ often probed consciences in public, and before he chastised the audience. Confession-going Catholics are unlikely to have murdered anyone, or robbed a bank, or worked for Cosa Nostra or the C.I.A. Their regular sins customarily (even those called mortal) are pedestrian: hatred, greed, various lusts, meanness, drunkenness or addiction, jealousy, laziness — all the capitals — plus failure to do what their state of life calls for. Sexual sins tend to be repetitive, yet deserve a priest's attention, not only because the Church considers them serious, but because once ingrained, they misshape character toward indulgence, affect family life and personal relations negatively. They often upset the balance between piety and faith. The Church is precise in the caution it gives to priests about sexual probes in the confessional, especially with women. Some priests overdo everything, but the most common failing is neglect in forming consciences. Probing, unlike counseling, need not take much time, if done skillfully. The particular sin of our culture is the "cover up" of evil, calling it sickness, leaving evildoers at peace with themselves, or offering meaningless general absolutions.

The Sacrament of Confirmation

Confirmation continues the initiation of a person into the body of the Church, as Pentecost fulfilled the promise of Easter. The Acts of the Apostles (especially 2:38) recalls how, fifty days after the Resurrection, those who believed with Peter and his company were first baptized, and then received "the gift of the Holy Spirit." This laying on of hands is rightly recognized by the Catholic tradition as the beginning of the sacrament of confirmation. Paul VI had reason to remind the entire Church of this, when he published the *New Rite*, August 22, 1971.

For the years most of the present generations have lived, confirmation was administered by a bishop to converts, to adults only partially reared as Catholics, and to children about nine years of age. (According to the 1990 *Code for the Oriental Churches*, confirmation is administered with baptism, even to infants, and regularly by a priest.)

According to the new 1983 *Code of Canon Law* for the Latin Church (cns. 882-883) the ordinary minister of confirmation is still the bishop, but the faculty for administering it is now given by law to priests (1) when they baptize an adult or a child of catechetical age (at least seven years old), or (2) when they receive people into full Communion with the Church, although baptized elsewhere, and (3) anyone in danger of death, if unconfirmed. Without special delegation from the bishop, a priest may not confirm other unconfirmed Catholics.

The only significant difference of opinion to arise about this sacrament is over the age of confirmation. According to the ritual, seven years is acceptable, but may be postponed to a later age to allow for additional formation and more mature choice by the *confirmandi* themselves. The postponement is usually recommended by those who are in favor of greater volunteerism within the Church and greater stress on mature choices. (This view stands in stark contrast to the practice in the Oriental Church, which is to confirm children when they are babies.)

Normally, parish priests follow the custom of their diocese, but occasionally one or another establishes his own preferred age as a norm for his parish. Some postpone the sacrament into the high school years. This can be upsetting to parents and to other priests: to parents, because many of their teenagers find ample reason to skip confirmation completely; to priests, who have to deal with, or who create difficulties for, an unconfirmed adult at the time of marriage. Since a span of ages for confirmation from seven to sixteen is abnormal, priests should follow the general custom of their diocese. Nowhere in Church documents does one find that confirmation is a sacrament for adolescence, or a time for the teenager to make a decision for or against the Church. The Catholic tradition places the sacrament closer to baptism and the Eucharist than to adolescence.

One other item is also worth mentioning, namely the unapproved translation of traditional formulas. For example, the "gifts of the Holy Spirit" are customarily enumerated as "wisdom, understanding, counsel, fortitude, knowledge, piety and fear of the Lord." The Church, co-opting this list from Isaiah 11:2-3 in the Old Testament, associated it with the grace of confirmation. Children of old memorized those gifts by heart and, while unlikely to understand the significance of each and every one of them, were impressed at least a little with the relationship of the bishop's anointing and their new status as enthusiastic apostles of the Church, *a la* the Twelve on Pentecost.

Changing the names of these gifts, like altering any section of Holy Writ, must be scrutinized with care, lest the proper sense of the Church's meaning be lost. New translations, often printed and distributed to young and old alike at confirmation time, rearrange the gifts as "wisdom, understanding, right judgment, courage, love, knowledge and reverence in your service." Notice that "piety" is retranslated "love," and "fear of the Lord" becomes "reverence." However piety is an act of justice, something we owe God as a matter of obligation, not simply an act of "love." "Fear of the Lord," powerful words of scripture, appearing there at least thirty times, describes the awesomeness of our relationship with Our Maker and Our Redeemer, not unlike that manifested by Moses on Mount Sinai, or by the Apostles on the Mount of Transfiguration, or by Thomas the Doubter falling to his knees after the Resurrection. Isaiah called fear of the Lord "a delight" and, from Judeo-Christian time immemorial, "God-fearing" was a reflected corollary of sincere faith. "Reverence," properly understood, might do, but not "reverence in your service," because the biblical word deals with man's attitude toward God, not with service. If wisdom begins with "fear of the Lord," why should *confirmandi* not be fully introduced to this religious sense?

The Sacrament of Holy Orders

One might think that this sacrament involves the local priest in only one respect. Depending on circumstances, he is likely to be one of the few persons most qualified to provide solid information on, or a unique evaluation of, a candidate for the priesthood. Seminary faculties usually know students in their academic framework, hardly a holistic view of "the man." The parish priest, who has close touch with most such applicants, is in a unique position to rate the person from a perspective few others have — family background, neighborhood associates, and style of life during holiday periods at home. In former days, when a pastor wrote routine letters of approval to seminary authorities, his chief offense might have been passing mediocrity on to the Church of the future. The Church can no longer afford mediocrities, especially during a time of crisis. The good pastor today is more an important actor on the seminary scene than he might have been in days bygone. And, if ever there was a time for his honesty, it is now.

There is a new burden, however, that pastors have today, one that hardly troubled their predecessors. In pre-Conciliar times, candidates for the priesthood walked in off the streets. "Father, I'd like to be a priest," called for encouragement, perhaps congratulations, occasionally some money, but little more. Whether the young man intended to become a diocesan priest or a religious, what followed usually transcended the parish priest's role. The boy went to the appropriate seminary, to be seen occasionally, and then to celebrate his first Mass in his home parish. But, for the parish priest, that was all there was to it.

But, now, the question arises: What part of the priesthood does he want to join? What seminary should he attend? Following the Council many strange things went on in some seminaries that debilitated priestly training and discipline. The seminary as we knew it was the creation of the Council of Trent, intended to improve on the quality of priests, certainly unlike those of the fifteenth and sixteenth centuries who helped bring on the Protestant Reformation. The seminary became a professional school for future priests, not unlike the schools that came later to turn out first-rate doctors, lawyers, and generals. It had a point of view different from a college, from a monastery, from a pious society. It stressed character, committed faith, probity of life, intellectual ability, disciplined respect for superiors and the laws of the Church, and the intention to live a celibate life devoted to the Kingdom of God. Particular individuals might aspire to be intellectuals, or given to asceticism, or preeminent writers, or outstanding community organizers, but the thrust of training for the priestly body was service to the Church, not self-fulfillment. By that time the Church was expansive enough to permit the creative person or the individualist to fulfill his private dreams while doing his ecclesial duty.

One priest, on the occasion of his golden jubilee, told the story of how, when he reported to his pastor after ordination in 1904, the older man said to him: "Hear you know a lot of theology. I don't care how much theology you know, I only want to know how hard you're willing to work for the people of this parish." The interesting sidelight is the presumption of the pastor that the young man's theology was as solidly Catholic as his priestly intentions.

Much of the revolution after the Council, not surprisingly, affected seminary life too. It was not merely the fact that ordinations per year fell from one thousand in 1967 to three hundred in 1992. The selection process changed, the type of candidates changed, dissenting university professors led to dissenters on seminary faculties, and the same individualism, subjectivism, and egalitarianism tht characterized American culture began to take over the training of priests. The incidence of homosexuality in seminaries was only the most startling aspect of the new situation.

Rome would not have called for an investigation of our two hundred fifty seminaries during the 1980s, nor a Roman Synod on the formation of priests in 1987, nor have issued an apostolic exhortation on the same subject in 1992, unless there was trouble in the ranks. These efforts have proved valuable, but the trouble had reached into high places of the Church. One bishop investigator, making his rounds of a major seminary in 1984, expressed displeasure at the stress on orthodoxy there, at the sight still of all those cassocks, and at the dominant presence in the bookstore of shelves of papal documents! Another bishop of influence, who after the Council took a broad view of change in the Church, thought seminarians who were not comfortable with such change ought to be rejected.

Recently the American hierarchy has issued an excellent document entitled *The Fourth Edition of the Program for Priestly Formation* calling for more rigorous selection of candidates and formation of them, both spiritually and theologically, with proper stress on orthodox belief and practice. How well it will be enforced, after ten years of investigation and worry, remains to be seen.

But, for the parish priest, the question remains, one that is often raised by conscientious bishops: "Where can I send my candidates so that they return properly trained for priestly service?" It is a poser for pastors, too, when one of his youngsters breaks the news of his intention. More than a few bishops think the number of "good" seminaries can be counted on the fingers of one hand, a claim resented particularly by religious, whose houses of formation have been charged with many of the violations of ecclesial protocol. Bishops tell other bishops, and theologians tell bishops, that most American priests do not believe in the doctrine taught by *Humanae Vitae*. If that be so, then it is the fault of most seminaries, because the priests who are trained in the alleged "good" seminaries do believe in the doctrine on contraception, sterilization, and abortion that the Church has taught from its infancy.

The point of these remarks is the suggestion that parish priests may have more responsibility for the sacrament of holy orders than they might think. It might serve them, therefore, to read the new NCCB booklet on priestly formation, and enquire diligently of the quality of particular seminaries, before they dismiss the young man who simply says, "Father, I'd like to be a priest."

An Afterthought

When all is said and done, it may well be claimed that the main source of priestly vocations is the parish priesthood. Some say, not without merit, that mothers first encourage sons to a religious vocation. Even if that is true in many cases, her motivation may rightfully be rooted in the admiration women have, or at least had, in the parish priesthood they experienced. The social and ecclesial forces responsible for the rapid and radical decline in priestly vocations have been analyzed ad nauseam, oftentimes with the object of changing the public or institutional perspectives of the state itself. But common sense based on Catholic truth may be the surer guide. A manly priesthood, trained properly for the fatherly role in the Church, and institutionally supported up and down the line of all dioceses, is still the more likely road to more and better priests. God surely gives the increase, but even his will can be frustrated by obstacles placed by his own representatives.

The Sacrament of Anointing of the Sick

This used to be, as everyone knows, "the last anointing." Priests always anointed more sick than the term "*extreme unction*" seemed to call for, probably because they saw that this sacrament helped Christians deal with serious illness, not exclusively with death. Catholics also knew it forgave sins if they could not confess them, and that it sometimes restored health. Witnesses to these effects were commonplace in any large parish, usually because most "sick calls" occurred in people's homes, not in institutions as they do today.

The Second Vatican Council, while repeating the historic understanding of anointing, simply widened the conditions under which the sacrament could be administered, and proposed a rite that would be devotional and meaningful. Paul VI in 1972 declared that this sacrament is intended for others than those at the point of death. "Danger of death" from sickness or old age, he said, is time enough.

The sacramental form was simplified to permit anointing of the forehead and palms, instead of the five senses. Priests are encouraged to repeat the sacrament if, after a temporary recovery, there is a relapse; on those also who are about to undergo surgery for a serious illness; on old people in weak condition; on those who are unconscious; and on children, if their physical condition warrants. Diocesan norms frequently encourage the communal anointing of the sick when it is pastorally appropriate, instructing priests to remind the congregation that only those who are proper subjects of the sacrament should come forward to receive it. There are communal anointings in which clearly comparatively few of the participants can be classified as "seriously" ill. In several instances, people who see a crowd will walk in off the street onto a line, and after the anointing ask the priest, "What is this?" The individual pastor should follow a probable, rather than a tutior opinion about serious illness, but he should make sure that the sacrament is not cheapened or denigrated by its distribution to people who are not sick at all, who merely have a cold or headache, or walk in off the street.

Visiting the Sick

The busy parish priest must budget his time, especially if he is the pastor of a large parish. And he must make decisions for service based on his sense of parish priorities and his own preferences. With the movement today toward distribution of Holy Communion by Eucharistic ministers to the sick of the parish, and to communal anointings of the sick, priestly visits to them can end up, if he is not careful, on his back burner. Obviously, the priest is absolutely needed only for penance and the anointing, and most of the ailing in his parish are likely to be well attended in those regards. Also, many of the aged or the longtime ill are not able to carry on satisfying conversations with a priest. Yet their sense of gratitude, and that of their family, is related proportionately to his caring enough to come — if only for a blessing:

"They shall lay their hands upon the sick and they shall recover."
(Or: "They shall be strengthened.")
May Jesus the Lord of Mercy
Through the Holy intercession of His Apostles Peter and Paul [and
  the Patron Saint]
Show thee favor and mercy
Restore thee to full health (or full favor)
Both inwardly and outwardly
And, may the Blessing of Almighty God,
Father, Son and Holy Spirit
Descend on you and remain with you forever and ever.
Amen.

The visit is as much a blessing for the priest, as it is for the suffering parishioner.

Endnote

1. TAN Books publishes a pamphlet, *Is It A Saint's Name?* [$1.95], but better are two books by Albert J. Nevins, M.M., *Saints For Boys* and *Saints For Girls* (Our Sunday Visitor, Inc., 1980), which have biographies and varieties of name forms.

Part Three

The Parish Priest

and Evangelization

Chapter Ten

The Beginnings of Evangelization

The job a man has supplies him with wages for food, clothing, and other necessities for himself and family. It is the most important thing in the world to him. A man's job is his life. Therefore, our economic world must accept the investment of a worker's mind and muscle as no less important than the money invested.

— Monsignor John Patrick Monaghan

E vangelization, the process through which the Church makes and remakes disciples for Christ, involves more than preaching. Good works in Christ's name are also required, and these vary with time and culture, even at the parish level.

Church historian Marvin O'Connell tells a story about a parish priest, an electrifying personality, if there ever was one, and a political operator of substance. This Irishman began his priesthood in Saint Paul, Minnesota during the Civil War, in a parish which housed thirteen thousand of his countrymen, many of whom were often arrested on Saint Patrick's Day by their own kind of cop. There was hardly an aspect of their lives he did not touch, mostly by helping them to earn money and use it wisely. While the priest had compassion on those day laborers, many of whom ended up in the poorhouse, if not in jail, he set a goal for himself, namely to "help them achieve the American dream through education and the proper use of their precious vote." This parish priest was John Ireland, who went on to become one of the American Church's most celebrated archbishops.[1]

John Ireland is only one of the tens of thousands of other parish priests in the United States, practically all of whom died without recognition by anyone. If they left behind them better people and better Christians, it is likely that they were personally involved in the human condition of their people. Rarely did they leave letters in archives by which historiographers might celebrate their accomplishments in posterity. Nonetheless, the Second Vatican Council provides new bases for modern parish priests to function in ways that were natural to the likes of the John Irelands.

From its earliest beginning, century after century, evangelization often began with loaves or fishes, or a bowl of rice. But if that worked to draw attention to the message, the matter did not end there. The Church never engages exclusively in the work of leading people to the world beyond the grave, although that is its reason for being. Church Fathers, following the example of their Master, knew that they must give evidence of their credibility, and sensed that they could not talk easily of heaven to hungry men, nor of God to men bent on violence. Their successors have the same understanding, only in our day the field of pastoral interest may include contemporary issues including the local welfare agencies, labor unions, school desegregation, the level of social payments, national health insurance, food stamps, the death penalty, a neighborhood riot, even atomic warfare. It is not surprising anymore to have diocesan or parish committees confront local politicians, help run public schools and community boards, or collect petitions for and against proposed laws as elements of their evangelizing mission.

Many Catholics may not see this connection between man's life here and his afterlife, but modern popes, from Leo XIII through John Paul II, have no such difficulty. They have developed a body of social doctrine which places the Church in the middle of all human problems, with a view toward facilitating people's eventual sanctification.[2] What Leo XIII said in *Rerum Novarum* (1891) was "so utterly new to worldly ears" that forty years later Pius XI conceded how the Church "was held suspect by some even among Catholics, and to certain ones he, Leo, gave offense." By the Second Vatican Council the Church stood on surer ground with its own. *The Pastoral Constitution On the Church in the Modern World* (*Gaudium et Spes*, 1965) made the salvation of the world an essential part of the Church's mission. The Synod of Bishops in their 1971 document *Justice in the World* spelled out the new mandate: "Action on behalf of justice and participation in the transformation of the world fully appears to us as a constitutive dimension of the preaching of the gospel, or, in other words, of the Church's mission for the redemption of the human race and its liberation from every oppressive situation."

The social apostolate, therefore, takes its place alongside liturgy, catechetics, education, family life, and spiritual formation as a regular part of the Church's evangelization procedures, even at the parochial level. This is a risky enterprise, to be sure, not because there are two right sides to secular questions, but because equally informed and properly motivated Christians may begin their analysis of a human situation with a different interpretation of facts, or draw different conclusions from common principle, for example, the propriety of freedom from government interference in one case, the need for government intrusion in another. Public disagreements about politics — peace in the Middle East, or race relations in Los Angeles — are always convoluted, since they involve conflicting claims far away, and the self-interests of opposing parties, some of which may be illegitimate.

In social matters there is also a real difference between "human rights" and "human interests." The right to organize a labor union is a valid right, based on the nature of a human being; it is an inherent right of workingmen to have as much reasonable control of the condition of their employment as they can obtain politically. The "closed shop," on the other hand, is a legitimate pursuit, a human interest, if you will, but not a natural right. Blurring this distinction between the rights as against the interests of opposing parties, fires controversy in all public debates over alleged racism, sexism, secularism, ordination of women, homosexuality, etc. The Church, *qua* Church, is mainly interested in defending human rights, and teaches about them, but leaves the defense of partisan interests to appropriate parties. For reasons such as these the Church establishes two conditions for its involvement in politics.

1. This apostolate is better carried on by laity than by clergy. In *Progressio Populorum* (March 26, 1967), Paul VI said: "While the hierarchy has the role of teaching and authoritatively interpreting the moral laws that apply in this matter, the laity have the duty of using their own initiative and taking action in this area without waiting passively for directives and precepts."

This freedom permits Catholics to be on several sides of social issues, while preserving the priests (who should be forming consciences) from a political factionalism, which divides the faithful unnecessarily.

2. This apostolate is designed to advance the kingdom of God, not purely secular ends. In his Exhortation on Evangelization (*Evangelii Nuntiandi*, December 8, 1975) Paul VI made this relevant point: "It cannot be denied that many Christians, generous people who are concerned about the serious questions liberation raises and who want to involve the Church in the liberation, think of the Church's mission and try to limit it accordingly — would have her restrict herself to political or social action without any concern for the spiritual or the religious. But, if this were a true picture of the Church, she would have lost her meaning."

Two years later the *International Theological Commission*, an advisory body serving the pope, examined the same question. While calling efforts "to change inhuman conditions ... a divine command ... God's will," the practice of faith "is not reducible to changing the conditions of society"; "Politics (for the Christian) is not the final ground that gives absolute meaning to all in life"; "in many individual circumstances it is possible for Christians to opt freely among different paths." The Theological Commission was gravely concerned about the perils to the Church's unity, not only from violent class struggles, but from Catholics refusing to celebrate the Eucharist with confreres of different political persuasions.

The parish, therefore, as part of its evangelization program, is justified involving itself in the social concerns of its own neighborhood and within the limits of its competence. The Church is not the diocese, nor is the parish priest a bishop. Its extraterritorial influence will always be modest, but important for the local community. In particular, the parish plays three complimentary roles: (1) educates, (2) renders personal service, and (3) advocates appropriate public action.

First: Educates. The parish can deepen people's understanding of the faith's social significance. Stress on personal morality and responsibility, on the abhorrence of violence and the use of peaceful means, on self-help and the prudent balancing of conflicting rights and interests, and on the temptations of affluence, are basic elements of Catholic education. Raising social consciousness is another. In certain situations all that the Church has to say to its people is what Christ said on occasion: "Carry your Cross."

The local Church may be the only voice families, workers or the poor have. Discerning who the poor are calls for education. Citizens who lack decent work and income, and "the new poor" (Paul VI's term), that is, "people who have trouble fitting into society," need special attention; and "minority groups ... who are denied equality before the law" need someone to raise the consciousness of the neighborhood. What institution better than the parish?

Second: The parish provides service. The American parish normally excels at this, often being the "middleman" between people and the well-endowed public institutions. A parish providing a name, an address, or a telephone number may only be the beginning service to its people. Parish priests with creative relationships to existing bureaucratic structures can be local heroes. It is not easy for simple people to break through the red tape of Catholic Charities, local employment and welfare agencies, union or industry groups, hospitals, homes for the aged, hostelries, public education officers, the police precinct, local political leaders. Knowing the right physicians, or the key person in the hospital emergency wards, helps immensely when the priest is the intervenor.

What about parish units of the Saint Vincent De Paul Society and Ladies of Charity? They cannot remain simply another parochial bank account. A band of parochial apostles visiting forty or fifty homes a week, and performing corporal and spiritual works of mercy are manna to the poor who find civic agencies cold and forbidding. In every parish, too, there are doubters who appreciate counsel, the ignorant who require instruction, the sorrowful who relish a little comforting, which may explain why many parishes pay people's rent, or provide Alcoholics Anonymous (AA) meetings, or organize people to clean up the neighborhood dirt. From out of consistent personal contact between parish priests and the "least of my brethren," parish community develops. Modern parishes, however limited are their resources, do this better than other institutions because they operate where people live.

Third: Advocacy and action. "Speak out on behalf of the poor," says the hierarchy. Or, "do something to liberate them from intolerable living conditions." The process of man's redemption, of which the Church is a vital guardian, must begin here on earth. The kingdom of heaven is foreshadowed today through the respect shown by the Church's ministers for mankind's humanity and for his sacred destiny. Advocacy and action will, at times, involve the Church in a little politics, but politics is legitimate participation in the struggle among competing groups for a voice in decisions of the commonwealth. In democratic society competing interests clash, and some causes at different times will win, others will lose. But, under the American system, those without a voice never win. The commonwealth's practices usually reflect the power held by those whom the power-brokers come to respect.

The Church, having fought many times to protect its own existence or institutions, or to safeguard a fundamental value such as the sacredness of marriage or human life, is no babe-in-the-woods at politics. Catholics are often uncomfortable with any kind of public brawling involving the Church, arguing that there are no preeminently religious issues at stake in crass politics. While this allegation can be true (e.g., if a Church body attempted to determine the price of steel, set the prime interest rate or the cost of a labor contract), supporting the helpless defends the sacredness of human life itself, in its living as much as in its dying. Few would contest this teaching of the Church's *magisterium*. Parishes may not have seeming power to improve regional or national social problems, but *a network of parishes effectively raising the consciousness of their own people, urging them to civic responsibility, can go a long way toward balancing public thinking which now tends to pragmatic and political, not principled or unselfish.*

Other elements in the Church's human thrust, which shape Church policy toward social action by the laity, include the following:

1. The Church prefers that reform of institutions goes hand-in-hand with a reform of morals. Advocacy is a two-way street — toward Church people's inner life as well as toward the external behavior of civic society. What does it profit to throw the rascals out, if new rascals take their place?

2. The Church prefers that properly trained laity lead the work of social reform, not priests nor religious. The secular world is the area of laymen's competence. Political choices by clerics tend to usurp that competence. Clerics and religious are not precluded, however, from action in cases of extreme need (e.g., when the laity are prevented), but even here, the 1971 Roman Synod calls upon us "to preserve ecclesial communion and reject violence, in words and deeds, as not being in accordance with the Gospel."

3. The Church expects Catholics to unite on political causes which promote, protect, or defend religious principles or the Church institution itself. The most clear examples of such issues, of course, are the protection of right-to-life, and the right of parents to choose non-public education for their children without social penalty.

It must be kept in mind, however, that religious activists labor under serious difficulties, not the least of which are differences of opinion among clergy and prominent laity about what is the authentic Catholic response to the problems of society. Furthermore, as a result of doctrinal divisions within the Church, we do not have a well worked out political agenda consistent with our principles. Social apostles find themselves, therefore, caught between papal/episcopal teaching, and the tendency of well-known Catholic academics and politicians to espouse the agenda of secular intellectuals. Catholics who adopt what looks like an authentic Church attitude are accused of trying to impose their personal beliefs on the country; as if that is not precisely what many Harvard University professors, editors of *The New York Times*, and leading lights of both political parties, try to do. Other Catholics bow to the pressures of the dominant opinion-molders by disassociating themselves from Church positions, some even collaborating in the frustration of efforts by fellow Catholics to influence the democratic process, frequently saying in public, "I am personally opposed to abortion, but do not want to impose my views on the commonwealth."

In view of this confusion within Catholic ranks, it is not surprising that Leo Pfeffer, the well-known antagonist of religious schools, years ago confidently proclaimed the victory of secular humanism in American society, asserting, too, that the present abortion fight is merely the Catholic Church's last hurrah.

If Catholics are to succeed in the political arena, they must (1) choose the right religious principles on which to make a stand; (2) form allegiances with like-minded groups, especially with those motivated by religion; though of another persuasion, and (3) be prepared for high-minded and skillful brawling in the political arena, including the media.

A Last Word

The Catholic Church is a mega-institution, with local units in every nook and cranny of the United States. No parish represents the entire Catholic community as a whole, but cooperation between its various organs is essential.

1. The larger Church should cede to the parish what belongs to its pastor and his aides, especially those services best performed on the local level. Diocesan agencies should not take referrals from a parish unless the priest or his staff has done homework, and can demonstrate that the problem exceeds its competence or resources. Emergency assistance for the needy, up to a reasonable amount, is the function of the parish.

2. Diocesan leadership should train priests in the proper use of existing social welfare resources. Priests must learn to deal with these agencies on behalf of their people from a position of knowledge and competence.

3. Agencies, like Catholic Charities, should bring their pastoral expertise to bear on the training of future priests. Pastoral training of priests should be as intense as in the preparation of social workers, psychologists, medical doctors and engineers. Not the least part of this training should be the study of the history, aims, techniques, constitutions of the Catholic societies the diocese expects parishes to organize and administer.

4. Future priests should at least know in broad outline the traditions of the Church, and what modern science can tell about organizational techniques, leadership qualities, administration and management procedures. Parishioners cannot expect all priests to be charismatic personalities or saints, but they have the right to expect that an ordained leader knows how to lead and to manage the trust given to him by the bishop.

5. The bishop should be in the position to know, and to evaluate what goes on in parishes, particularly if he wishes to raise standards of performance. In some cases, it appears, many of the bishops' favored enterprises are poorly managed year after year.

6. In their turn, pastors should bring to the attention of the bishop inadequacies in the way which diocesan agencies serve them.

In one parish years ago a group of mugwump Democrats, calling themselves "Minute Men," took upon themselves to rid the neighborhood of a local Congressman, whom they called a "Commie." Gerry-mandering had placed this individual in a community whose interests he represented badly. It was fun to watch the pillars of the parish Church fight two battles at once — the Congressman and the local bosses who had tapped him — and in the long run to win.

Priests tend to forget how many Catholics, besides having a developed moral sense, also have political know-how, which they would like to put to good use on behalf of their communities, given half a chance. If clergy are on their side, well and good, but they sometimes prosper if the clergy merely stay out of their way. When the "Minute Men" were doing their favorite thing, priests were not sideliners, but neither were they on the picket lines. The street parades were ecumenical to the core, not clerical feasts. The Church helped most in providing meeting space to union organizers, strikers, morality-in-media activists, and interracial leaders, when the cause seemed righteous, even if not *per se* religious.

Some parish priests are squeamish, not knowing what the chancery thinks. Normally chancellors and neighborhood pastors have the good sense to know what is fitting to their kind and what is *verboten*. (No one in olden days would have scheduled a debate between abortionists and right-to-lifers right below the tabernacle upstairs.) If priests then were inclined to be politically shy, the newer kind somehow have an idea that wearing the Roman collar confers ward-heeling skills, or dubs them potential would-be mayors of the city. There is good reason why a sensible parish priest would stir up his people for a worthy cause, especially since Christ was a pretty good agitator in his own right. However, Christ had His Father's priorities in order, and so did that Father John Ireland, who learned the hard way not to find salvation, even on earth, in political machinations: "I certainly am not going to undervalue laws, science and industry; in their own place they merit and receive our plaudits. But to make them the means of man's real progress, to call them progress, is the sheerest of follies. They are all outside of man, and do not reach the root of his evils, his own heart."[3]

Endnotes

1. Marvin R. O'Connell, *John Ireland and the American Catholic Church* (Saint Paul, MN: Minnesota Historical Society Press, 1988) pp. 94ff.
2. The social encyclicals are impressive: Leo XIII's *Rerum Novarum* (1891); Pius XI's *Quadragesimo Anno* (1931) and *Divini Redemptoris*

(1937); Pius XII's *Summi Pontificatus* (1939); John XXIII's *Mater et Magistra* (1961) and *Pacem in Terris* (1963); Paul VI's *Populorum Progressio* (1967); and John Paul II's *Laborem Exercens* (1981) and *Centesimus Annus* (1991).

3. Marvin O'Connell, *op. cit.*, p. 99.

Chapter Eleven

Going Beyond
the Poverty Line

To the Question: "Can you draw me a composite of a poor person?" I give the following answer. Surprisingly the first ingredient is not black, but female. She will be non-white, either black or Hispanic, over sixty-five, and not part of a family unit. She will live in the rural South and because her education is limited she will mainly be unemployed or employed only intermittently at the most marginal jobs that just do not pay, such as plastics, which simply cannot compete with the price and quality of imports.

— Nicholas Kisburg, International Brotherhood of Teamsters

There is hardly a subject about which there has been more wasted talk since Vatican II than how to turn the poor into good Catholics. Part of the difficulty is that we have people in positions of influence who think it more important to make people less poor than more or less Catholic. Other voices heard include those who consider it colonialism to disturb native or inherited belief systems, and those who would rather talk of African-American rights, Hispanic rights, Indian rights, sharecropper rights, fruit pickers' rights, or homosexual rights, than of the Apostles' Creed. Then, there are the multiculturalists, who are deeply into anthropology, and say that preaching the gospel in Hebrew, Greek, Roman or European terms is fraudulent. They would rather hold seminars for the next quarter-century about new doctrinal formulas (about Christ's divinity, e.g.), than go out and do what the Jewish Peter and Paul did for the Greeks and Romans, or do what the English monk Boniface did for the Germans.

A New Problem?

Obstacles to preaching the gospel have always existed. Even for Christ. Who else did the early priests address when the first foreigners landed on American soil? The rich? The educated? The disposed? No, mostly the poor, the untutored, and hostiles. In the early years of this country, the original missionaries, including bishops, walked into alien territory, sometimes among peoples whose languages they did not understand. And we know the results.

In years bygone, priests did not round up converts by the thousands and rush them into tents for a charismatic visit with the Holy Spirit. In city slums priests often baptized members of a discriminated-against minority by the hundreds several times a year, and ushered them quietly into parish life. While contemporary priests sometimes bemoan their present inability to cope with the Hispanic migrations, others manage very well by doing very ordinary things, like being concerned about the state of their faith, and of their souls.

Great oaks may grow from little acorns, but part of our new problem in evangelizing the poor is that elites are waiting for a macro-plan, devised by experts, to do the job overnight. Another explanation for depressing results is the lack of well-trained native priests for incoming native populations. During the nineteenth century ethnic groups brought their own priests and, however much later Americans (and bishops) complained about national parishes, they served the Church as bridges between the lifestyle and Catholicity of one culture to another. Also, those who favor homogenization and detest separatism are occasionally at war with others would hyphenate immigrants forever. Whatever *we* think, Mexicans, Puerto Ricans, and South Americans are different Spanish types, who simply want to be Americans. Blacks from Nigeria or from the British colonies are not the same as blacks from Mississippi or New York. Koreans are not Chinese or Japanese, and so forth. Finally, as these "outsiders" grow to become one-third of the American population early in the twenty-first century, the Church faces its worst shortage of American-born priests and religious in a century.

We are also running into a new ideological problem. Anything that smacks of "paternalism" or "*noblesse oblige*" is out, even for parish priests. Charges of "Uncle Tom-ism" can be intimidating for well-intentioned white priests from a middle class background working in a slum. Now, in certain quarters, they are expected to act more like liberation theologians than as pastors. Blaming nativists for local difficulties is in style. Catholics often did the same in the nineteenth century, when some of their problems developed out of their own vulgarity, or their drunkenness, or their loose morals. Only Saint Paul's Archbishop John Ireland — as far as I know — was bold enough to blame some of the anti-Catholicism of the time on the conduct of Catholics themselves. Father Theobald Matthew's Temperance Society, for example, was aimed specifically at Irish drunks. Priests of that day, according to historian Theodore Maynard, were instructed to debar from the sacraments saloon keepers who sold liquor to drunks, or who permitted drunkenness on their premises. The crime statistics were heavily loaded with Catholics.

But priests, then, had one advantage in their favor. Customarily they belonged to the same ethnic group as their diocesan miscreants. Irish or German or Polish pastors had an easier time throwing a rhetorical rope around their carousers, and Italian pastors over their anticlerics, without fear of being tarred and feathered as enemies of the tribe. Even apostate Catholics took for granted the right of the priests to correct their failings. Crusading against sin was not simply a Protestant fetish. Catholic pastors were good at it too, preaching not only against the vulgarities of their congregations, but about the white collar crimes of their upwardly mobile parishioners. Upper-class Catholics, whose manners were often better than their morals, and whose religion was latitudinarian enough to incline them to look down their noses at the crude pieties of their immigrant pastors, were often arrogant. Some priests joined their clubs, but others were their severest critics.

New Immigrants and a New Game

Similar battles go on now, but the rules of intra-family war have changed. The public no longer has a clear idea of who is on what side, even within the Church. In determining what to do about the new immigrants, the country's mores may count more than Catholic morals, mores being the norms of behavior sanctioned by society, not necessarily those commanded by God. In our time, many Catholic opinion-molders grant everyone freedom to follow the Church's moral code, but they also look upon this as something the priest must not impose.

Political correctness, not well-established moral norms, is at times the determinant of acceptable social behavior for the masses. Sexual aberrations — illegitimacy, adultery, homosexuality — are in many quarters looked upon as peccadillos, and "doing one's own thing," even when to the extent of being vulgar or becoming a public nuisance, is condoned. On the other hand, popular ethos has turned certain free choices into social sins. Anyone who threatens a neighbor by smoking in public is quarantined, but killing one's child in the womb represents a sacred pro-choice freedom, especially for immigrants who have too many babies anyway.

These cultural changes, which pour over ghettos as much as on gold coasts, have evolved out of several philosophical assumptions which took scholarly roots more than a generation ago in American universities. One argues that God, if there is a God, consigned the management of man's universe to his creatures and, that in the process, the primary social value is free choice. The second takes for granted that all institutions, including the Church, are inhibitors of freedom, and that all authority figures are enemies of equality. "Discrimination," a neutral Greek word which etymologically only means "judgment," preferably good judgment, takes on a punitive significance, when governmentally defined. Defenders of the secular mores can exercise discriminating judgment, but not apologists for Judeo-Christian morality.

What This Means for Parish Priests

Present American mores make it difficult for Catholic priests, especially those dealing with immigrants day by day. Those who want the priest to tell everyone what to do about eliminating poverty and its causes do not want him to say anything about what people should do in bed. In olden days, newspaper headlines would hardly have featured "Pastor Fires Irish Drunk," nor would the city's aldermen have remanded him for trial. Indeed, public opinion of that day would normally have agreed that priest showed good judgment, discriminating wisely between what was good for the community and what was not. Furthermore, those priests had clerical neighbors who were of one mind about the Catholic moral code. Today, however, good pastors may be in hot water with government, with media, with fellow priests and, additionally, be shepherds of an ethnic group other than the one into which they were born.

Secular forces, now arrayed against Christian belief, more powerfully than anything the Protestant Crusade ever mustered, pressure priests to think that their parishioners are entitled to special privileges, or to dispensations from obedience to public laws. Contemporary priests are subject, also, to threats rarely faced on the docks or in the coal mines of yesteryear. And, if they have been trained in a seminary, whose professors looked at the gospel charge "Seek first the kingdom of God and His righteousness" as an opiate to frustrate the underclass, they may not know the difference between their mission and that of the local mayor. With that kind of world around them, priests who think that forming character or saving souls is their job may become lost souls themselves.

The "Poor Parish" Considered Abstractly

There is a little difficulty in the phrase itself. What is "poor"? At the end of his life, my father was asked, "What kind of an estate are you going to leave behind?" To which he responded: "Money? Nothing. Property? None. Only my six children."

In the language of the streets, the poor parish is one in a ghetto with dirty buildings and as much as half its population (at least a quarter) earning below the putative poverty line. Unemployment is high, especially among women and the young, the marriages possibly not marriages at all, certainly not often valid by Catholic standards and, today, the number of live infants born to wedded parents is likely to be surpassed by the number of out-of-wedlock deliveries, plus abortions. Mass attendance is well below par, the children are poorly catechized, a good deal of sexual hanky-panky goes on among the teenagers, the people use the street as if it were their private backyard, and they are loud, often angry.

Remember, however, slums may not only be places. Sometimes slums are people. A great many economically "poor" (i.e., low on money) are clean, well-mannered, God-fearing, hard-working, parents of children educated beyond anything their weekly pittance can reasonably afford. On the other hand, in other, more antiseptic neighborhoods of the well-to-do, one may find by the legion various kinds of slummy people — corporate bandits, grafters, white collar criminals, traitors, alcoholics, sodomists, adulterers and fornicators, irreligious pornographers, and pedophiles, as the evidence shows. Whose poverty are we talking about? The pastor of a "middle class" parish usually finds that most of his constituents lack the blatant vices of Cannery Row or Snob Hill. But even he, if he digs deeply enough, will find his share of "poor" people, whose vices reflect the reference group which gives them their civic identity.

The Church has all kinds of children everywhere, and her families, the "little houses of worship," are far from saintly in all respects. The Church is also like a grab bag, into which the parish priest reaches for whatever methods are likely to work on Cannery Row, Snob Hill, or in middle America. He must not neglect those who appear housebroken to Church discipline nor those who ask little from the Church; but the problem "cases" are the ones which will preoccupy a good part of his time. Still, within every parish, no matter what his audience, the priest finds sacraments, liturgy, the Bible, litanies and music, devotions for Church and the home, quiet moments and processions, Holy Hours and retreats, societies for pious and for Catholic activists, programs for young and for old, specialists and enthusiasts, many saints and a lot of sinners. If he is prepared for his role, he does not need experts to spell out his priorities, nor to tell him his agenda. Clearly, he needs priest friends and collaborators in the chancery office or the seminary, a good array of up-to-date reading material and, of course, a parish council that reflects the total parish, more so than the neighborhood's special interest groups. He also has the tools of his priestly trade, the Church's basic resources, culled and cultivated over the centuries. With these in hand, every priest of the streets should have the wherewithal to deal with the many incomplete Christians he finds in his parish.

Somehow, we have allowed specialists to break the Church down into its statistical parts. In the process, we have forgotten the Church's "wholeness." Experts are said to be good at analyzing problems, but they are not necessarily qualified to solve them. Once upon a time Harry Truman, facing a critical decision for the nation, was advised to bring in a half-dozen experts. To which the president is said to have replied: "Hell no, they'd only give me six different opinions, leaving me to decide anyway." This decisiveness, based on his sense of who he was, and what the nation needed, is what made him, to the surprise of his betters, an outstanding president. Furthermore, experts have their own fads and follow the trends of their given time. The in-program of one decade is readily displaced when a new theory, based on a different research model, emerges. The view that evangelization is aided by merely changing the poor's environment is a myth. One does not have to read many social science texts — the index of the bishops' documentary service *Origins* has much to say about the socioeconomic environment of various poverty populations — to realize how much stress is laid on saving the world as the way to save souls. (More will be said on this in another place.) Suffice to say here that, since the parish priest is not going to save the world of his parish in his lifetime, he had better be content with saving souls as best he can. And for that the Church has a great deal to say to him. Especially about what the pastoral leader of a "poor" parish should do.

"The Buck Stops Here"

He can spend his time weeping or gnashing his teeth. He can waste a lot of time studying the problem or attending seminars on poverty,[1] or he can go to work, remembering that when priests do not walk the first mile toward the Church's objective, it is for the reason they did not take the first step.

Among the things he must consider, the following deserve special attention:

1. He must make sure his priorities are in order. The priest's job is to uplift his people to "know, love, and serve God in this world and to be happy with Him forever in heaven." Priests may not be able to make them rich, or even promote them into the middle class, but they can catechize people, and inspire them to be better than anyone else expects them to be. They can instill in them a sense of the presence of God by getting them to Mass on Sunday, by baptizing their babies and by carrying their loved ones to their final resting place this side of eternity.

Muddled thinking sometimes gets in the way of obvious work. The poor are still easier to reach than the rich, largely because the underprivileged have a sense of their incompleteness, no matter what their race or native tongue. Choosing de-povertization over evangelization as a priority may have appeal to a certain type of modern ideologues, but it never worked as superior evangelization when the Church *was* the State. What makes anyone think that clerics today can develop wealth or create jobs for their poor? Hopefully, they can pray and moralize, provide direction and an outstretched hand. But it is the state, government being only one of its parts, which has the resources and competence to advance the worldly well-being of its citizens. The Catholic contribution to poor people's prosperity is to uplift their life while trying to deepen their spirituality, to develop their God-given talents (we all have some) and to inculcate the habits of thinking and behavior necessary to their upward mobility, often in an unfriendly cultural atmosphere. Our parochial schools did this beautifully for a century, assisted by those Catholic social service agencies which succored the blind, the lame, the deaf, and the exceptional child to overcome the handicaps which inhibited his or her growth.

The final word on this subject will never be said infallibly. However, it is important for the Church to build up people's hopes, as well as their virtues, to improve their morals and their lifestyle, so that they may take advantage of opportunities, to develop their self-esteem and habits of work. It is not to the Church's advantage to allow parishioners to wallow in envy and sloth, simply because they are still on the lower rungs of the economic ladder. Indeed, priests should help them resist political opportunists who infect the poor with resentments that can only frustrate character development. Nationals of every kind are naturally given to preferring their own kind, to ethnocentrism, as it is called in academic circles. This is quite different from wallowing in the people-hating ideologies political opportunists work to multiply. Hating does not help a teenager finish high school.

2. He must acknowledge the magnitude of the problem without allowing it to depress him. One can go from study to study — we have never seen so many statistics — and discover that after forty years of conscience-raising, the vast majority of poor minorities are still not practicing Catholics, especially the ones who, by infant baptism and attention already given, should be merging into the Catholic mainstream. We have even begun to blame Protestant sects for stealing Catholics away from us, when all the evangelicals do is steal our pious practices, ones which we copyrighted, but rarely use today. After forty years we should realize that the success of Protestant proselytizing is not where the Catholic evangelization difficulties began.

3. He must create a milieu for the poor that will make them open to, and friendly toward, the local parish. This takes time and involves tedious work. Father Ronald Marino, a Brooklyn priest who deals with immigrants and migrants exclusively, explains our sometimes failure to find social or religious support from the "poor" parish: "The one underlying factor is the knock on the door. It's something we Catholics don't do very often." Closed churches, unused parish properties, telephones poorly answered or answered not at all, priests invisible on public streets, unfamiliarity with local customs or the local language, hardly help the parish's public image.

4. He must go and do whatever he can, and do whatever is required. We don't need any new outreach organizations. Or additional instruments of so-called cultural impenetration. A curse of contemporary political life — whenever officeholders are facing a critical problem — is the creation of another line on a flowchart.

What the poor need are priests and parishioners sympathetic to them who realize the difficulties standing in the way of the underprivileged, and who have the ability and interest to become a team of apostolic-minded coworkers in the highways and byways of the neighborhood. We need a priest willing to be his parishioners' "Father."

If his audience is bilingual, he and his staff must be bilingual, too.

And, just because his flock is underprivileged, he need not neglect what it takes to run a good parish anywhere. His program must have the same sacramental, educational and welfare elements as the parish on Lake Shore Drive. If he has Sunday Mass, and the reception of the sacraments uppermost on his mind, his people will hear his message, even if they respond slowly. He may have different pious exercises than his cathedral, but what else should you expect from a parish priest anxious to have his people worship God comfortably.

Everyone says catechesis is almost impossible today, but then such critics may have been spoiled by a large parish school filled with obliging and overworked nuns. Go back to the nineteenth century when the children of Catholic immigrants were all public schoolers, and when lay catechists, such as they were, had less education than today's parents. Priests, poorer then than now, were just as frustrated; but dogged too, digging children out of farms or five story walk-ups and, as a rule, forced to instruct personally potential teachers of the under-catechized young. They had no Catholic college graduates in their parishes. In 1892, one pastor became so unhappy with what his Sunday School teachers were producing, that he set up his own School of Theology. Priests like him became so successful with their public school students that they often postponed building a parochial school, at least until the bishop put his foot down. In an off-the-cuff remark on catechetics, John Paul II was quoted once as saying: "We must start all over again." Unquestionably, in some places, that is precisely what has to be done.

Granting the success of such priests and the three Baltimore Catechisms which capsulated the essentials of Catholic teaching, catechesis in those days meant more than rote learning, or the discipline of a children's Mass. Evangelization also meant Catholic witness. Drilled into the Catholic body at an early age were the corporal and spiritual works of charity and mercy, and the natural and theological virtues, too. Children took faith, hope, and charity for granted, but the nuns surely gave them what-for if they failed to understand the importance of prudence, justice, fortitude, and temperance.

The seven corporal works of charity — feed the hungry, give drink to the thirsty, shelter the homeless, clothe the naked, visit the sick, console prisoners, and bury the dead, mostly based on Matthew 25:35ff. — were compiled by Lactantius around the third century. Primitive Christians, looking upon spiritual needs as belonging to a higher order, went further to recommend seven other works to the faithful: instruct the ignorant, counsel the doubtful, console those in sorrow, correct those in error, forgive injuries, bear wrongs patiently, and pray for the living and the dead. The phraseology may be ancient, and practice did change with the times, but parish societies were created specifically to make these virtues viable on any street where Catholics lived.

Later on, in the middle of the nineteenth century after the rise of Marxism, works of justice were added to the Church's array of demands on believing Christians. The general principles of Catholic social action apply to a pastoral mission among the poor. These will be discussed elsewhere in this book.

For the moment, however, the ABC's of the Church's social involvement, even at the local level, call for character and religious formation by the priest, along with sociopolitical activity by the laity, and within an ecumenical framework, where possible. While the parish will not be a catalyst for reform on world-shaking issues, there are welfare families, single parents, bad housing, filthy streets, abortion clinics, school boards, parents' rights in education, crime, drugs, and so forth that keep a social action committee very busy.

Endnote

1. An early study entitled "Catholic Survey of the Puerto Rican Population in the Archdiocese of New York" (George A. Kelly) was completed in 1953. Forty years later New York distributed a "Pastoral Plan on Hispanic Ministry," which was more detailed and, in some respects, painted a gloomier picture of the Church's difficulties in poverty stricken areas. *Origins* (August 22, 1992) devotes an entire issue to the African-American family.

Chapter Twelve

Walking the Highways and Byways

We exhort you again that, as pastors of souls, you do not restrict your zeal to those who already take part in the life of the Church, but go in search, with no less zeal, of the wanderers who live far from here. These are, as you know, exposed to grave danger, but not irremediably lost. Many, perhaps, most, can still be won to and brought back to the right path. Everything depends on getting in touch with them.

— Pius XII to the Pastors of Rome (1946)

Parish priests have preached the gospel on street corners, in Protestant assembly halls, and in saloons, and they also have done it the hard way — going house to house.

It is not possible to say when American priests stopped visiting their people at home, but, by and large, they have. Oh, there are many instances across the country when "Father drops in for a visit," but is the visit for purposes of evangelization? There are suburban parishes which are teeming with Catholics where families have never seen a priest walk their streets. Priests are busy, but not where the people live.

Priests do not *have* to visit homes for the purpose of evangelization, but when the American Church was growing, they did a lot of it because, among other things, there were few or no telephones. And the Church gained from it. The visits we are talking about, however, are not just for a chat, or to kill a little time, or for a party. We refer more to the example of Jesus dropping in at the Temple "because he was about his Father's business." The call is made for a clear religious purpose.

Perhaps times have changed so much in the direction of worldliness that the sacramental side of a priestly visitation has been lost, on the laity's part, too. But there is something to be said, still, for the aura in which those meetings used to be held. The house was cleaned at his coming, for one thing, and there was almost a church-like atmosphere during the conversation. A great respect was shown to the priest, and he also was conscious of the basic goodness of the people he was meeting, and the burdens of daily life they were carrying.

Of course, priests kept their distance from the people in those days. They were well indoctrinated during their seminary days about the dangers of familiarity. (A disposition modern priests might relearn to their advantage.) One does not want to overdramatize an event that many times was pedestrian, but there were occasions when the laity seemed to think that they really were welcoming Christ to their homes, and the priest himself sensed the special aura in the visit.

It would be ridiculous to maintain that such occasions are the only way, or the best way, of making disciples, or of keeping them. Laity do well at this sort of thing, if properly trained, and religious women — the ones who made a vocation of it — best of all. But no one should discount the long-term value of a priest in someone's home "for purposes of evangelization." An experienced priest can light up a household when he is there "only for a drink." But "the Father's business" type of visit remains a steady memory, even for family members who were absent at the time.

It is presumed that the priest knows, or soon learns, how to comport himself on that occasion. Being comfortable in his own role, and at home with priestly speech, while being friendly at the same time, are great blessings. The stuffed shirt was, and is, no more helpful to the Church or its mission than the Joe Collegian type who bounces around the parish these days in sports clothes.

Where the priest works makes a difference, naturally. In a village or a rural area there are not as many barriers, except distance, between a priest and his people. "Come on down" is an easy invitation for the priest, as it is for everyone else, unless the town just does not like priests. But, once in place, priestly visits "for purposes of evangelization" are the same.

My first assignment brought me in touch with an Irish lady worried that she might be doing wrong by attending Mass in my little parish, which was situated just two blocks from her apartment. Technically, she belonged instead to a large parish eight blocks away. Her conscience had been disturbed a few days earlier when her proper pastor, out on one of his home visitations, climbed four flights of stairs to ask why she was not on his parish list. The priest in question was nearing seventy years old, and was the dominant figure in the neighborhood, known triumphantly as "Big Bill," because he knew virtually everyone. And "knowing everyone" is an important part of the local evangelization process.

A good example of this occurred during World War II, when the young bishop of Florida (essentially one diocese, then) directed that all Catholic homes in his diocese be visited by priests. The pastors resisted at first, but actually handled the house calls quite well. But after the war one heard little of the subject, except from religious communities of women who replaced priests, or from priests in places like Philadelphia, where visits still occur. By my time, when our churches and schools were overcrowded, the norm seemed to be "people coming to priests." When taking over a pastorate in later years, around 1970, it was impossible to motivate curates to do any serious visitations. Parishioners of twenty-five years' standing had never seen a priest cross their doorstep, and young priests insisted the people preferred it that way!

Defining the Terms

Maybe the words "parish census" are inaccurate because they suggest statistics, and parish priests are not in the research business. "House calls" may be better, but even doctors have given up that practice. However, though a priest is rarely on emergency calls any more, his day-to-day work is to bring men and women closer to Christ through the parish, and to inspire them to a higher way of life.

Regular parish visitations, whether carried on by priests, religious, or laity, establish that "Catholic connection." It is home missionary work at best, and community building, too. By these methods the faithful are often motivated to become fervent or apostolic, the lukewarm or indifferent nudged toward the sacraments, and even the Church's enemies, if one succeeds in getting through the door, can at least be touched by the visit. Some of a priest's memories may include seeing the breakdown of reserve when the host begins to explain his or her estrangement from the Church. In any event, the by-products of a regular system of parish visitations are likely to result in the baptism of children, validation of marriages, instruction of the ignorant, confession for the lapsed, or conversion of the unconverted.

A parish priest can, of course, get to know a lot of people in other ways: by standing outside of church on Sundays, by interviewing the parents of all children to be baptized or confirmed, or who enter school for the first time, by attending all wakes, wedding receptions, riding with families to the cemetery, and so forth. You get to know a great many people if you do these things routinely year after year. However, in the examples cited, the people want or need something specific. The situation is quite different when it is the priest or his representative who goes out to say hello to "the elect," or to find the lost sheep. In either case, the parish attains visibility in places where people live.

The Big Obstacles

We speak here about obstacles, not excuses. Anyone can duck a hard job, especially for a lame reason. Old-time priests, ordained at the turn of the century, had no such privileges, they averred. Rain or shine, they were sent out to distant farm families by horse and buggy, or to climb four floors of a slum to meet a drunken dock worker, hardly given a choice by the system. Only a few years ago, an Irish immigrant priest, bored by the rectory habits he found on his arrival, turned his parish into an Hispanic mission simply by barnstorming the Puerto Rican and Dominican tenements day after day. As he used to explain: "My confreres think the command 'Go out into the highways and byways' is better fulfilled by staying home."

If, after World War II, priests in urban areas seemed rectory-bound, and semi-idle, it was in part because the world outside was changing. The use of the automobile, movement to the suburbs, the rise of Levittowns and huge welfare centers, often separated Catholics from their priests by more than geography. Even sick calls moved from homes and rectories to hospitals and chaplains.

When making a judgment about parish visitations, two things must be kept in mind: they take time, and they take priests out of the rectory. The mental attitude of priests themselves, and their priorities, may be more determinative than anything else of what does or does not go on in a priest's life. Priests are creatures of habit, and habit may beget activism — or the ruts in which many are content to function. Of course, lack of interest may also be due to the way budding priests are trained, to the seeming lack of interest by bishops in the personal visits of priests with people. It is also difficult these days to get anyone to follow directives, and what one priest will not do, another better disposed priest may not do either, if only to keep peace in the house. Sometimes, it is argued, modern parishioners want to be let alone, but this claim sounds like an excuse, not an obstacle.

Most Catholics live in highly concentrated urban, exurban, or suburban areas. They are strangers, living among strangers, as much to their church as to the family who lives in the next street. Face-to-face relationships are not what they used to be, nor as numerous. People, if they choose, live anonymously, even to the local priest, especially if they are wayward Catholics. The approval or disapproval of the priest, or of the confessor, or of a neighbor, once an encouragement to piety or a restraint on waywardness, is no longer a social force.

An ongoing plan of "house calls," which establishes direct and personal contact between a parish and its people, is one way of making parishioners less anonymous. If new residents of a parish do not report to their priest, it might be desirable for the priest or his delegate to report to them.

About fifty years ago the Apostolic Delegate to the United States instructed the American bishops, on behalf of the Holy See, to have parish priests keep an "accurate and current census of the faithful entrusted to their care" and to take up such a census in every parish "no matter what the difficulties or the outlook." That probably was the last instruction of its kind in this country.

How to Make House Calls

It makes no difference how a parish priest accomplishes this, or has it completed, as long as it is done with consistency. It is preferable, however, to have a system, one that entails appropriate procedures:

1. Decide who does it. The first thing the priest must decide, once he has tapped the thinking of those who work with him, is: Who is responsible for it? In former days you could count on religious women, but their numbers are few these days. Those who did this well, like Parish Visitors, Helpers of the Holy Souls, Missionary Helpers of the Sacred Heart, were great evangelizers, especially with the underprivileged and the forlorn. Usually better trained for this work than priests, they often entered homes where no priest was welcome, but their role was of a precursor, like John the Baptist. The instruction from the Holy See made it clear even then that substitutes for the clergy were not to be seen as valid replacements. Visiting homes was an essential element of the priest's ministry of the word.

A great deal is said today about "partnership parishes," places where priests pass to others what once was priestly work. In one respect, the term is meaningless. A parish cannot survive without partnership with people. The clergy remain solely responsible for the well-being of "the flock," no less than the bishop for the diocese, or the pope for the Universal Church. So, if the pastor harnesses his Saint Vincent De Paul Society or his Legion of Mary to be his parochial assistants in this matter, that becomes the way to go. Parishioners may treat lay representatives with less reserve, since fallen-away Catholics sometimes resist the ministrations of a priest. However, the priest or the priests must stay close to the project lest the visited Catholics become mere names on someone else's index card. It is one thing to note an invalid marriage on a form, but quite another to hear the stories or remember the faces of the ones so married.

2. Surveying the territory. To those who have done it, part of the fun of parish visitations is deciding where the Catholics are. In this connection, the nature of the community and the condition of the housing are factors of importance. Names of regular donors to parochial and diocesan collections, families of Catholic and parochial school children, and other obvious sources, when properly collated, are good starting points. The local telephone company, correctly approached, can provide lists by streets of names, addresses, and telephone numbers, which contain

"Catholic" names recorded nowhere else. Every parish has parochial loyalists on every street, or in every town, who can be trained to report otherwise unidentified Catholics. The longer that parish workers have resided in the place the more likely they have good information to share. As the visitations proceed, the names of additional Catholics will surface. By the end of each year, the parish office should have a list of all known Catholics arranged alphabetically, by avenue or street or town, with name, address, and phone number.

3. Letting everybody know. Regular announcements of the parish program of "house calls" are important, because they provide nonthreatening information and good reasons for cooperation. Telling parishioners that the priests are scheduled to bless homes in a given area, in a given month, is generally well received. On the other hand, suspicious parishioners may think that the parish is only looking for more money. Insofar as it can be done, such resistance can be short-circuited only with honest talk. It also helps if the first calls are made to "safe" parishioners whose account of the visit to neighbors is likely to be favorable.

Judgments must be made eventually about how the visits will proceed (house by house, village by village, random style, divided among priests or lay teams), and whether it is to be ongoing or limited to a specific time period. It is always helpful to have a specific goal. A project to be completed in two months of a given year is only slightly different from asking three workers to make ten house calls a week, thirty weeks a year, with a view to covering the entire eighteen hundred families in two years. The options for the parish are many, even within a system.

It is always courteous, preferable, and in some places absolutely necessary, to make an advance appointment by telephone. Due to the increase of crime and violence, many people are wary of inviting an unannounced stranger into their home.

4. The desirable information. The amount of accumulated information to be sought depends on whatever the priests hope to accomplish. (In the old days parishes had their census card printed to suit those purposes, with a place for the *name*, *address*, *phone number*, and *date* clearly visible at the top.)

Whether formal or informal, the process should result in a wealth of information recorded during the visit or thereafter. Any or all of the following items, phrased as precisely as possible for the sake of accurate responses, should be kept in mind as useful things to know later:

- First name(s)
- Relationship(s), (e.g., son, aunt, etc.)

- Age at last birthday
- Highest grade of schooling (1-16)
- Religious affiliation
- Occupation
- Actual or estimated monthly rental value of residence (a better index of income and, more likely, answered better)
- Baptism
- Confirmation
- Easter duty this year (phrased to avoid evasion)
- Number of Sunday Masses attended in previous four weeks
- Number of Communions received in previous four weeks
- Marital status (M, S, W, sep., div.)
- Where and when married (for validity)

5. Ringing the doorbell. Preparation for the calls should involve an open discussion among the priests and/or the workers about how to enter Catholic homes properly, especially those of relative strangers. The opening minutes of such visits are important, taken up first with an introduction explaining the friendly purpose of the visit. The impression created at that moment signals the success of the entire encounter, or its lack. Time saved with fervent Catholics can be used profitably with the lukewarm or the lax.

The atmosphere of the Catholic home in which little piety is evident will be obvious immediately by the manner of the greeting, by the reluctance to admit the visitor, or by embarrassed silence. In such homes the caller must be careful. Once admitted, he or she should be casual and relaxed, especially since an estranged Catholic is likely to be distant, or even hostile. Discussing the weather, the health of the baby, or anything and everything that will ease tensions, are helpful openers. During the early part of the interview, informality should be the rule, with the visitor edging up to the sensitive questions carefully. In difficult cases he may have to terminate the interview and return another day. A Catholic wife may not like to speak in the presence of her non-Catholic husband. At no time should the visitor, even a priest, censure anyone. If all goes well, he may find the last words of a difficult interview will be consoling: "Thank you. I didn't want you to come, but now that it's over, I'm glad you did!"

The work for the parish created by home visitations may be more time-consuming than the visits themselves, in baptisms and marriages alone. But so are the rewards. Legendary parishes are those which are people-oriented, which give direction to human lives, shape consciences, raise hearts and minds to God, know how to deal effectively with evildo-ers, which are always respected, sometimes loved, but never forgotten even by those who never liked the Church.

Making "house calls" is simpler when everyone is doing it. Be-cause they have become a rarity, discussions about them tend instead to be complicated exercises in pop-psychology, about motivation, personal tastes, qualifications, and so forth. Granted, not every parish worker, in-cluding a priest, is good at meeting people, any more than every doctor has a good bedside manner. Yet this is part of parish work. In broken Catholic situations, additional Church documents or sermons do not work. The one certainty that remains with the parish that walks the streets is the stored memory of friendly faces, the consoled lonely hearts, the malcon-tents who came to take a new look at the Church, the parents who thanked the priest, and the Living Body of Christ in a corner of the world no one thought was there.

The Extras

Part of the advantage of being people-oriented is that it moves the parish priest to organize the best roster of parishioners, active or inactive, that he can assemble. Its value is incalculable for several reasons:

For personal letters. Why should not a parish priest, especially a pastor, send a personal note once a year to everyone on a notable occa-sion, probably Christmas, or perhaps on the death of a beloved priest. A little costly, perhaps, but worth every penny of recall it gives to the luke-warm, and dollars of appreciation from the *fideles.*

For parish announcements, especially about Sunday Mass, its im-portance, of a parish mission or special event like the blessing of couples, mothers, children, etc. The announcement can also contain a little bit of pastoral wisdom or a sermonette, if the priest is good at that sort of thing. Announcements, too, of what he is doing for them (this time not asking) may surprise a good many.

For thank-yous. Hilaire Belloc once said, "The Grace of God is in courtesy."

In any event, the action or gesture that establishes contact in a per-sonal way between rectory and people, even if it is only through the postman, is a work of God. It reminds those out there that the priest cares.

Chapter Thirteen

The Parish Army:
Societies the Old Way

Now there are varieties of gifts, but the same Spirit, and there are varieties of services, but the same Lord; and there are varieties of activities, but it is the same God who activates all of them in everyone. To each is given through the Spirit the utterance of knowledge according to the same Spirit, to another faith by the same Spirit, to another gifts of healing by the one Spirit, to another the working of miracles, to another prophecy, to another the discernment of spirits, to another various kinds of tongues, to another the interpretation of tongues. All these are activated by one and the same Spirit, who allots to each one individually just as the Spirit chooses.

— Saint Paul to the Corinthians (1 Corinthians 12:4-11, *The New Revised Standard Version, with Apocrypha*)

The best parish priest I ever knew could not, according to a diocesan wag, "organize a fist fight." His altar boy society was one of the worst, and hardly anyone showed up for his high school club. But if he thought his parish should be properly represented at the Cathedral on a given Sunday morning for a bishop's event, two hundred teenagers at his call would come out of the shadows and join him on the pilgrimage. He was "Father Parish" personified, who knew everyone, and to whom everyone came when they were in trouble. He just was not an organization man.

Yet, if you take a look at the typical Sunday bulletin, what do you find? Beyond the little ads, most of the space is occupied by references to the Parish Council, the New Parishioners Committee, the Young Adults Committee, the Youth Committee, the Finance Committee, the Friendly Visitors, the Leisure Club, the Women's Guild, the Divorced and Separated Group, the Social Justice Committee, the Saint Vincent De Paul Society, RCIA, and so forth. Apart from priests, the parish church just cannot get along without organizations and committees of laity. If, as it is said, the army crawls on its way to victory on its belly, the Church lives and functions through its societies. And why not? They have been there from the beginning, with the first widows and the early virgins. And for three hundred fifty years at least, popes have been saying that lay apostles are an essential part of the Church mission.

For reasons of simplification, parish societies can be divided into three categories — those involved in *contemplation, cooperation*, or *celebration*. All Catholic groups have their contemplative side, in the sense that their reason for being has to do with piety. They exist, whatever else their purpose, to help sanctify members, even if the members spend most of their time staging the annual parish show. All Catholic groups *DO* something, even if their function is dominantly worship. The Nocturnal Adoration Society, primarily contemplative, may supply most of the parish's liturgical activists. The *Legion of Mary*, an important cooperator with clergy in making parish visitations, holds weekly meetings which are highly meditative and prayerful. "The celebrators," those in charge of the parish's social life, are unlike Rotarians because, when not creating parochial fun, they gather from time to time around the altar to help forge a pious Christian community.

Parish organizations change with the times, with the needs, and at the inspiration of a bishop or a pastor. The large Holy Name and Rosary Societies of another era reflected the Church's concern for Catholic piety in a Protestant culture. But we cannot, willy-nilly, move in new directions without having a good grasp of the reasons why certain apostolates perdure, even if the names change, and others rise only to die an early death because they were badly organized. Something can be said for looking backwards, so that we can go forward with the learning we acquired from the experience of those who have gone before.

Priests can become cynical about parish organizations (some of which can be sources of parochial friction), or can become bored with them if they see the same faces month after month. Still, parish societies, when properly run, are the eyes and ears, arms and legs of the local church. Their derring-do for the faith, and the laity who evolve into leadership roles with clergy, provide warm memories for a priest in the twilight of his life.

Parish societies serve four purposes: (1) they tap leadership; (2) they intensify faith and moral life; (3) they help parochial morale; and (4) they train apostolic-minded activists.

Parish societies attract only a small proportion of churchgoers, and priests come to expect that, but these leaders influence the parish mood through the social events they sponsor. Historically, their most significant contribution to parish life was the inculcation of good sacramental habits within the family. This purpose is still valid, even if the organizations which pioneered the piety are outdated. Today's specialized groups of married couples and their teenagers, single parents, the divorced and separated, therapy groups and political activists, senior citizens, can profit, without abandoning their specialized focus, from the lesson older groups leave behind, because once upon a time they helped form Catholic consciences and stimulated the frequent and worthy reception of the Eucharist.

A world specifically male or female, a family world, a teenage world, a children's world, exist everywhere. There is no reason, therefore, why on one Sunday each month the pastor cannot call each of these distinct worlds together for common worship. Many older priests fail to understand why "the children's Mass" was virtually outlawed simply because nuns were no longer around to keep peace or count heads, as if other proctors could not have been found to keep alive the importance of children learning from an early age the discipline of Sunday Mass. Even careless parents learned a lesson when they were reminded week by week that their child was expected at the 9:00 A.M. Mass. Consequently, reconsidering a weekly Mass specifically for men, women, teenagers, etc., may well be in order.

The Specialized Apostolates

Every age, every nation, creates the specialized bands of laity the Church needs to carry on its mission. Not even the most energetic priest can resurrect a dead apostolate, especially if the reasons for its demise are unclear. But, if a parish priest is caught up in new trends or new movements, it is important that he analyzes its purpose, nature, and constitution to determine: (1) its potential for Catholic formation and good works, and (2) its chances of survival. There may be some value, therefore, in surveying a few earlier "specialized apostolates" to discover their secrets, and to judge whether their *modus operandi* have relevance to new creations.

In the last century four particular Catholic groups had significant influence on the lives of Catholic laity:

The Christian Family Movement (the youngest) involving married couples trained for social action; *The Sodality of Our Lady* (the oldest), a Jesuit association, mostly of women in the United States, directed toward the spiritual formation of its constituency, with a view of impelling them to the performance of certain Church works; *The Legion of Mary*, a group of men and women whose primary interest is religious conversion; *The Saint Vincent De Paul Society*, Frederic Ozanam's society of men committed to exercising the corporal and spiritual works of mercy among the poor.

The Christian Family Movement founded in 1943 collapsed after Vatican II for all practical purposes because its lay leadership became doctrinal dissenters, and were disavowed by their founding priest. *The Sodality of Our Lady*, a women's society in most parishes, went out of business because, in spite of the fact professional groups of men did exist, it was abandoned by Jesuits after the Council. *The Legion of Mary* continues to exist and, although it never enjoyed widespread use, is less discussed today, and seemingly less an apostolic element of American parish life, although its original value to the Church's mission continues. *The Saint Vincent De Paul Society* is still on the docket of many parishes but, for some strange reason, its internal discipline has generally been abandoned.

These four apostolates, whether short-lived or durable, had or still have qualities of enduring value for priests who contemplate new approaches intended to make the Church's contemporary mission more effective. The itch to do something new is always tempting, especially if it coincides with a cultural trend. But the word "apostolate" has a specific Catholic meaning, and learning from old hands is not a bad idea, even if the intended lessons are ignored.

The four groups under study here have a number of valuable things in common:

1. They were leadership groups, organized for a specific Catholic purpose, created to exercise significant influence on the internal life of the Church or of the world.

2. They were small in numbers, with typically from twelve to twenty members.

3. In different ways, and with different emphasis, members were subject to an intensive formation process, trained first in what the Church traditionally has called "contemplation," before engaging in apostolic endeavors proper to the association. In some respects they were "charismatic," before that word came into Catholic vogue.

4. Priests were vital to the process and, of necessity, devoted a good deal of time to the formative aspects of the enterprise, as did the members themselves.

5. The teaching of the Church, and thinking with the Church, were vital to the effectiveness, and to its utility as an apostolic arm of the Church.

6. The success of the association depended on how well "the book" was followed. Each society had a detailed program with specific rules about meetings, officers, forms of activity, and accountability for doing what the movement was created to do.

7. A significant number of the membership exercised influence within and without the Church far beyond the areas of their association's particular field of interest.

8. At every point the movement was under the supervision of hierarchy.

In essence, these specialized groups represented the Church's idea of "lay apostolate" — the organization of the few to exercise major influence on the many. They might also be called "the yeast" of the Church, and their members "the leaven" of the world.

While they were usually called "lay organizations," these societies were intrinsically tied to the parish/diocesan Church, and most of them engaged in the Church's priestly work (i.e., formation and salvation), although there was a social component to each of them, for example, works either of social charity or social justice. Anticlericalism would have been inconsistent with the society's intrinsic ties to the Church's hierar-

chy and mission. Neither did they exemplify the so-called "free apostolate," one Catholic in spirit but totally "lay" (i.e., free of clerical control),
such as the "labor groups" of old or the "right to life" groups today. In the
"free apostolate," resistance to clerical control is understandable, since
Church authority neither subsidizes the work nor takes responsibility for
its conduct.

Let us look at each of these movements in some detail for the lessons in Catholic potential and/or danger we might learn.

The Christian Family Movement (CFM), an offshoot of Canon
Cardijn's youth activity, called first for Bible study, worship (liturgy),
and ultimately action on the social milieu in which the members lived.
Teams of married couples met weekly in family situations, with a priest
present, to observe a specific issue, judge its significance to the well-
being of the human family, and decide on a course of remedy within the
couples' competency. CFM couples often became the underpinning of
the vibrant diocesan family life programs of the post-World War II era,
especially its Cana and pre-Cana conferences. Its official purpose, defined as the reform of industrial and community institutions, was unat-
tainable because of the "couple" constituency in the movement. Having
a large family, which was characteristic of the membership, was one such
frustration. Indeed, critics often defined CFM as "Can't Find Mother."
As CFM grew to maturity, and contrary to the intentions of its founder
(Monsignor Reynold Hillenbrand), younger priests, seizing the "lay"
aspects of the movement, cultivated an antiestablishment motif in the
membership, even against the Church's pastors, to enhance their own
clerical roles against their superiors. By the close of Vatican II the national leadership of CFM had become doctrinal dissenters.

The Sodality of Our Lady's prescribed program followed a fixed
"book," unlike CFM's, which used a different manual each year. Stress-
ing devotion to Our Lady and attractive to Catholic women (although the
Latin word "sodalis" simply means "companion"), *The Sodality* engaged
first in Christian formation, and in various Catholic activities as the consequence. Sometimes large in number — as many as two hundred members — its fundamental "action" involved mostly Church works: worship, devotion to Our Lady, family life, parish ministry, works of mercy
and social service.

The handicaps under which it labored, besides its title, was that
diocesan leadership, including priests, did not recognize the genius of its
formative mechanisms. This may explain why priests gave it little time

and, in too many cases, it became a "monthly Communion" society. Following Vatican II, the Jesuits reorganized what they called their "Marian Congregations," those "founded after 1584," into what they now specify as "The Christian Life Community." New "general principles" were approved by the Holy See in 1990,[1] emphasizing "the pressing need of local communities (usually of twelve members) to work for justice through a preferential option for the poor and a simple lifestyle which expresses freedom and solidarity with them." The suggested spiritual formation is not dissimilar from the earlier Sodality, although its focus is now more social activist than formative. The word "priest" is not used in this new manual, but each Christian Life Community is told to have "an ecclesiastical assistant" responsible for doctrinal and pastoral concerns "in virtue of the mission given him by the hierarchy, whose authority he represents." According to the new "book," failure to observe the approved norms is reason for suspension, and eventual exclusion by the National Community. While collaboration with the Society of Jesus, with hierarchy, and "a Church connection" is taken for granted, the word "parish" does not appear in the founding document. This probably explains why the reorganized Sodality is not well known.

The Saint Vincent De Paul Society may be the best structured group of these four, explaining why it has perdured so long and is still relative to the spiritual and social demands of the Second Vatican Council. Founded by a layman in 1833, it is still lay in nature, intensely religious for those who follow its program faithfully, parish organized, and devoted totally to alleviating the bodily and spiritual burdens of the poor.[2] Originally established as a men's society, a special "Ladies' Society" is permitted, but is to be entirely distinct. The program demands weekly spiritual reading in concert, prayer and worship, detailed evaluation of domestic difficulties, and immediate remedy. In well-run councils, men give up two nights a week, one of which involves personal visits to parochial homes. The so-called "cases" may originate with the spiritual director, or women religious, or by personal appeal from distressed parishioners. More often than not they extend beyond corporal works of mercy to dealing with children or adults in need of catechesis or the sacraments, with invalid marriages, marital difficulties, or special neighborhood concerns. First-rate Conferences are also involved in the political activities of the community.

The Saint Vincent De Paul Societies vary in effectiveness from diocese to diocese, and from parish to parish. Funded originally by upper-class men who used their own money, the typical Society today uses "poor box money," that is, church money. In some cases the contributions are negligible, in others are so impressive (perhaps $40,000 annually) that the monies are siphoned off for other parish purposes. The Society has tended, in many places because of clergy disinterest, to become a "private club" for cronies who meet weekly for gabfests, card playing, perhaps even a little beer. The "club," whatever its format, tends to make the poor come to them for "food tickets," an embarrassment in itself for those proud poor whose needs are not generally known. Finally, the "club" may be nothing more than a "bread and butter" association, unconcerned with those who are poor spiritually, those families perhaps more needy than ones who have their rent paid.

In recent years, as a result of declining interest or neglect, women have been accepted into membership in what is now a "mixed" Conference. Kelly's Law is relevant here: "Except where marriage or family life is the object, women entering a society of men tend to drive out the men." Through no fault of the women (who by constitution are entitled to their own Conference), the manly aspect of the work tends to disappear, and in mixed company men are inclined to let women do the work.[3]

Given the impetus of the Second Vatican Council, one would think that the Saint Vincent De Paul Society is a modern parochial "must." Instead, it is withering, even though its tradition is completely compatible with added "works of justice" and its methodology, properly used, is invaluable to these new challenges. Pastors should no longer tolerate "clubs" bearing the Frederic Ozanam name. Instead, they should reorganize this apostolate "according to the book."

The Legion of Mary[4] is another small group movement which, from its origins September 7, 1921, has stressed sanctification and conversion of lapsed Catholics and the unchurched. It is also a parish organization *par excellence*, which emphasizes training and formation, weekly meetings, prayer, learning, and apostolic works to follow initiation. The various Legions comprise men only, women only, young only, or a mixed audience. Meetings include prescribed prayers, instructions by the spiritual director and mutual discussion of the weekly activities.

The specialized works of the Legion of Mary include any or all of the following: hospital visitations, visiting homes, conducting a parish census, disseminating Catholic literature, running a parish library, working with the young, teaching Catholic doctrine, checking on school attendance, adult education, reaching out to soldiers and sailors, promoting frequent attendance at Mass and the sacraments, working for the missions, attending wakes and funerals to lead prayer, etc. Legionnaires are barred from soliciting funds or providing material relief to anyone.

Pope John XXIII once said: "*The Legion of Mary* presents the true face of the Catholic Church." Its founders guaranteed that no branch can fail that works faithfully according to the rules. Their advice remains the same today, as it was in the beginning: "If unprepared to work the system exactly as described in the handbook, please do not start *The Legion* at all." Variously scattered throughout the United States, The Legion is attracting the interest of Latin and Asian immigrants, but is not as popular in our country as it might be, perhaps because its military structure and its Roman nomenclature is seen as counterproductive, and in need of updating. Still, its essential formative procedures and its apostolic mission are vital adjuncts to the enterprise of a zealous pastor.

General Summary

Every parish needs organizations. Years ago, the *Confraternity of Christian Doctrine* described itself hyperbolically as "not just another organization, but the parish organized." No one special apostolate is that. But special apostolates taken together are, although the majority of parish priests do not seem to appreciate the need, even in this hour of their shortage.

General parish societies seem to be out, and *ad hoc* meetings of parishioners may be in, for example, to serve an occasional purpose of the parish priest. Blessing throats, distributing ashes, celebrating wedding anniversaries, blessing children and mothers, singling out selected parishioners for church honors, are likely to meet more people's needs than old-line organizations. But, even the pope needs a Curia, the president needs a cabinet, teachers need their honor students, and police need their SWAT teams. The parish priest needs his disciples, whether they be twelve or twenty-four in number, and they constitute the Church's specialized apostolates.

A parish priest cannot effectively administer his parish without them, these "elites," properly selected, whom he forms into thinking Christians, ready to go out into the byways. Whatever form those apostolic groups take, they must be trained, learning not only the lessons of their elders, but how to eschew the mistakes of their predecessors, and be fully Catholic from the beginning.

The American Medical Association would never, at least almost never, allow a surgeon to cut into a patient's body unless he had been closely disciplined over many years in training, practicing under supervision; a submarine commander knows in the same way just how many fathoms he may descend without breaking his vessel in two; NASA spends years training an astronaut to repair a shuttle module on earth before he is allowed to do so in space. The formation of priests to appreciate the lay apostolate, to teach them the theory of various movements and their specific mechanisms, to supervise their techniques in a parish setting (as in a laboratory), to have them know how to choose candidates, be familiar with the tools of formation, to acquire skill at running a meeting, or how to inspire confidence and when to give it, to be faithful to the Church himself and how to instill that in others, to know how to correct and counsel, are as important to a priest as space school is to an astronaut. Some priests have a natural talent for skilled leadership. But there is little justification in throwing them into the pond of parochial life without teaching them organizational skills as well. And, in the process, to discover those priests who are incompetent for that role.

In the old days, the so-called "pastoral theology" courses for deacons were a joke, consisting primarily of an older professor (of scripture perhaps), telling stories of what the real priesthood was about. Following the Joannine Council, "field education" became customary, sending deacons out to a parish in their last year to learn the tricks of the trade, perhaps to take a university course or two. But, during the recent Roman Synod on priestly formation, bishops expressed unhappiness with the results. And John Paul II in *Pastores Dabo Vobis* called for stricter controls. Many current parish priests, trained badly themselves, are not the proper teachers for the artistry under discussion, and many universities, given their present makeup, may do the aspiring priest more harm than good. In actuality, field education often means sending a deacon to a parish to do assignments which the resident priest is no longer interested in doing. If the seminary is a professional school, full training of future priests for dealing with the lay apostolate is an overdue responsibility.

Endnotes

1. Statements of these principles are available from *The National Christian Life Community of the U.S.A. (NCLC)*, 3601 Lindell Blvd., Room #421, Saint Louis, MO 63108 (314) 533-3183.

2. *The Manual of the Society of St Vincent De Paul*, originally available from 64 Grafton Street, Dublin, or a local particular council, is now out of print, at least for many American dioceses.

3. Some pastors may disagree, and assert mixed councils can and do work. It is not possible to argue with success. Still, the genius of the Vincentian "book" is its stress first on personal spirituality forged in weekly meetings. Since the Church recognizes the difference between male and female spiritualities, Frederick Ozanam's manual may still have the right idea.

4. *The Official Handbook of the Legion of Mary*, originally an Irish publication, is usually available from the diocesan headquarters.

Chapter Fourteen

The New Ministries

The parish community must become involved
with the neighborhood and its problems to
witness Christian concern for a better life for
all and its work for justice at the local level.
Parish life should provide challenges and
opportunities for the believing community to
confront sin, suffering, and injustice within
and beyond the local community.

— National Conference of Catholic Bishops
Bicentennial Statement (1977)

M ore "new ministries" have been created in the Church since 1965 than had been established in the previous half-century. Many of these lack ecclesiastical supervision or approval. We now have ministries to the old and to the young, to the married and to the divorced, to priests and to former priests, to men and women, to homosexuals of both sexes, to the privileged and underprivileged, for the altar and for the streets — all of which claim or cherish a deputed role in the service of the Church, and the right to function within Church structures, or the tolerance so to do.

This phenomenon cannot rightly be attributed to the Second Vatican Council, which drew a clear line between "priest" and what today is called "minister." Conciliar documents reserved the Latin word *ministerium* for the activity of the clergy. Indeed, two years after the Council's close, when the *New Catholic Encyclopedia* was published, the only reference to "ministry" was under the heading "Protestant." Yet the terminology, in official as well as popular circles, was speedily eviscerated of its traditional meaning. In common parlance, the words became interchangeable.

It is worthwhile to remark that, for want of more precise terminology, the "new ministries" soon fell into "humanist" and/or "transcendental" categories. Ministry to the married, to the divorced and the separated, to the homosexual, to social liberation, to alcoholics, drug addicts, gamblers, and so forth, come to be looked upon primarily as "psychological" support systems for troubled people, although the transcendental is not excluded for those who insist on a religious component. "Marriage encounter" is a good example of ambivalence, with its stress on better communication between spouses and the tendency there to downplay discussions of contraception, divorce, worthy reception of the Eucharist, etc., lest they frustrate open communication. Alcoholics Anonymous (AA) and Daytop are hardly religious ministries of themselves, although their founders had religious motives and gave a "Christian" orientation to the program, which unbelievers in their midst would like officially to extrapolate from both methodologies.

The new "transcendental" groups would surely include Eucharistic and catechetical ministries, which are numerous; Bible and ecumenical prayer groups; care of the sick; and bereavement associations, all of which have Catholic coloration.

Somewhere in between are the "base communities," the small, intense parochial or regional groups of Catholics that organized either in the interest of developed personal piety plus Catholic action, or the Christianization of the social order, pure and simple. *Cursillos* would be an example of the former, liberation communities the latter. Paul VI takes up "base communities" in *Evangelii Nuntiandi*, pointing out the differences between those rooted in the Church, and those (even if organized by priests) that are driven by Marxist ideology or given to violence against both state and Church.

It is not possible in a summary treatment to give in-depth coverage to all of these specialized ministries, except to say that, if Catholic, they should be fully Catholic. Nor should one segment of the parish — age group, sex, nationality, etc. — dominate the apostolic scene of the parish. It almost goes without saying that, whatever the ministry is, if it is parochial, having growth in piety is a purpose. (Humanist groups may surely function on parish property, but the Church is not responsible for the activity, except perhaps to make sure that it is not antisocial or anti-Catholic.) Initially, the parish priest must select as leaders those whose faith and piety are recognizable to others. Having leaders of marriage encounter who are known to be sterilized or in a bad marriage is hardly good parochial witness to the Church's faith. The Eucharistic ministers, the ushers, the lectors, and the acolytes, who are the most prominent "apostles" on display week after week, should also be above reproach.

Small Beginnings

Before treating several of the new major ministries, recommended or mandated by the pope and/or bishops, it might be of some interest to examine, as an example of Catholic principles at work, a few difficult but new apostolates.

The *Cursillo de Cristiandad* is worth analysis because it is Spanish in origin (1949) and a helpful tool for dealing with newcomers to the United States. Twenty years from now forty percent of the work force in the American West will be Hispanic. At this moment, the median age for the Spanish population is only twenty-five years, most of whom are unconnected with a Catholic parish, many already converts to evangelical or pentecostal Protestantism. While the *Cursillos* are not a post-Vatican II creation (existing on the East Coast in the 1950s), they are good examples of a bishop/pastor-oriented organization of enthusiastic Catholics who, after a short course in Christian living based on faith, are trained to spread the Church's way of life. The participants — either men or women, as many as forty — are first brought together for three days, during which, with priests present, they work to achieve together a deeper appreciation of life in Christ. The *Cursillo* usually opens on a Thursday evening and closes Sunday night. Priests give five meditations and five talks (called drills), the lay leaders adding ten mor drills to apply in their life in the world what the priests taught. Small groups intensify the discussion. The central act each day is the Holy Sacrifice of the Mass, but other devotions — Rosary, Stations of the Cross, Visits — are part of the process. All told, the *Cursillo* has become an interesting mixture of piety, personalism, and pastoral activity. It is available in both English and Spanish, and the *Cursillo Manual* is used for weekly meetings. Juan Hervas, bishop of Ciudad Real, Spain, was its founder and the movement presently has headquarters in New York, Michigan, Texas, and California.

Courage is another movement begun only a few years ago by Father John Harvey, O.S.F.S., to minister to homosexuals, active or nonactive, who desire to live a fully Christian life. While no biological factors predetermining homosexuality have been discovered (although predispositions are not discounted), so-called "Gay Rights Activists" have, through potent political clout, persuaded many Americans that their alternate lifestyle is legitimate. However, many confessed homosexuals identify instead with the heterosexual lifestyle, feel that their life is encumbered by a same-sex attraction, have no deep resentments against the Church, and wish to lead a full Christian life.

Courage appeals to these homosexuals, and its program is based on the Letter of the Congregation of the Doctrine of the Faith to Catholic Bishops of the World ("Pastoral Care of Homosexual Persons," October 1, 1986), which said in part: "Although the particular inclination of the homosexual person is not sin, it is a more or less strong tendency ordered toward an intrinsic moral evil; and thus the inclination itself can be seen as an objective disorder."

Father Harvey reaches out to these persons, the younger the better, to fashion among them a mind-set on, and a method of, practicing chastity. Courage does not attempt to change their orientation, but in weekly meetings it works for *psychological healing*, that is, teaching them in practice to avoid serious temptations to homosexual lust; and *spiritual healing*, daily prayer spiritual direction, and the sacraments. In this, Courage is different from another group calling itself *Dignity*, which assumes that chastity among homosexuals is unlikely, if not impossible, and works instead to support the homosexual lifestyle, as long as it is responsible, not promiscuous.

Father Harvey's headquarters is at Saint Michael's Church, 424 East 34th Street, New York, NY 10001.

A number of similar ministries to special groups, such as *The Divorced and the Separated*, exist basically as support groups of decent people caught up in very sad situations, sad not only in the light of Christ's teaching on the indissolubility of marriage, but in view of the frequency with which some canon lawyers today, not always implicitly, assure divorced and separated Catholics that annulments of unhappy Catholic marriages are by no means impossible. Any Catholic program must, like Courage, have its doctrinal base. John Paul II, in *Familiaris Consortio* (Nos. 83-84), while calling on priests to discern the difficulties Catholics endure in this state, makes it clear that priests are not to remarry divorced people improperly, and that those invalidly married a second time are excluded from the worthy reception of the Eucharist. The difficulty for the law-abiding parish priest is that the Catholic bishops' documentary service, *Origins*, occasionally gives space to ministries to the divorced and separated, which are little more than "dating services" for lonely hearts, already bound to an indissoluble sacramental union.

Major New Ministries

Several ministries, directed to specific audiences, are not always well known to everyone in the parish, but are important because the hierarchy has demonstrated a unique interest in their contribution to the mission of the Church. These would include: (1) the initiation of adults, (2) youth ministry and catechetics, and (3) separated brethren.

The Rite of Christian Initiation of Adults (RCIA)

The Congregation for Divine Worship instituted this rite on January 6, 1972, as a method for receiving adult converts into communion with the Church. Sixteen years would pass before the English translation was approved and the program mandated by the American bishops for use by their pastors. The ritual emphasizes the communitarian aspects of Catholic membership, prescribing that newcomers be introduced to the Church in a sequence of steps.

First, the inquiry and initial excursion into the sweep of the Catholic commitment.

Second, selection of candidates for the catechumenate — a preparatory period originated in the early Church, to test the intention and suitability of those interested in conversion. Specific prayers and blessings are proposed for the initiation, after which a more formal period of instruction in the Word of God begins.

Third, a period of purification, preferably during Lent, a formation process, if you will, which goes beyond cognitive learning and individual participation, culminating with the reception into the Church, through baptism, confirmation, and the Eucharist.

Finally, the full assimilation of the convert into the life of the parish during and after the Easter season.

(The ritual may be adapted for the reception of baptized, but uneducated Catholic adults, validly baptized non-Catholics entering full communion with the Church, even for teenage youth, as circumstances warrant.)

Questions are frequently raised about how widely RCIA is used in other parts of the world, but it is expected over time to prevail in the United States. Pastors must remember this mechanism, which comprises education, worship, and community life, is to be adapted to local circumstances. It presumes sufficient numbers, yet sometimes a parish will not have enough. The program usually runs from one Easter-Pentecost season to another, but some candidates are not available for that long a period. It is communitarian in scope, while converts, at times, are private persons who do not fit comfortably into public appearances. These are challenges more than they are difficulties, ones which the proper administration of RCIA can handle. The president of the National Conference of Bishops, sensing resistance from some quarters, has assured parish priests that RCIA is not another package "dumped" on them from above, and is manageable. Another archbishop finds it hard to reconcile the rite's community priorities with the private administration of the sacraments, sanctioned both in law and in practice, but this should not be a problem either. The genius of the Roman Rite is found precisely in the freedom it grants to pastors. Liturgical divines look upon "baptism by immersion" as the more perfect symbol of what Christian initiation is all about, a practice born in the days when converts lived near the Sea of Galilee, and might walk to baptism in sandaled feet and a loose garment. In spite of these beginnings, pouring water on the forehead has also been standard liturgical practice in both East and West for most of Church history. All sacraments, including the Eucharist, are preferably administered in a community form, but are still licit when done privately according to pre-scribed rubrics. So it is with RCIA — pastors have a substantial amount of leeway.

If one reads commentaries in *Origins*, especially by academics, about what RCIA is supposed to be, he will find some calling it an attempt by the Church to get away from the "Father Smith instructs Jones" type of convert, the one of old, ostensibly awash in cognitive learning. Ante-RCIA priests were surely imperfect in many ways, and if they were into convert-making, it was their shortcoming as cognitivists that was the more observable fact. Their ability to draw a neophyte into the Church, how-ever, was pretty good. In those years there were well over one hundred thousand converts baptized in the United States each year, most of whom remained active Catholics. The academics are correct, however, on the value of RCIA in extending the length of preparation and accenting the social aspects of Christianity. RCIA could still fail, if the priest in charge overdoes the emotional and social aspects of conversion, and is ambigu-ous about the intellectual content of the faith. This has been a failing of modern catechetics. Many converts are attracted to the Church because they want to marry, or are already married to, a Catholic. Others seek instruction because they sense that the Catholic Church is "true," that it is the Church of Jesus Christ, and it is God's will they take this step.

The Church has come a long way from Pentecost, to become a highly intelligent body with a proud history, to have reasonable explanations of its faith, acquiring in the process a long list of Catholic apologists from Tertullian to Gilbert Keith Chesterton, to Walter Percy and Flannery O'Connor. Not every bookkeeper, not even an overeducated sociologist, visiting a rectory for the first time for purposes of conversion, compre-hends the theology expounded by Henri De Lubac or Germain Grisez. Nonetheless, they must come away from RCIA with the deepened con-viction that the Church is "true." Otherwise, their emotional ties will hardly sustain the piety the Church expects them to acquire, and which they, if truly convicted, will manifest, even when there is no one around to no-tice.

Youth Ministry and Catechetics

John Paul II came to Denver in 1993 and rallied more thousands of young Catholics to song, to prayer, to fellowship, than had ever been seen in this country anywhere, at any time. He told them they were the hope of their nation and the Church. He praised their young years and their idealism. The holy man from Cracow went on to warn them how thieves and robbers of faith and morals are waiting to devour them, to smash their dreams, and to lure them to seek first the kingdoms of pleasure, comfort, and money, while turning their backs on things that make human life worthwhile — family, service to others, and love of God. As only the young can, they roared their approval during the open-air meetings and manifested their faith and their piety in the hushed silence typical of that moment when John Paul II raised the Host and the Chalice before them to say: "This is my Body." "This is my Blood."

And, then, they left in small groups, by the fifties and the hundreds, by bus, by rail, by plane, on foot, these thousands of eager, enthusiastic adolescents and young adults, who for a year at least had spent hours and hours of their time in their local dioceses, and dollars of their own and parents' incomes, to come see and to greet, to be blessed in turn, by the Vicar of Christ on earth.

As darkness covered the last night in Denver, and silence reigned again, Colorado became once more the home of the Denver Broncos.

Perhaps this is what our young Catholics need today, more than ever before — the spectacular presence in their midst of a holy man, exposing and espousing the gospel of Christ with flair and fervor, with the charisma of a pope. They had heard much of what he said before. But this time the Vicar of Christ said it in their presence. That made a difference. Street-talkers call them a generation of "rock and rollers," or worse, "religious illiterates," so it is not by accident that John Paul II came to Denver. He has been aware for some time that Catholic youth in the Western world, particularly in the United States, have been detached from their Catholic roots, and are in danger of losing their souls to Mammon. To inspire young Catholics to rethink their image and their future, this pontiff came to Colorado.

Priests have never had an easy time working with the young, even when families were strong and religious plentiful. But when one speaks with parish priests today, he discovers a large amount of pessimism. Once upon a time, priests, face to face with the restlessness of male adolescents, would console themselves with the thought: "They'll come back later when they marry the right girl." Priests are not saying this so much any more. And the problem may now be the girls. The loose link between the Church — its religious faith and practice — and the children of so-called Catholic baby boomers, is well recognized. The present disaffection is bad enough, but the state of the Church a century from now is a major worry. Few consider "these kids," as they are sometimes called, really bad, but the Church surely is "foreign" to the "playboy" culture which these youngsters sop up like a sponge.

It is appalling, from a Catholic point of view, how little regard so many of them have for the sixth commandment, how much money they spend on frivolities, the vulgarity of their speech, the trouble their parents have obtaining obedience, and the dangerous experiments they undertake early in life "doing their thing." In a continent as vast as America, brighter spots exist, to be sure, but it is ever more difficult to keep the young "down on the farm" when, from watching television, they think that "Paree," so often depicted there is at hand. Not uncommonly, twenty-five-year-olds, well out of their teens and after a lifetime of Catholic schooling, when asked about the Church, openly confess to a priest: "I haven't thought about those things in years."

As far back as 1972 the American bishops, in their well-respected pastoral *To Teach As Jesus Did*,[1] spelled out the challenges of "youth ministry," what they called the disenchantment and alienation of youth. At that point they outlined the threefold objectives of the Church's "youth ministry": (1) to involve Catholic youth in Church life; (2) to foster their religious education; and (3) to encourage community involvement on their part through what the bishops called "peer group ministry." That pastoral was visionary in expectations of good results at all levels of Catholic education. Particular help was solicited from theologians and institutions of higher learning. Twenty years later, it is clear that bishops have not succeeded in directing Catholic educators toward the goals set for them by the *magisterium*. It should not be surprising, therefore, that at the parish level, "youth ministry," which is a freer apostolate than an institutionalized school, should fall short of the demands of *To Teach As Jesus Did*.

Youth ministry is at present one of the most depressing works facing parish priests. The depression is deepened by the fact they are really engaged in re-saving the saved. They can gauge the scope of their problem by looking down from the pulpit on a Sunday morning for an eye count of eighteen-year-olds in attendance. And, if the priest is old enough, he can remember earlier days when roisters from an all-night Saturday fling would slink into the back pews for a 6:00 A.M. Mass, before they dared go home to be greeted by their mother. The worship might have been imperfect, but the intention had a piety of its own.

Our present dilemma is compounded by the fact that "youth ministry" was once the work of the Catholic school. That system may have had its critics outside the Church, and some "Americanists" inside, who decried the separatism. But it produced results for God and country. From parish school to college campus, the children of foreign-born Catholics moved on to become intelligent believers and pious churchgoers, and patriotic Americans. Because parish schools existed, Catholics in public schools benefited from the Sunday religious instruction and Released Time programs staffed by the schools' religious. From World War II through the post-Korean War period, Catholic family life grew stronger. Priests and religious by the legion were involved in teenage lives, even if it was only at a CYO gym or dance. Many boys of public high schools married girls who had completed twelve years in nuns' schools. The Junior Holy Name Societies and the Children of Mary might have been jokes by World War II, but only the worrywarts would have considered their teenagers to be alienated. Somehow, the young were so saturated in Catholic neighborhoods that if they didn't get doctrine in a classroom or around the altar, they picked it up by osmosis on the streets.

This system is now withering away and Catholic family life itself has seen better days. If building a school is no longer the dream of an aspiring pastor, closing one down has become the ineluctable reality for his elders. The parish is thrown back, therefore, on the uncertain devices for reaching the young that plagued pioneer priests more than a century ago, with no seeming dogged plan of recovery on the national agenda, which might not be enforceable, if there was one. What makes it psychologically worse for parents is that the results of the old system are in evidence in their own continued and committed Catholicity, and priests who once were saviors for the parents now seem helpless or unconcerned about the state of the soul of their children. (The priests often are more helpless than unconcerned.)

Youth ministry, developed after the Council, is thus far not an adequate substitute for what went on before. Conceived to bring or keep youngsters (ages eleven to eighteen) and young adults in the fold, it suffers from some disagreeable facts of life: (1) there are less and less qualified religious around, and a paid youth minister, even if the parish can afford one, is hardly a comparable substitute; (2) the vast majority of young Catholics now attend public schools and "the religious illiteracy factor" is no myth; (3) the culture itself is pervasive, and defenses against its religious agnosticism, its sensate nature, and its hedonism in particular, are hard to override or counteract. There is a lot of loud Catholic moaning these days about our young following the mores of the streets, not the norms of conduct expected of Christian believers. But the cultural problems of the young have a deeper root. When the pope speaks of an original sin by first parents — worthy of God's judgment requiring redemption by his Son made man by the Holy Spirit, born of a Virgin Mary, who died but rose from the dead, founded a Communion of Saints under pope and bishops, leading to heaven, hell, or purgatory — does he have support, outside of religion, for those convictions from any public figure of his stature? And, within his own Church, while these truths are not denied, their force is muted when stress is placed on the humanity of Jesus and on making us better humans as the goal of his life's work.

At the present moment, therefore, there are only a few things that can be said with certainty about youth ministry apart from its built-in frustrations:

1. Youth ministry, however else it is defined, must mean catechetics, and someone in a parish with a particular genius at making it work. Since high school students are reluctant to come for "instruction" outside of a school setting, the parish priest might "bootleg" it in through lectures of another kind, perhaps *ad hoc*, which appeal to their fantasies about fulfillment, career, or marriage, an especially important topic in this age of AIDS. The right outside speaker, of some stature, may be more appealing than a familiar face.

Of course, it helps if the parish is in other respects the center of community life. Some parishes are veritable beehives of activity, and of their nature draw more bees constantly, who thereby sustain their "Catholic connection" socially, if not intellectually.

2. Catechetics should become an offshoot of the parochial life. A lot of nonpracticing Catholics, even the young, come to parties, shows, and ball games. Some priests, by their demeanor, have the ability to turn a hoedown into a religious event, by the way they bless an audience, by their storytelling, by their holiness. John Paul II ended a meeting with young people visiting his summer home at Castelgandolfo by getting them to sing religious songs with him. "Holy God We Praise Thy Name" or "The Battle Hymn of the Republic" in the right place might leave a lasting impression.

We underestimate the teaching possibilities of social life, as we overestimate its bonding qualities. When Chicago's Bishop Bernard Shiel created the *Catholic Youth Organization* at the onset of the Great Depression (1930) he intended sociality and fraternity, not catechetics, for poor Catholic kids, many of whose fathers were unemployed. Praying before basketball games was impressive (before Notre Dame decided it was in poor taste), but it was not intended to enlighten anyone. Perhaps, today, social affairs, including athletics, may be one of the few opportunities to catechize by indirection. There are many occasions available to lift minds and hearts to God, if the priest seizes the day or the night, and knows what to do when he gets it. One pastor has nine hundred high schoolers in his CYO, and many of them made Denver in 1993.

3. Then, appropriate staff, either in the form of a youth minister carefully chosen and dedicated, or trained volunteers, fill an important role. The minister is a replacement for a priest, but hardly a substitute for the priest who likes kids. Still, volunteers are the kinds of people who continue to make the Little Leagues and the Scouts the successes they are.

One parish bulletin, under the heading "Youth Ministry," reads: "There are 40 adult volunteers and over 200 young adults enrolled. Activities such as amusement park visits, ski trips, dances, retreats, and discussion groups are organized to experience God in a new and different way."

4. An offshoot of this activity should be the "peer group leadership" — buzz groups — which meet on and off church premises to discuss Catholic issues and do Catholic things, such as by influencing friends to return to Sunday Mass. This is a variation of the old *Young Christian Workers* approach which was suggested by the American bishops in 1972.

5. A parish rally, from time to time, *a la* Denver, featuring a Catholic hero, is another good idea whose time has come. Once upon a time an Irene Dunne or an aging Bing Crosby helped the cause simply by proclaiming their Catholicity publicly. But now we need "little J.P. II's" who attract the young, while demonstrating an ability to discuss the faith intelligently and correctly.

All good priests savor the full implementation of the American bishops' 1972 agenda, and many places do succeed admirably, even though they observe the somber mood of their own pontiff who, in speaking of catechesis, uses the word "rediscover," as if a pearl of great price has been lost. One priest, in charge of twenty thousand Catholics, recently moaned aloud with his pope, but keeps trying: "For the moment, in parishes like mine, the ball game is lost. The TV morality has become our morality. Good parents no longer command their teenagers' religious life, nor their thinking. And they have lost power to get them to Mass, let alone a CCD class. I might get more to listen if they were sure ahead of time that I was going to tell them what other parishes, or some religious coordinators, let them think, that is, counsel which merely reinforces their lax approach to worship and to their free and easy sexual appetites or lifestyle. Once teenagers know that this parish will teach only what John Paul II teaches, you can write the program off as a dead duck."

This particular pastor has placed his finger on a problem that goes beyond any parish. His college students may read the *National Review*, not the *New Republic*, yet they have also learned to think "religiously" with the mind-set of the *National Catholic Reporter*, instead of *Our Sunday Visitor*. It may be helpful, therefore, for every priest to read Monsignor Michael Wrenn's *Catechisms and Controversies: Religious Education in the Post-Conciliar Years* (Ignatius Press, 1991). Once religious educators began to teach the young Catholic to be human, that being human was itself Christian, and that the way to humanity was through personal experience, it was only a short step to the end of what one nationally known religious educator disparagingly called "handing on shop-worn formulas, tired customs and trite devotions." The die was cast at that moment for parish priests also. One tireless pastor, hoping against hope, turned to parents. Given his interest and catechetical expertise, he decided to undertake a "home study program," offering it to the parents of high school children free of charge, with all the appropriate teaching/learning tools. He did not receive a single reply.

Catechesis is especially trying for the parish priest who must deal with a highly unstructured situation. His starting point, however, might be a rereading of John Paul II's *Catechisi Tradendae* (No. 69, 1979), an exhortation early in his pontificate, where he reminded pastors: "The parish remains, as I have said, the preeminent place for catechesis. It must rediscover its vocation."[2]

If all he can do is keep trying and praying, then that is what he must do.

Ministry to Separated Brethren

The controversies which erupted after Vatican II rarely argued against ecumenism, once the Council's decree became Catholic policy (November 21, 1964). The prayer by the Council Fathers made sense that "little by little ... all Christians will be gathered in a common celebration of the Eucharist." John XXIII probably had the Greek and Russian Orthodox

Churches uppermost in his mind when he promoted this cause, because of his personal experiences with them in Eastern Europe, and his faith in their nearly common creed and similar sacramental system. Eleven years later Paul VI, having already established good relations with Athenagoras, Archbishop of Constantinople, confessed: "The Catholic Church and the Orthodox are united by such a deep communion that very little is lacking to teach the fullness authorizing a common celebration of the Lord's Eucharist." The Eucharist, the touchstone of unity, is the final stage of a truly ecumenical Church.

While the pope's primacy of jurisdiction continues to obstruct the path of East-West reunion, more substantial differences in both worship and teaching seriously complicate dialogue with Protestant churches and Jewish congregations. Still, after the Council, the three popes and those bishops in union with them began to reach out, without caviling, to these separated brethren also.

The original decree failed to provide specific direction beyond prayer and good will, study and dialogue, and sensitivity to doctrinal differences. But concrete steps on the Catholic side came in short order — relaxation of earlier restrictions on mixed marriages; permission for their celebration on, or in, a sacred setting; at times before a minister of another's faith; the establishment of diocesan ecumenical commissions to promote cooperation and proper meetings; Catholic recognition of the validity of certain baptisms by non-Catholic ministers; and the elimination of indiscriminate Catholic conditional rebaptisms. "Communication in spiritualities," as Rome called it, also advanced the cause — sharing in common prayer, common use of sacred places and objects, and certain kinds of worship together, including the reception of Catholic sacraments under special circumstances, the occasional participation for reasonable cause of Catholics in non-Catholic religious services, and the effort to receive Episcopalians into the Church under acceptable conditions.

Most of the original initiatives toward better ecumenical relations have come from Rome, and the significant immediate results have been the theological discussions between Catholic bishops with their consultants and their Orthodox, Lutheran, and Episcopal counterparts. The agreements have been notable, but they continue to fall short of what the Holy See considers acceptable. Papal jurisdiction, the priesthood, the Eucharist, and certain prescriptions of moral law, remain items in controversy. The breakup of the Soviet Empire, and the subsequent efforts of Rome to reinvigorate Catholic churches in the old Eastern bloc, have also created new tensions with the Orthodox, who see this activity as poaching on ecclesial domains historically theirs (at least in recent times). Nonetheless, the forward movement of ecumenism continues.

Dissident theologians express frequent dissatisfaction with the progress, blaming the pope's and the Curia's insistence on Catholic teachings and/or structures which they prefer to see abandoned by the Church. Some think that the Catholic Church should become a loose confederation of Christian communities, sharing worship and the Eucharist, without radically altering the belief systems of participating denominations. Realistically, this is not likely to occur.

For the most part, local pastors have not been involved in these top-level negotiations, nor in the public controversies. By and large, however, Catholic and Protestant pastors continue to break bread other than the Eucharist, attend each others' services when the occasions are convenient, cooperate on civic matters of importance, such as Right-to-Life, and in many cases have cemented strong bonds of personal friendship.

The pope has called ecumenism "a pastoral priority," and pastors at the grass roots level are making a local contribution to the Church's new universal vocation. In some respects, American priests have an easier time than foreign missioners who often deal with more deeply entrenched rivalries, to say nothing of high cultural walls between them and other Christian ministers. Cardinal Johann Willebrands has been the Catholic voice worldwide on building bridges to Protestant, Jewish, Buddhist, Moslem, Confucian, Taoist, and native African religious leadership. Dialogue, and more dialogue, is a major theme of his, sensitivity on proselytizing members of other persuasions in an unchristian way is another, strengthening mixed marriages (forty percent of Catholic marriages in the United States) is a third, shared prayer is as vital to ultimate union as any other contribution. Local pastors can do all of these things.

Fundamental to better relations are, of course, honesty and sincerity. Faith differences may not be papered over, especially by anyone familiar with the nuances involved, and shared Eucharist is the end of the road, not the beginning. The best representatives of all religious bodies recognize what is involved, namely truth and right — in the Catholic case, about Christ's divinity and his Presence in the Eucharist. The best and the brightest know the ecumenical cause is not advanced only at high levels or rarified theological discussion, but by what Rome said in 1975: "It is at the level of the local Church that the spirit of ecumenism must find its concrete expression."[3]

To recap the Church's best thrust by local pastors in this area, the Secretariat's suggestions are somewhat inclusive:

- Sharing in prayer and worship
- Common Bible work
- Joint pastoral care, for instance, in prisons
- Shared premises
- Collaboration in education
- Joint use of communications media
- Cooperation in the health field
- National and international emergencies
- Relief of human need
- Social problems
- Bilateral dialogues
- Meetings of chief pastors
- Joint working groups
- Councils of Christian churches

A word of advice from the Secretariat reminds local pastors: "It has to be kept in mind that while these fields of action offer many opportunities of ecumenical collaboration, they also entail problems and difficulties which have to be solved in the light of Catholic principles of ecumenism."

The unmentioned problem may not be so obvious in Rome: The very busy pastor is likely to have little time to devote a great deal of his day to this important new apostolate. As bishops have discovered, there is a risk in delegating someone else to do their work, but there is also a risk in getting up in the morning. The good parish priest — in this case, as in so many others — must remember that he, not anyone else, has responsibility for improved ecumenical relations. But since there is no timetable for the proper reunion of Christian churches, he may comfortably wait on God's Providence for someone else to savor the fruit of his labors.

What About Married Deacons?

While married deacons belong to the clerical state and are hardly a "new" ministry, in the sense the word is commonly used, the point should be made that, properly chosen, trained, and used, they are a pastor's most valuable coworkers. Some of them do not preach well, and so should be used sparingly in the pulpit; but many have extraordinary human talents for teaching, administration, and organization. One hears frequent complaints from them that they are not used properly. Some pastors have them organize parish retreats and marriage encounters, train ushers, lectors, and Eucharistic ministers (many of whom are under-trained), and occasionally one or the other is so uniquely endowed (and otherwise free) that he becomes, to the pastor's relief, the parochial controller, RCIA director, or parish attorney, accountant, etc. Since many of them have rich secular backgrounds, and are better trained theologically than other ministers, married deacons have much to contribute to easing the burdens of overworked priests.

Liturgical Worship in the Absence of a Priest

Catholic communities without a live-in priest are not rarities in Church history, although there are places like the United States where for many decades a priest has always been available for every eight hundred baptized Catholics. It was not always so, however. Back in 1868 when the future Cardinal Gibbons was young, the new Vicar Apostolic of North Carolina quickly discovered from one of his priests that six widely scattered "stations" in his state, where thousands of Catholics lived, were without priests. About the same time, foreign missionaries to Japan, which had been closed to the West for at least two centuries, came upon (thanks to Commodore Matthew Peary) closets of Catholics in places like Nagasaki, priestless for twenty decades, but still Catholic. Recently, John Paul II, extolling the impressive growth of the Church in Africa, recalled the debt we owed to the lay catechists of earlier days who kept Christianity alive in local kraals, waiting for the return of itinerant priests, whose visits never came when expected.

Liturgical worship without a priest is no ideal, of course, because the Church is recognized mainly in "the breaking of the bread," which requires an ordained priest. Even the lay Catholic communities of old were, at best, holding patterns for his eventual return when he, like Christ before him, would mediate the Lord's sacramental presence among believers. That Sunday worship in the absence of a priest is becoming more common in the United States, may surprise Catholics accustomed to crowded Churches, but it is a fact of modern religious life. These same Catholics, however, over the years have had rich experience with, or at least knowledge of, family worship, prayer meetings by apostolic groups, even in a parochial setting, and pilgrimages of one kind or another, led by laity. These were not substitutes for Sunday or daily Eucharistic liturgies, to be sure, but they were legitimate worship of God and bonding experiences for the participants.

By 1988, when the shortage of priests in the West became noticeable in selected areas of established Catholic centers, the Holy See decided to regularize these celebrations. The Congregation for Divine Worship issued its "Directory For Sunday Celebrations in the Absence of a Priest," which is available from the United States Catholic Conference. A deacon normally should preside at such services in his alb and stole, seated in the presidential chair. In cases of necessity, a lay person or religious may be so delegated by the proper pastor to lead services from a chair situated outside the sanctuary.

The ritual normally includes the following elements: (1) morning or evening prayer from the Liturgy of the Hours; (2) scripture reading; (3) the deacon preaches his own homily; the lay person may read one prepared by the parish priest; (4) the distribution of Holy Communion by properly commissioned Eucharistic ministers; and (5) thanksgiving, which may take the form of a psalm, a hymn, or a litany.

The proper leader should relate this celebration to the Eucharist, and the congregation before him or her to the parish church. If, in days of the horse and carriage, Catholics yearning for Mass walked miles and miles, Sunday after Sunday, it is not beyond imagination that today's Catholics might properly go out of their way to travel to Sunday Mass, and consider this particular celebration but a substitute for the real Presence of Christ through his chosen priestly mediator. The Directory is very clear that this celebration must never be a simulation of the Sacrifice, nor use any of the Mass's special prayers or blessings.

The Holy See, since 1965, has learned how often liturgical innovations have been misused and abused, even by priests, occasionally with the oversight of a bishop. Indeed, the abuses are often imitated purposely, namely to denigrate the doctrine of the Mass as Sacrifice, of the ordained priesthood, of a male priesthood, of the role of hierarchy in determining the nature of fitting Catholic worship. The faithful, caught up in properly approved innovations, do not know when first they are exposed to departures from liturgical norms. In due course they take "the wrong" as "right" and can be made to feel resentful when errant leaders begin to resist attempts by the bishop, or by Rome, to reestablish worship in the Catholic mode.

Recently, one of the country's respected bishops appeared on a television news program to explain (and defend) the Church's doctrine on a male priesthood. He was quite good. No sooner had the reporter concluded the interview, than the network panned over to a "priestless parish" in his diocese, administered by a woman, dressed in alb, standing behind a main altar, conducting a Communion service that, to the untrained eye, had all the appearances of a Eucharistic ritual. The camera then left the altar scene to interview the lady in question, and varied parishioners too, as to how shameful it was that women could not be ordained priests, how the failure to do so was creating tension in the Catholic community, and how in view of their recent religious experience with liturgy without a priest, it was the pastor, when he did arrive eventually for Mass and other sacramental administrations, who was somewhat of an intruder.

All violations of rubrics, if extended and contumacious, usually end up bringing disorder to God's house, and a certain amount of sinful behavior, apart from the injury they do to the sacredness of the Church's worship. Parish priests are responsible for seeing that rubrics are observed, even when they are distant from the place where worship is conducted with their authority, but in their absence.

Endnotes

1. *Pastoral Letters of the United States Catholic Bishops, Volume III, 1962-1974*, published in 1983 by the United States Catholic Conference, pp. 306ff. Most official documents prescribe goals, without reporting on the effectiveness or noneffectiveness of recommended or actual programs.
2. See Monsignor Michael Wrenn and Father Robert Levis, eds., *John Paul II, Catechist* (Quincy, IL: Franciscan Press, 1980), a commentary on the papal exhortation.
3. "Ecumenical Collaboration at the Regional, National and Local Levels" (February 22, 1975), issued by the Secretariat for the Promotion of the Unity of Christians. In Austin Flannery's *Vatican Council II, Volume 2, More Post-Conciliar Documents* (Costello Publishing Co., 1983), pp. 153ff.

Chapter Fifteen

The Parish
and the Family Apostolate:
Doctrine and Priorities

> Young married couples should learn to accept
> willingly and make good use of the discreet,
> tactful and generous help offered by other
> couples that already have more experience of
> married and family life. Thus within the
> ecclesial community — the great family made
> up of Christian families — there will take
> place a mutual exchange of presence and help
> among all the families, each one putting at the
> service of the others its own experience of life,
> as well as the gifts of faith and grace.
>
> — John Paul II, *Familiaris Consortio*

The intended object of this chapter is to explore with priests what the Church says about the Catholic family and what they should be doing about it. The duty of the clergy to watch over the family and the right of married couples to defend their vocation are clear and paramount. Holy orders and matrimony are directed to the commonweal of both the *Ecclesia* and *Ecclesiola*. However, Vatican II-influenced renewal in this area will likely begin when Church teaching is reintroduced to the Catholic community by priests who themselves believe that teaching to be true.

Let us review where we are, how we came here, and how the full mind of the Second Vatican Council can be recaptured with the help of the bishops and parish priests to whom is entrusted the care of the faithful. What is said of bishops applies to parish priests, and vice versa.

State of the Question

A recent study by George Gallup and Jim Castelli concludes that the Catholic Church "has lost much of its credibility on everything related to sex."[1] An official of Planned Parenthood, during the push to foist condoms on public school children in the hope of combating AIDS was no less blunt. Joan Coombs, in *The New York Daily News* of June 4, 1987, simply declared the Church hierarchy "doesn't have a whole lot to do with the reality of Catholic lives."

Twenty years ago, Catholic academics hoped to solve many marital problems by legitimizing the use of contraceptives. Contraception, we were told, would enrich and solidify marriages, diffuse tension within marriage, delimit the growing reliance on abortion and help solve the population problems of the poor. Instead, as we know, our Catholic people are not notably happier, our divorce and abortion rates approximate those of the United States at large, and in the meantime we have acquired a surfeit of over-copulation among our young without benefit of marriage. A 1985 Gallup poll indicated that Catholics are now more tolerant of premarital sex than Protestants. These developments have occurred within the Church with surprising serenity, considering the fact that we are dealing with sins that few people confess anymore, and about which there is a grand silence among the Catholic clergy.

Let us place these issues where they belong, or should belong. John Paul II, on July 18, 1984, said that the roots of the Church's sexual morality are in the deposit of faith itself. Even the doctrine on contraception, so often scoffed at today by important clerics, is part of the "moral order revealed by God."[2] Three years after that statement, the pope continued to insist that the Church's teaching on contraception was not a matter of free discussion among theologians. He scorned them for "leading the moral conscience of spouses into error."[3] *A fortiori*, the divine displeasure with fornication, self-abuse, divorce, adultery, and homosexual lust, must remain a matter of moral concern for faithful Christians, especially for those who have been appointed to preach and teach in Christ's name.

Apart from divine displeasure, there are troubling human questions. The justification for the Catholic sexual revolution has been reduced to the much abused word "compassion," to reduce guilty feelings among Catholics. Compassion for those who engage in illicit sexual practices; for wives overburdened with too many children; for husbands denied their marital rights by puritanical or dictatorial spouses; for children reared in combative homes, the stress allegedly caused by sexual tension; for families groveling in poverty because of too many children; and so forth. Sociologists and psychologists were called upon by theologians after 1965 to "prove" the damaging effect of the Catholic sexual ethos on human lives.[4] But twenty years later, liberated though Catholics seem to be, dissenting theologians do not speak much about the growing social concern over the results of liberation: broken homes, children without mothers, children without fathers, children with illegitimate children of their own, mothers without husbands, surrogate mothers, test tube babies, slaughtered fetuses, men who want sex without marriage, women who want sex without motherhood, and a generation of young people, including Catholics, taught not to frustrate their sexual impulses but satisfy them fully but safely — meaning with condoms.

We also face what one politician called "the spread of filth campaign" — pornography, pimps, dirty movies, pederasts, peep shows, massage parlors, violence, and dope pushers. And, of course, the growing rates of venereal disease and now of deadly AIDS, a direct result of unnatural sexual activity, mostly among men.

From the Beginning

The point to be made first is that whatever the social situation, Mother Church must preach God's word on marriage and family life, even if unbelievers or not-so-faithful Catholics turn a deaf ear to its significance. Whatever else is to be said about the Christian teaching on marriage or sex, therefore, must begin with Genesis (see Chapter 2) and its reaffirmation by Christ himself. Who more authoritatively than Christ spoke of "two in one flesh" (i.e., monogamy), "what God has joined together let no one put asunder" (i.e., indissolubility), that marrying another man's wife is adultery, that lusting is adultery of the heart, of the sinfulness of not only killing but of evil thoughts too (see Matthew 5:28). Where did Saint Paul obtain the idea if not from Christ that sexual immorality — whether it takes the form of fornication, adultery, or homosexuality — is anti-ethical to the demands of Christ's kingdom? Why did the early Church demand public penance lasting a lifetime for adultery and abortion, save that these were understood to be grave offenses against Christ's own norms for Christian behavior? During those first centuries masturbation, contraception, pederasty, sterilization, and copulation with animals all came under a similar censure. We speak, therefore, not of human traditions originating with unenlightened or ignorant people (a description that hardly fits the New Testament authors), but what God had deigned and joined from the beginning and for no man to deny or sunder.

If these reminders represent the negative side of God's word, they merely draw dramatic attention to his positive teachings on marriage and family life. Adultery is a grave offense against marriage because it contravenes the "till death do us part" commitment which marriage entails. In today's anti-family American environment, such long-term or irreversible commitments are countercultural. Yet, if young couples on their wedding day do not believe in the bone of their bones that indissolubility is what Catholic marriage involves, they are in peril. Our parents knew this truth with their mothers' milk, but their grandchildren are not so sure, sometimes even after sixteen years of Catholic education. They are uncertain because many priests and religious have lost confidence in the human benefit of eternal promises.

We may have to begin all over again, as John Paul II once reminded an audience, to reintroduce the world, and Catholics too, to the truth and the value of Christian marriage. This is what Paul VI tried to do with *Humanae Vitae* in 1968, without much success. John Paul II attempted the same with *Familiaris Consortio* in 198, only to have his classic Catholic remarks scorned and turned aside in Washington, D.C. by prominent and so-called Catholic family leaders.

The Christian Family: Nature and Mission

The distinctive note of Christian marriage is that it comes from God. It is not a human invention, but a postulate of God's created order. God calls his creatures to do many things, but the vocation to the married state is one of the most exalted. Why? Because marriage is a sharing not only in God's life but in his love, and in his creative power. A man and a woman who are married are called upon to manifest God's love by loving each other, the overflow resulting in the gift to others of God's life, which God first gave to them. Men and women of true faith must be taught to see their marriage bed as a consecrated center of true Christian love, not a playground for egotistical pleasure seeking. Their home is "a little Church" dedicated to building up the Mystical Body, rich with little children dear to Jesus, where God is worshiped daily, where the example of parents is reflected in the piety of their young ones, as much as in their civilized development. Home is memorable more for these things than for its artifacts and tools of amusement, or for eating, drinking, sleeping, and merrymaking. In the truly Christian home husband and father complements wife and mother in the gifts they bring to their common life, and in the contribution they make to the Christian manhood and womanhood of their offspring. That Christian home is not an arena of competition, domination, or raw upward mobility, where few children are to be found, where husband and wife vie with each other in their distaste for parenthood.

Most religious people, and not a few good pagans, have seen or been part of families which realized this dream. Most young married Catholics, after leaving the altar, hope it will be realized for them. Yet more often than not, young marrieds may not be particularly inspired by what they see going on in the lives of professed Catholics; or worse, they may look upon the Christian dream as downright silly or simply unworkable. Christ had a similar effect on his contemporaries, and he sounds pretty impracticable compared to the pseudo-psychologists of our day. So before couples ride the marriage train too far, they have to see again and again the Christian vision, and be brought to recognize the hard-rock reality that marriage is a sacred work. Reconciling the opposite sexes takes work, having babies is the hardest labor of all, paying for their birth and their rearing involves a long life of work and going without. Dealing effectively with pain, suffering, and death, with sin and the effects of sin, calls for Christian character, and this entails a lifetime of prayer, penance, and piety. From an early age, young people need to be prepared to deal with these normal contests of life and with the temptations of idols, whether they be contraception, divorce, abortion, lust, consumerism, improvident marriages (especially by those of tender years), invalid marriages, parenthood denied, latchkey households, etc.

The Church never stops its preaching on family life. It recognizes how easily lust takes over, unless the sexual appetite is channeled toward the purposes God wrote into its structure "from the beginning." This discipline, however well-internalized by individuals, calls for social supports. Without support by Church and state, the family is easily overwhelmed by destructive forces from the outside. Saint Augustine was quite right in his affirmation that "no one can be ready for the next life unless he trains for it now," but few of us remain virtuous long if everyone around us forces on us a different lifestyle, while our own value system remains unenforced.

Church Support System

Whenever the Church preaches to the world, it is important that its own house be in good order. The Catholic community is never perfect, of course. Still the Church has had remarkable success at times and in many places, bringing its faithful up to standards of belief and behavior first set by Christ himself. The network of agencies, social and religious, under Catholic auspices in the United States, engaged in health, education, and welfare, is one of the largest of its kind in the country. In 1962 two-thirds of our Catholics considered the use of contraception as mortally sinful[5] and, for the vast majority, divorce of a sacramental marriage was unthinkable. One is reminded of how early Christians were described in the second-century letter to Diognetus: "They marry and have children, but they do not kill them. They share meals but not their wives. They live in the flesh, but they are not governed by the desires of the flesh. They pass their days on earth, but they are citizens of heaven. Obedient to the law, they live on a level that transcends the law."[6]

It does not require a compilation of statistics or bookish footnotes to suggest that Catholic teaching on sex, marriage, and family life has lost its force. Not only is John Paul II a lonely voice crying in the wilderness, but there are important clerics who wish he would stop talking about sex completely. Technology, they say, has separated sex from procreation, from marriage, even from heterosexuality.

227

It would only waste time to explore the smugness of those Catholic opinion-molders who seem gratified that Catholic family life is now no different from that of other Americans. The decline of their Catholicism as a cultural force in their lives, the election of self-interest and self-fulfillment over duty and commitment, the flight from generous parent-hood, the alienation of the young from the Church, are not simply the result of Americanization, but in large part of the abandonment by priests of their role to preach the Gospel in season and out, popular or no, and to defend fidelity, fertility, and indissolubility as proper and God-given norms for all Catholic couples, newlywed or not.

The First Catholic Response

Obviously, the Church must once more address her own people with renewed seriousness. The general public, which has more experience with liberated sex than Catholics do, still listens when the pope speaks. Witness, for example, the attention John Paul II's office received when the Holy See spoke out on surrogate motherhood and homosexuality. While the secular world was acknowledging that the questions the pope raised called for examination and discussion, Catholic spokesmen could be heard telling fellow religionists that these statements were not infallible, were historically conditioned, possibly erroneous, and that Catholics would make up their own minds anyway.[7] We priests have, therefore, a major catechetical task ahead of us, one that goes beyond questions of sex and marriage.

John Paul II, at one point, expressed the view that a contraceptive mentality involved a break in a person's relationship with God. In the contraceptive world there is no place for God. Worshiping oneself, one's needs and one's fulfillment to the exclusion of God's dominion and providence is an old form of idolatry revisited. If contraceptive-using spouses fail at preventing God's intervention in their married life, they frequently defy God in another way — either by aborting the baby he gave them, or by resenting the baby God clearly wants them to take unto themselves. The contraceptive mentality finds justification for fornication, adultery, and homosexuality — all mortal sins. Those who use contraceptives also have low rates of attendance at Sunday Mass, rarely go to confession, do not confess contraception, and feel free to receive the Eucharist, a sacrilege by any normal Catholic determination (see *Notre Dame Magazine*, Summer, 1987). These actions are superficial indications of how little the sacred in life, those things which appertain to God, touches the innermost core of their being. So the answer is not so much to persuade contraceptive-using or sexually-liberated Catholics to give up their sinful practices, but to get them to make a true and sincere act of Catholic faith in God himself.

Twenty years ago the charge leveled against the Church was that it sent people on "guilt trips." Removing guilt, even of the normally non-neurotic variety, became a crusade within the Church. More than ten years ago Karl Menninger wrote a book entitled *Whatever Became of Sin?* He knew sin was not in hiding, and thought that the Church's doctrine of original sin was the only dogma of faith for which there was empirical evidence. Menninger really was asking not about sin, but "Whatever Became of Guilt?" Remorse following wrongdoing always had been the necessary internal control of errant behavior. The Church has never ceased sending its faithful on healthy guilt trips — today making them feel guilty about their racism, their anti-Semitism, their warlike attitudes, their sexism, and so forth. Since Vatican II, we have rightfully created a Catholic climate which makes the faithful conscious of their failings as members of society.

Catholics today often are embarrassed because they make a great deal of money or have voted against the Teamsters Union or have joined the downtown athletic club. Why are they embarrassed? Because they have acquired a sense of guilt about the violations of proper social norms, developed and preached by their bishops. But where is the embarrassment when a Catholic politician leaves his wife and marries another or, though married, is known to have a girlfriend? A young sixteen-year-old today has few qualms about discussing her active sex life on a street corner, or about carrying condoms, or about having a baby out of wedlock. Indeed we Catholics have almost begun to boast about our relaxed annulment procedures. How often anymore do we speak of motherhood? Or of the larger family, so praised by Vatican II and the last six popes? We have developed an easy tolerance of our sexual aberrations, but also shame about those aspects of family life which once were the proud boast of the Catholic community. Since the fundamental mission of the Church is eternal salvation, the least we expect of clerics is that they begin once more to preach what the Church has always considered essential to it. Sermons, lectures, seminars, and conferences with a coherent message built around the doctrines contained in *Humanae Vitae* and *Familiaris Consortio* are matters of urgent necessity, if the Church believes what it preaches. The faithful may not, likely will not, be converted overnight, but vigorous preaching of solid Catholic doctrine will help establish the Catholic norms against which all Catholics are called upon to make the conscientious decisions for which they are responsible before God. Such preaching must begin somewhere, in some parishes, by some priests. Without that, nothing else counts.

The Second Catholic Step

Preaching and teaching by themselves will not renew the Church's family system. We must restore pride in the Church itself as the Body of Christ — the one Sacrament of salvation, true and Catholic. A great deal is made these days about community, usually from those who look upon the Church as people more than Christ's Body, who denigrate the so-called institutional Church and who seek to form small elite or disparate groups within the Church for the purpose of sifting out from its cultural accretions the meaning of the pure gospel of Christ. In the normal course of events, community follows institution. It does not precede it. Whenever two or three are gathered to work together, there is an institution, whether they are Christ and the Apostles in the upper room, Mother Teresa in a Calcutta boarding house, or the devil in his workshop. The family is such an institution and its Christian work is enhanced best by that other institution called the Church, the home being where the family should find its best inspiration, its best encouragement, support, and protection. For all practical purposes this normally means the Catholic parish. Mr. and Mrs. Average Catholic admire the pope on television, and are still in awe at their bishop when he comes to confirm. But the parish is the House of God with which families regularly have direct contact. Most couples show little interest in activism, even with their pastor. But sleepers, too, need to sense the Church's presence in their lives, and this usually means contact with the local parish. A Family Life Action Committee in every parish might, just now, be an idea whose time has come, although it is an old proposal. Some few must devote themselves to supporting couples who aspire to meaningful Christian married life.

Many years ago, Father John L. Thomas, S.J., posed some of the contemporary questions for which a parish-based family apostolate should seek limited answers:

1. How can American Catholics maintain their marriage and family ideals in a society which not only refuses to accept these ideals, but which

almost evangelistically seeks to eliminate them from the conscience of everyone?

2. How do individual Catholics deal with social institutions (e.g., the ever present three-room apartment) or with social practices (e.g., easy sex) which either oppose or fail to support our Catholic family ideals?

3. When may our people conform to the dominant culture, and when must they stand against the group?

4. What can we do, not only to enlighten Catholics about the radical implications of their own religious philosophy, but to develop that "inner strength" in Catholic marriages which will withstand secular pressures?

5. What can Catholics do to redirect current patterns, customs, and practices relating to family life?

6. How do we deal with family life problems moe effectively when the basic authority of the Church in family matters, and other social issues, is questioned by important segments of the laity?

The typical program normally contains some of the following elements, many of which can be parish-based, rather than at the diocesan level:

1. Marriage preparation: conferences for teenagers in and out of high schools, retreats for the young adults, lectures on family life, to which the single are invited.

2. Family spirituality: Cana conferences, marriage encounters, days and nights of Recollection, Communion Masses, family Holy Hours, family retreats, blessing of mothers, blessing of children, etc.

3. Parent education: "teaching parents to teach," a much neglected apostolate.

4. Special events: golden and silver wedding celebrations, Catholic family suppers for newlyweds, and for couples ten years married, etc.

5. Marriage counseling or "the apostolate to the sick Marriage," at which the priest acts first, and the parish later, as a referral agency for troubled souls.

6. Natural Family Planning. Every parish should have, or be associated with, an NFP teaching unit. For further information and assistance consult either of the following:

(1) Your diocesan director of family life.

(2) Mr. and Mrs. John Kippley, Presidents, The Couple to Couple League, P.O. Box 111184, Cincinnati, OH 45211, (513) 661-7612

(3) Sr. Miriam Paul Klaus, M.D., 8514 Bradmoor Drive, Bethesda, MD 20817-3810, (301) 897-9323

(4) Miss Mercedes Wilson, Foundation of America, P.O. Box 1170, Dunkirk, MD 20754-1170, (301) 627-3346

(5) Mrs. Kay Ek, Diocese of Saint Cloud, 305 North 7th Avenue, Saint Cloud, MN 56301, (612) 252-4721

(6) Dr. & Mrs. John Billings, 21 Milfay Avenue, Q. Vic. 3101, Melbourne, Australia

The Church's Third Mission

As the Church works to shore up the family life of the baptized, it may not shirk its responsibility to deal with the family ethos of contemporary society, that which is wreaking havoc on the family life of more than Catholics. Couple-to-Couple Leagues, base communities, charismatic groups, Right-to-Life Associations, like the old Cana groups and CFM, serve many Christian purposes, not the least of which is support and defense of involved Catholic families in an anti-family world. We need to encourage more of whatever associations deepen the faith of family members. But protective and defense mechanisms are not enough. For at least three hundred years popes have been speaking about the Church's apostolate to the world, and the world seems to get further away from its Judeo-Christian roots. The Second Vatican Council was supposed to place the Church in the middle of the world, with a view to its evangelization, at the least to make the world less hostile to religion. The most notable effect of these efforts seems instead to have been the secularization of the religious life of Catholics. The Christian culture of the Western world is on a downward slide now that priests have removed their Roman collars, nuns their veils, and so many Catholic spouses are taking off their wedding rings. The only things people are advised these days to keep are their condoms.

What are we Catholics going to do about the situation? How do we preach over the heads of opinion-molders and reach our fellow citizens?

While the root causes of our neo-pagan environment may be traced to those universities which spawn cynicism, skepticism, and amoralism, and to the media which market these vices, the American family must come to see that its most immediate enemy today is government. Breaking the ties that bind has become almost a national pastime, with government the ultimate and chief umpire. Whether the rubric be "freedom," or "privacy," whether the actors are in the courts, the bureaucracies, or the legislatures, the scales of justice are being tipped toward abstract persons, and away from citizens' necessary and natural associations, of which the family is primary and most vital. We have moved from divorce for a cause to "no fault" divorce. The number of Americans living in non-marital "families" is increasing and the attempts to "demaritalize" the family are no longer camouflaged. In 1981, the name of the "White House Conference on the Family" was changed to a conference "On Families" as a result of pressure from the homosexual lobby. Jimmy Carter lent presidential respectability to the rejection of the nation's historic understanding of family as heterosexual and marital. Catholics abet this process when they insist that a loveless marriage is a dead marriage, and when Church tribunals discover belatedly that a sacramental marriage never existed after twenty-five years of common life and six grown children. One allegedly Catholic theologian goes a step further by defining marriage as "the ultimate form of friendship achievable by sexually attracted persons."[8]

The hitherto privileged position of the family to the meaning of a free society, recognized through the Christian era as untouchable by the state, as the primary educator of the young and their most important school, the ground and center of public virtue itself, is being challenged by those who ask: "Is marriage necessary?" The single most important buffer against state domination of personal lives is under fire by a government which wants more control of family failure, ignoring its own role in the denigration of the family. It is not surprising that the withering away of the family would be the objective of every socialist state, yet a similar result is not impossible in an omni-competent democratic state whose norms of governing are utilitarian and antireligious. Affirming the importance of government to social well-being is not equivalent to endorsing a democratic government's domination of the family. Seventy years ago, in 1924, American bishops expressed outrage at the thought of federally-sponsored child labor laws, thereby giving Washington authority to intervene in parents' decisions. Today, contemplated laws which would create children's rights against their parents hardly create a stir.

Nor are we embarrassed any longer when public law pretends men and women are the same. Common sense should dictate otherwise, but we remain strangely passive as government flattens roles and occupations, redefining the feminine in completely masculine terms — of office, rank, contest, achievement, success, and failure. The stereotype of the oppressed housewife and mother appears everywhere as part of the orchestrated effort to persuade the American public that women are to be honored for the salaried work they do, not for their motherhood. One feminist theologian recently re-exegeted the New Testament to claim that it is Mary's role as Christ's first disciple that gives her special status in the Church, not the fact that she is the Mother of God.

The family unit, especially its intended permanence and procreative significance, is now looked upon by many as an oppressive structure for the simple reason that it involves a relationship with a lordly male "for better or for worse," and potential pregnancies over many years besides. The family is seen as oppressive, especially because it enshrines man-woman differences. By politicizing the complaints of frustrated feminists, organizations such as the National Organization for Women seek to use governmental power to gain for them what they are not likely to gain through the ballot box. Indeed, many of the modern limitations on heterosexual marital life have come not by a vote of the people, but by the fiat of a judge, an agency, or a politician. It seems sensible to suggest that any parish Family Life Action Committee be pointed in the direction of the diocese, and through diocesan influence to the affairs of the nation.

Catechesis: The Truth, the Whole Truth

John Paul II has a favorite catechetical thrust: Catholics have the right to be taught the Church's authentic message, wholly and entirely. He repeats this demand because he knows that today Catholic teachers are frequently silent on those aspects of the gospel which many moderns are reluctant to accept. If culture tends to make cowards of us all, it makes us especially cowardly in our time about vigorously proclaiming the full Catholic doctrine and policy decisions on sex and marriage.

The following are a few areas which call for bolder teaching by priests and bishops:

1. Motherhood. Some years ago, after a sojourn in India on behalf of family planning, Germaine Greer, the early birth control advocate, gave a lecture in Dallas which shocked some of her friends. "I have gone to India," she said, "thinking there were too many of them and returned home deciding there were too many of me." The author of the 1970 best seller *The Female Eunuch* and of a later book entitled *Sex and Destiny* (1983), complained that Western society is anti-child. Without abandon-

ing her advocacy of planned parenthood, Miss Greer nonetheless regretted her own barrenness: "I chose not to have a child when I could have. Then when I thought I could fit one into my life, I found I couldn't conceive." [9]

It is a strange anomaly of the present Church situation that so many Catholics live by the norms of Germaine Greer the younger, than by the norms which have characterized Catholic family life in any country where the Church was effective. It is only a generation ago that Catholic moralists instructed fertile Catholic couples that they fulfilled God's command to "increase and multiply" if they brought three or four children into the world. [10] Indeed, the better educated Catholics of that era were convinced of that demand and frequently had larger families, couples described later in *Gaudium et Spes* (No. 50) as having "a generous heart." Today the expected 1.8 children from American marriages falls far short of what Christians usually meant when they used the word "family." Less than ten percent of young American women expect ever to have four children. Most will settle for two. [11]

Consequently, if the American woman is likely to have the first of her two children in her early twenties and the last before she is thirty, there are serious marital and familial, to say nothing of moral, problems ahead for practically all Catholic marriageables. If the Christian woman's role is, as John Paul II says, an "irreplaceable value," what are we Churchmen doing to change a mentality which dishonors motherhood as a vocation and makes it instead an exercise in self-satisfaction? What we have here, if we are speaking of people who claim the faith, is a Catholic couple's relationship with God and attention to Divine providence.

By way of conclusion to this section, something should be said about woman power. Germaine Greer went to India and discovered the kind of power Indian mothers exercised in their local villages and in city neighborhoods, even as their husbands patrolled the civic community as if they were budding Rajahs. Most of us who grew up in Christian families could probably have enlightened her on this subject. Rare was the mother of a family who was not the heart and center of her home and of her parish. Catholic mothers were a power to be reckoned with because they knew who they were, and so did their husbands, who generally were not the macho-male types feminists like to decry. A pastor may well get along without a curate, but could not have survived without the women — the single and the married — who contributed most to the priestly ministry and in a large amount to the neighborhood social action. The eternal feminine rocks the cradle and rules the world, not the female eunuch. A generation ago the psychological affliction which imperilled our nation, according to writers such as Philip Wylie and psychiatrists like Edward Strecker, was not Ramboism but Momism — women in the home, women in the schools, women in the welfare institutions, and the rising influence then of women at work.[12] By 1960 the National Catholic Welfare Conference (predecessor of the USCC) was concerned enough to publish a booklet called *Father, the Head of the Home*, as if Catholics needed that reassurance from Washington, D.C.

When we speak, therefore, of woman power we must make sure that it is not manpower that is sought as the special quality of woman, and the emasculation of men which Strecker says began under "Momism." Nor does it help the cause of women as women to have "femachos" speak for them. Women surely have the right to rival men in the public arena if they wish and if they can fulfill their marital and maternal responsibilities. But mothering is power enough for most women, especially if their men are accomplished in their own right and are satisfied with their role as fathers of the family. When elites speak of women hurting because their wants are unfulfilled, one should ask which wants and what women. Mary Joyce said it well: "Women need not hunger for authority when their special gift is for influencing everything. That's their best power."[13]

2. Fatherhood. Saint Augustine, in addressing fathers, was wont to call them "my fellow bishops." He conveyed the idea that they were heads of their families much as the bishop is the head of the Church, with primary obligations in the family to teach, to rule, to sanctify. We speak glibly of marriage today as a fifty/fifty proposition, when in truth it is a union of a one hundred percent man with a one hundred percent woman. Augustine was only building on Saint Paul's formal dictum, "Since as Christ is head of the Church and saves the whole body, so is a husband the head of his wife" (Ephesians 5:23). Almost twenty years ago Stephen Clark's monumental study *Man and Woman in Christ* (Servant Publications, 1980) reinforced what has been a Judeo-Christian tradition "from the beginning," namely that within the domestic community (we are not speaking of society generally) there are complementary roles to be played, with the husband responsible for the overall government of the family without the wife being his subordinate, and the mother responsible for all those areas which pertain to the internal life of the family, without the husband being voiceless. This division of labor is looked upon as God's creative plan for the family.

If boys growing up suffered under "Momism," tending to accept domination by women, they are taught by feminism to look upon women more as sex partners to be played with than as mothers who need their protection, support, and leadership. Christian marriage with its propensity to child-bearing quickly roots the man in the father's role from the earliest days of his boyhood training. That very concept of manhood and fatherhood has been under attack in recent years — first from the business and professional community which demands commitment to the job more than to the family; from the economic system itself which has made the two-income family almost a necessity to reach or maintain middle-class respectability; and from the ideology of feminism which legitimizes manly traits in women, while sanctioning a certain feminization in men.

The Church does not need George Gilder (*Sexual Suicide*, 1973, *Men and Marriage*, 1987) to know that women by virtue of their mother's role are more important to society than men, and a civilizing force of children and husbands. Even a woman's more pervasive and more erotic sexuality is a superiority used to good advantage within the historic family. But if the manly and fatherly role is denied, or made a matter of indifference, then it is the males who are liberated — to eschew what they think is the drudgery of home life, to distance themselves from commitment to one woman, to see sex as a toy, to turn homosexuality into another outlet for pleasure, to prove their virility not by domestic and social achievement but by sexual prowess.

If men to be men need fatherhood to fulfill their God-given manly nature, and as more than an incidental experience, women are most contented in the arms of a man whose love goes beyond sex to the care and protection of her children, on whom she can rely, making it possible for her to develop her own womanhood.

It is important for the Church, therefore, to defend and promote the child-centered family, and the importance of men and fatherhood to that family. In their many economic proposals the Church should call for the revision of tax laws to allow families with dependent children to keep more of their income. Some way must be found to distinguish, in our tax laws, family-oriented workers from child-free careerists, with economic incentives favoring a family's single-wage earner.

3. Natural Family Planning. This has been discussed earlier, but it is well to be reminded that never before in American history have Catholics had it so easy with regard to the necessities of life. Never has there

been more known about the natural spacing of births. Never has there been more practical help available for Natural Family Planning. Never has the teaching of the Church been more clear, never better defended. Never has the moral bankruptcy of the contraceptive movement been so obvious and the social ill-effects of its widespread use. Never before in the history of any country has there been less reason for those who profess faith in Christ and his Church to turn away from Catholic teaching on marital love and birth control.

Yet, twenty-five years after *Humanae Vitae*, more than half a century away from *Casti Connubii*, the vast majority of married Catholics use contraceptives, and Natural Family Planning remains a stepchild of the Church in practically every parish.

One other thing: The serious sins that most Christians are likely to commit from their earliest days involve marriage or sex and actions related to either. The sixth is not God's first commandment, but sins against marriage or sins involving lust are more commonplace than blasphemy, heresy, murder, or treason. Furthermore, as Saint Thomas Aquinas long ago demonstrated, untrammeled lust often leads to loss of faith: "Blindness of mind, lack of balanced consideration, inconstancy, precipitation, love of self, hatred of God, excessive clinging to the present world, and horror or despair of the world to come."[14]

For this reason the Church has always preached moderation in the use of sexual powers, insisting that Catholics be trained from their earliest years in the virtue of chastity. The tragedy of our times is that sexual sins have been reduced to premoral evils or peccadillos, of little account in the formation of Christian character. Yet since sexual sins are of their nature seriously sinful, they have an important bearing on eternal salvation.

4. Eternal life, salvation, sin. The Night Prayer of the Church on Sunday reads as follows: "Lord Jesus Christ, when tempted by the devil, you remained loyal to your Father, whose angels watched over you at his command. Guard your Church and keep us safe from the plague of sin so that we remain loyal to the day we enjoy your salvation and your glory."

Open the liturgical books of the Church at any point and you are likely to come across sentiments similar to these — a Christian prayer for eternal salvation and a plea for Christ's help in rising above our sinful nature to reach this beatitude. "God made us to know Him, to love Him, to serve Him in this life and to be happy with Him forever in the next." The penny Baltimore Catechism said it right. As we read in Hebrews

13:14, "For there is no eternal city for us in this life but we look for one in the life to come." The spiritual life of Catholics calls for a way of life that more and more is free of serious sin. Once the Catholic is in sin he is expected to reconcile with God through the sacrament still called penance.

Are we turning away from our doctrine on sin to calm the guilt feelings of sinners without regard to Christ's express command?

Summary and Recommendations

The Church's social agenda seeks to solve a Church dilemma: How to uplift people's social class without destroying what enriches and ennobles life itself — an appreciation of family and children. This is important because at stake is the family life of middle-class American Catholics, those great-great grandchildren of once poor and relatively unlettered immigrants, and the family life also of the new poor whose Catholicity is traditional but undeveloped and often marginal.

Positing the truths of the Church, and the state of American culture, a number of things are worthy of consideration by parish priests:

First, there must be a recatechesis of the faithful concerning the nature of eternal life and Christian commitment to the Church's way of achieving it. Eternal life is the motivation and sanction. Christians striving in this life must come to value both the goal and the striving.

Saint Paul spoke of it as follows: "For there is no eternal life for us in this life but we look for one in the life to come" (Hebrews 13:14). Or, as he told the Philippians (3:14-15): "I strain ahead for what is still to come; I am racing for the finish, for the prize to which God calls us upwards to receive in Christ Jesus."

Modern teachers who tell our young people that the important Christian value is how they live this present life, should pay attention to Saint Paul: "If our hope in Christ has been for this life only, we are the most unfortunate of all people" (1 Corinthians 15:19).

"Do you really believe this?" — an important question not unlike the one asked by Paul VI in his 1975 exhortation *Evangelii Nuntiandi* (No. 76), and by Christ in the Upper Room (see John 16:31). Secularization has given our people an earthbound view of life. If this remains the case, there is little reason that they will believe anything else Christ and the Church have to say, unless it is to their convenience.

Second, we must recatechize our faithful on the divine vocation of marriage, the central place of children and parenthood in that calling, and the vital importance (for Christians at least) of the sacred norms to fulfillment in this life and reward or punishment in the next.

To do this well the United States bishops, perhaps in collaboration with the Congregation for the Doctrine of the Faith, must assess the present status of authentic teaching within Church institutions and initiate whatever remedial steps are necessary to see that correct teaching is the rule in the Church.

Parish priests must preach and teach, sanctify through the liturgy and the proper administration of the sacraments, and govern the Catholic community. But their preaching is in vain if this community is ungoverned, if false teachers prevail without restraint, and sacraments are administered sacrilegiously with no complaint from the pastors. In recent days political scientist George Weigel reminded bishops of Saint Augustine's concept "*tranquillitas ordinis*," a negative concept to be sure, but one without which sinful men cannot live in peace. As Weigel phrases it: "Order keeps things from getting worse than they would be under conditions of chaos and anarchy."[15]

What is so different about insisting that only fully committed believers teach and supervise the Church's pastoral mission, especially among the poor whose family life is at the moment reasonably intact? What is so heinous about quarantining the carriers of heresy, which is what "pick and choose Catholicism" really means, in a Church professing to proclaim Christ's truth? We are not dealing anymore with a sick situation calling for therapy. We are dealing with an evil situation which demands the corrective action of which Christ himself was the prime mover.

If we do not move in this direction with deliberate speed, then the universal catechism will turn out to be another Church document filed and forgotten.

Third, the Church should initiate a national crusade on behalf of *Natural Family Planning* — not only to teach our people how to be married and Catholic when child spacing is indicated, but to educate the vast body of religious Americans what authentic married love is and why marriages based on this kind of love are more meaningful to them, more perduring, and more fruitful for both Church and society. For the Catholic people alone, NFP promises this much at least — a married life in conformity with God's law.

Fourth, and this surely will be the Church's most arduous task, the Catholic community must bring its corporate influence to bear on the public institutions of our society, especially on the government, on the media, and on those who fashion the secular mind-sets of the country's public leaders. There is the critical matter of freedom of religion. In the last forty years religionists have allowed themselves to be antiestablished out of public life, with religion reduced to the status of public oddity. The approved, acceptable public role of an otherwise avowed religionist is capsulated in one affirmation: "I believe in Jesus Christ but...." Here the adversary is government and its various subdivisions or bureaucracies. No longer must we permit the media to trivialize or treat contemptuously the teachings and sacred authority of the Church.

As a last point, we must draw on that segment of the Catholic university world which still is or wishes to be institutionally committed to the Catholic Church and its faith. One of the tragedies of our times is that the aspiring Catholic Harvards have become more Harvard than Catholic, and of little use to the Church in confronting the neo-pagan and statist ideas that presently prevail in the higher regions of American society. What we must never forget is that there are a large number of Catholic scholars who believe in the truths of their faith and are quite willing to defend them.

If we can still speak of the Catholic lay apostolate, and we can if we mean "Catholic" as well as "lay," then parish priests must give their support to these kinds of faithful and permit them to take the Catholic cause into the marketplace, where they, not clergy, will demand respect and get it, after they first fight for recognition.

With a fully developed alternative to the present secularized organs of opinion-molding, our Catholic parents can hopefully once more take pride in their Church and the quality of their family life, even if it is not mainstream secularized America.

Endnotes

1. *The American Catholic People* (New York: Doubleday and Co., Inc., 1987), p. 183.
2. John Paul II, *Reflections on Humanae Vitae* (Boston, MA: Saint Paul Books and Media, 1984), pp. 9-10.
3. English *L'Osservatore Romano*, July 6, 1987, p. 12.

4. Eugene Kennedy once argued that the moral distortions in Catholic life were due to "people's acceptance of the Church's moral authority on the way they live their moral lives" (*America*, August 22, 1970, p. 87). Jesuit Francis Buckley attributed them to "moral conformism and the acceptance of authority" (*I Confess*, 1972, p. 53). Sister Marie Augusta Neal thought it improper to impose any "doctrine or values or commitment" (*Discovery Patterns Book*, 1969, p. 92). *Time Magazine*, September 3, 1971, p. 41, in a review of what was wrong with sacramental confession, stressed its disastrous effects.

5. Cf. Andrew Greeley, *Chicago Studies*, Spring 1963.

6. Letter to Diognetus (usually attributed to Justin Martyr in the second century), F. X. von Funk, *The Apostolic Fathers*, pp. 397ff. This citation is used in the Church's *Divine Office of Holy Men and Women*.

7. Cf. *Origins*, May 28, 1987, pp. 21ff.

8. Dennis Doherty, *Dimensions of Human Sexuality* (1979), p. 130.

9. See *Newsletter* of the Fellowship of Catholic Scholars, June 1984, p. 8. In her 1971 *The Female Eunuch* (New York: McGraw-Hill, Inc.), she looked upon the family as the "prison of domesticity" and " patriarchy's chief institution.

10. John Ford, *Contemporary Moral Theology: Marriage Questions* Volume 2 (Newman, 1963, pp. 420-421).

11. *Statistical Abstract*, 1987, p. 65.

12. Philip Wylie's *Generation of Vipers* (Marietta, GA: Cherokee Publishing Co., 1979) and Edward Strecker's *Their Mother's Daughter* (1956).

13. *National Catholic Register*, March 22, 1987. The initial ethnic family was "father headed and mother centered" in which the father generally exercised executive command while mother managed the household and oversaw the division of labor among the children [Charles H. Mindel and Robert W. Habenstein (eds.), *Ethnic Families in America: Patterns and Variations* (1976), p. 415].

14. *Summa Theologica* II, II, q. 153, a. 5.

Part Four

Parish Priests:

Administrators and Diocesan Officials

Chapter Sixteen

Priests: Administrators and Money Men

My Dear Father:
I wish to offer you my heartfelt congratulations and assure you of my good wishes
and prayers in your work as pastor of Sacred
Heart parish....
In regard to the material condition of the
parish, I am pleased to report that all the
buildings are in excellent condition. There is
no debt on the parish and there is nothing in
the treasury. You will find that most of the
parishioners intelligently appreciate that it
costs a great deal of money to maintain the
parish property and the parish organizations;
that there are four priests and eighteen sisters
constantly at their service; that there are ten
other persons employed in the school, the
Church and the rectory. You will also find that
they are Catholic-minded and Catholic-
hearted enough to contribute in proportion to
their means to the considerable and constant
expense of maintenance.

— Archbishop Francis J. Spellman, May 21,
1939 (letter to his successor as Boston pastor
on the Sunday he left to take over the See of
New York)

When Francis J. Spellman went to bed on May 23, 1939, after a long day of welcome to New York and the completion of his first official business there, he found a huge basket of red roses in his private quarters, with a letter tilted against the wicker, which he mistakenly thought was another greeting. It was a hello, all right, but from a group of bankers informing him that they held $28,000,000 in mortgages on various churches and institutions of his new archdiocese, and what was he going to do about it? He was not amused, naturally, lost a good night's sleep, and his first act the following morning was to undertake the immediate refinancing of the archdiocese.[1]

What's an Administrator?

No pastor walks into a parish expecting to find on his first day that he is badly in hock, or to come out remembered only as an administrator. Even if the parish is known to be in debt, or to need a new church or expensive repairs, hope springs eternal in his bosom that raising money or paying bills will not be what keeps him awake nights. Still, when he rises on the second day, however much his church may be a seat of prayer and a font of grace, he knows that storekeepers, electricians, tax collectors, and certainly bankers, will continue to look upon his parish as simply another account. And it's the pastor's duty to keep that enterprise financially viable, so that its benefits to people's lives continue to be provided.

Things are much tougher today for pastors than in Cardinal Spellman's day, tougher for the poorer parishes than the rich, for the larger parishes, the changing parishes, the multiethnic parishes, certainly for places where the cost of upkeep outstrips the ability of a declining Mass attendance to carry the burden. The annual fuel oil bill for one cathedral-like church was $10,000 forty years ago; a few years ago during a cold December the bill came to $10,000 for just that month; today the church is closed. The decline in the number of priests and religious, inflated prices and higher wages, tax burdens, and pension costs are all part of the picture. The other element making it difficult to balance the parochial budget is the loss of productivity commonplace everywhere as a result of widespread individualism, subjectivism, and egalitarianism. Whatever problems a Father Spellman-type had in 1939, and money was scarce then, his pastor's authority was unchallenged and he could tailor his costs to income with greater ease, because he had so many people working almost for nothing who were absolutely dedicated to the cause. And he did not have to worry about their tender psyches, or about diocesan mediation procedures.

One pastor of a large parish with 500 baptisms and 200 funerals *per annum*, 700 children in the school, and a budget well over $1 million calls himself "a manager, an administrator, personnel officer, chief of maintenance, financial officer, and hotel manager." He might have added entertainer and bandmaster, maître d'hôtel, CYO director, and likely nursemaid, too. A great deal is made of shared responsibility, but the more committees, the greater likelihood that Murphy's law and the Peter Principle begin to work at the same time, guaranteeing chaos because someone has risen to his level of incompetence.

We once had a mayor of the City of New York who had the answers to all municipal problems: study them. He was succeeded by a mayor who took such accumulated research seriously, only to leave the city on the verge of bankruptcy simply because, drawing board or no, he forgot to control the special interests. If the country's metropolitan areas are in a state of chaos or semi-chaos, it is because we have given government over to specialists rather than holding proper officials accountable for the efficient management of their areas of responsibility. For too long society has sat idly by while lawbreakers humbled elected officials by simply saying no to the law. Serious analysts attribute the disintegration of social order to the loss of nerve at the highest levels of government which, once debilitated, negatively affects the authority of officeholders down the line of institutional structures.

There are three levels of authority in any society: policy making, tactical decisions, and execution. All kinds of interplay goes on between interested parties concerning where an institution ought to be going and how it plans to get there; but, when objectives and direction have been decided, it is the function of the executive to get things done according to the will of the people or their representatives — or, for pastors, the will of God and/or those bishops who are in union with the pope. And among the things that bishops and their parish priests must worry about, one is money, the subject that makes some people think that religion is little more than a "racket."

American Catholics, however, even the post-Persian Gulf War kind, are not so cynical, or so post-Christian. They have seen what their money, given to the Church, has done for their upward mobility and for their faith. Those old enough to remember World War II have also witnessed the unselfishness and modest living of priests and nuns who built the Catholic infrastructures, of which Catholics have been so proud, and which today seem to be in so much trouble. So long as they observe the same dedication and restraint in their leadership, money talk by priests will be accepted as a natural element of the priestly mission, one that must be handled carefully because, like power and sex, it tends to corrupt those who need it, or those who handle it.

We will deal with this subject, therefore, with discretion, and with a certain willingness also to tabulate the bills that come with running a church, and to count the wherewithal it takes to pay them.

Depending on where the priest lives, he will find himself, especially if he is a pastor, with a host of administrative problems from quarters above and beneath him — ambiguous policies, higher and higher diocesan taxes, burdensome regulations concerning use of public halls and/or buildings, interference with his judgment by Church bureaucracies, ethnic or racial conflicts among parishioners, unusual school costs, emergency expenditures for repairs, high salaries to employees who are often disruptive or troublemaking, and the other difficulties which invade the church from a distressed secular culture.

But if people reread Bishop Spellman's 1939 letter to his successor at Newton Center, Massachusetts, they will find certain priestly administrative responsibilities remain constant — everywhere and down the years — buildings, programs, and staff, the management of which is easier when there is enough money, and when the pastor is frugal.

Paying the Bills

Catholics are not the most generous benefactors of Church enterprises that the country ever saw. Protestant and Jewish congregations, they say, do better because their fund-raising and fiscal management are in the hands of competent laity who have ways of pressuring their peers into giving, far beyond anything that clerics can do. And do better keeping a tight hold on the purse strings when dreamers, with fancy or trendy programs in mind, push the local church or synagogue into deficit financing or toward fiscal irresponsibility. Giving a dollar to the parish is still an old Catholic habit, even though today's middle class earns ten, twenty, thirty times what their grandparents brought home. Those doughty laborers of old, and the menials, built cathedrals and universities with nickels and dimes that only looked like dollars. The Church's poor in those days had numbers on their side, and later on an abundance of religious who, for room and board only, contributed their lives to Catholic works. If parish priests seemed to multiply collections the way Christ did loaves and fishes, it was merely to increase the pittance that kept those saints building, evermore, the Church's schools and hospitals the people were demanding.

Furthermore, our early American pastors were not happy with the Protestant precedent and its "trustee system." Landed gentry tried to lord it over them, as they did Protestant vicars, telling them what they could and could not do, who they could or could not hire, especially for matters like catechesis; lorded, that is, until trustees met up with the likes of New York's John Hughes, who made it clear that he, not a committee of successful businessmen, succeeded the apostles. The Catholic Church was and surely is congregational, that is, "the people of God," but it also has a hierarchical structure, responsible directly to the Lord. In the Catholic scheme of things at least, the buck of ecclesial responsibility stops at the pastor's door. And however inadequate he might seem, the parish priest of those days could only nag, not tax. Catholic Mass-goers were glad for this limitation on a pastor's power, but inevitably they gave him enough to help the Church grow.

Catholic attitudes have changed little since the nineteenth century, and paying church bills is no easier, only now the pastor has to raise more money than ever. The withering away of religious communities, the demand of those who do remain on church staffs for professional pay, legally binding entitlement programs, the decline in the spirit of "volunteerism," collective bargaining, and the high cost of running anything, have diminished the desire of many priests to become pastors. A new pastor in 1970-1971 found out how costs could rise in a given year, from $1,750 a week to survive in 1970 ($350 short of need), to $2,800 in 1971 (when he paid his way). The pastor in 1992 needed $10,000 weekly to maintain his income-outgo balance.

Before we go any further, let us say what this chapter is not about. It is not about all those things the diocesan finance office (most dioceses today have one) can and will tell you in one memorandum after another — concerning payroll tax requirements or withholding and paying taxes, all of which are mandatory, and for which the pastor is personally responsible.[2] Nor will we discuss who a pastor may or may not hire legally, or the various penalties imposed on employers careless about these public laws. Father Government is today a strict disciplinarian, even when its administrators are pious Catholics.

Describing what local bishops demand of pastors is also unnecessary, since there are too many varieties of bishops. Even the type of investments or insurance policies available, and required of pastors under somebody's law, call for specific knowledge from bankers, brokers, or diocesan officials, not simply from a book. (Most dioceses discourage stock investments, although from time to time parishes have stocks willed to them.) Further, since the amount of tax-exempt property presently available for sale or leasing is large, in contrast to the days when churches were mainly buyers or lessees, pastors nowadays, over and above obtaining episcopal permission to negotiate such arrangements in the first place, must follow the policies determined by diocesan lawyers.

In any event, every pastor responsible for the economy of a substantial parish likely has already hired a competent accountant who guides him through the maze of regulations, who assumes the workload of seeing that those rules are obeyed to the letter. Additionally, the new *Code of Canon Law* prescribes that every pastor establish a finance committee, composed of members with competence in the management of money and who, without negating the final decision-making by the pastor, hopefully provide sage and prudent counsel at regular times during the year.

With these technical matters out of the way, let us proceed to examine more closely what is required of the pastor as "chancellor of the parish exchequer."

The Pastor Must Care About Money

Priests are still mindful of the "Dollar Bill Monaghan" types who made Catholic folklore so interesting a half-century ago. Members of the "brick and mortar" generation, they came to be despised later by the purist products of their own schools who grew to prefer charismatic or social action priests, not crude fund-raisers. (Unless, of course, the money went into their causes.) Some pastors surely allowed money to get the best of them, or found their niche in life as money changers. Glorying in their reputation for having successfully kept the spiritual in the background did not seem to disturb a few. It's strange how little credit is given to a pastor who, when called upon to establish a new parish in his late fifties, dies a quarter of a century later, leaving four thousand children in the schools he built, and money in the bank besides. To disdain such an accomplishment hardly does credit to the beneficiaries of that largesse. At a diocesan level, who talks anymore with approval of a J. Francis McIntyre, who came to Los Angeles as archbishop (1948-1972) and watched his Catholic population grow from 600,000 to 1,750,000, who built 200 diocesan institutions to service those developing needs, mostly schools, and paid for them all before he retired?

No priest in his right mind wishes to go to God known as "Dollar Bill." But "Freddie the Freeloader," who piles up debts for successors or the bishop to pay, is no great model either for God or man. The day of the pastor sitting in the corner of his room peering at his parish accounts under a green eyeshade and by a gooseneck lamp, may be gone; but the good pastor today, as before, must have a general idea how much money the parish has in the bank, what he owes, what he needs to raise, and whether he can afford to borrow.

Some pastors spend an inordinate time on money, almost as an escape from preaching well, visiting people, or coming to their rescue. Some priests would rather tinker with books than pastor the people. They personally do the shopping, check the plumbing, replace broken windowpanes in the school, and spend hours of time computing tax deductions. None of these chores is objectionable if its object is cost reduction. Far better to have a penny watcher than a profligate who instructs his delegates to "order it," without ever asking the price. Priests deal with people's money, which is hard for them to come by and worthy of a banker's care, especially at a time when everyone in state and church think they have a right to a piece of it. The priest who does not care, especially the pastor who overspends wastefully, is a poor sort of shepherd.

Keeping Costs Down

If you know your annual income, you ought to know what you can spend month by month. There was an old pastor, once, whose first assignment after World War I brought him to a parish whose annual income was $900 a year. A pastor's salary, in those days, was $900.

Naturally he survived, but as a member of a generation of clerics later called "cheap," he learned young the value of money by not having any of it. Years later he took over a church whose annual income was $50,000, but one which on his arrival had $10,000 in unpaid bills. His nuns immediately asked for a new set of desk-chairs for the first grade, so that they could divide the student body into learning groups. The pastor's answer was "No, not now." The nuns, far from playing dogs-in-the-manger, were creative enough to con the local grocery store manager out of one hundred orange crates which, properly painted, served as moveable chairs for almost three years, until the needed chairs could be afforded. These nuns belonged to an era when postponed gratification was a fact of everyone's life, and they lived with a pastor who did not spend what he did not have. We need to recover that kind of restraint.

The budget breaker common to today's parish may be the cost of a good parish staff, or of the parish school. Once upon a time it made little difference whether the cantankerous cook was fired or the lazy priest. Both came cheap. Today a live-in priest, religious, or cook (in metropolitan areas at least) probably costs the parish $50,000 a year, when you total salary, board and room, insurance health care, and pension. One priest walked into a parish where Mass attendance fell in a year from twenty-five hundred to eight hundred, and income from $300,000 to $100,000, because a new church was under construction. Yet the same nine employees from the old church were still on the payroll! Six of them had to go. The choices were not easy and the first casualty was an aged parishioner whose parochial salary supplemented his two decent pensions. What was his ongoing job? To watch the church during the daytime — the church which was no longer there! Dealing with that kind of a situation is a pastor's nightmare. Tact is needed, as well as judgment, and he must provide explanations, due notice, and severance pay. But payrolls must sometimes be trimmed.

The Catholic Church is recognized by many as a good employer, a fact testified by the devotion of its longtime employees. Yet, it is also known for its lousy salaries, a subject ofttimes addressed in rectories and chancery offices everywhere. "You get what you pay for," they say, and this surely is true of the Church enterprise. Still, churches are not subsidized institutions, the latter often corrupted by the infusion of government money, even when it is transferred to poverty-vowed religious. The voluntary parish, on the other hand, its school and service to the neighborhood, survives only on the contributed lives (not just the services) of laity and religious. In such unsubsidized situations a pastor's payroll costs can be a heavy burden. A good teacher or a good cook is worth gold itself. But working in a Catholic setting also has a bonus quality, even an economic one, if the alternative is employment in a Fort Apache-type public school or in the kitchen of a Roy Rogers restaurant. No pastor need feel obligated to match market rates, if by careful selection of em-

251

ployees and mutual understanding with candidates, he strikes the proper balance between their personal needs and those of the parish. (His problem, then, may lie elsewhere.)

The other side of the cost factor is unproductiveness. It is better to have one well-paid, but useful and devoted secretary, than two incompetent clerks, one of whom is a notorious time-waster whenever the pastor is off the scene. To fire anyone is not easy, especially today when lawsuits, accusations of impropriety, and violent reactions to pain, make headlines. Yet it can be done, sometimes best when a recognized staff supervisor other than the pastor prepares the way. Whatever the mechanism, getting a good day's work for a good day's pay is necessary. Some priests should not be pastors because they have irritable and overbearing personalities or, quite oppositely, because they are so timid that mayhem goes on in the rectory or school before the matter gains their attention. Furthermore, the pastor who foolishly develops "pets," who are singularly blessed with short hours, unexplained holidays, bonuses, etc., is destined for employee trouble. Meaningful performance standards must apply across the board. Sometimes, the "pet factor" is not the result of a conscious act. We all tend to favor those we know well, or who have served us faithfully over many years, particularly if they came with us from a previous assignment. Still, close friends on the payroll can be dysfunctional when the parish staff is fairly large, but intimately connected in their daily work. Probably no other cost depletes funds more rapidly than contract laborers: the painters, the plumbers, the electricians. Here the balance between competence and money outlay involves delicate choices. If you hire a cheap roofer to solder the gutters around the church, you may wind up with a five-alarm fire, and no church. On the other hand, blessed are pastors with a knack for finding the right people to make beautiful vestments or classy altar linens, to repair utensils and machinery, or to clean and polish, well below commercial costs. Having one handyman on the parish payroll full-time who is competent at various trades is also a wise investment. Do you know how much money can be saved if such an employee paints one room at a time week by week? If the parish is also endowed with talented volunteers willing to take direction, its overall operation can be "spit and polish" from one end of the year to the other. Buildings, even without vandalism, begin to look seedy and rundown over time — a dirty wall here, scratched pews there, lights out where lights are needed, chairs in need of repair, and so forth. Nothing adds more to a pastor's reputation as a good caretaker than church walls free of candle smoke, clean public toilets, a neat altar scene, and polished floors. If he relies on hit-and-miss labor because it's cheap, or he turns to contract labor spasmodically, the parish suffers one way or another. This is especially true when a parochial school is a large part of the plant. Preventative maintenance of the school during the summer months under the watchful eye of a first-rate "parish engineer" can save thousands of *ad hoc* dollar payments during the year. (This presumes, of course, that the school's upkeep is directly under the pastor's jurisdiction, as normally it should be.)

The parochial school is becoming, more and more, an economic burden to parishes. Once upon a time, because of the lifegiving contribution of well-educated religious women, the cost of an elementary school surfaced around $50 per child *per annum*. Today that cost circles at $2,000 or more. Many parents cannot afford this tuition, although many of the poor in or near slum neighborhoods do, to keep their children out of the public schools. Even when the parish subsidizes the overall costs, the tuition (which at one time was nothing, or a dollar a week) may range from $750 to $1,500, still too high for families with more than one school-age child. Apart from the pastoral component of the problem, the priest has to keep his eye on the expenditures incurred by principal and teachers. "They think we're made of money," many pastors say of certain school staffs.

The wise pastor places a cap on the size of the parochial subsidy and creates a "St. Mary's" parent-teacher association (PTA), responsible for closing the gap between parish subsidy plus tuition income, and the ultimate annual cost of the school. Responsibility for the cost of Catholic education becomes a shared experience, with parents as well as teachers given a stake in keeping salaries realistic and closing out non-necessary expenditures. If a large parish income is $1,000,000, of which the pastor commits ten percent each year to the school, and tuition brings in another $100,000, it is the responsibility of the PTA to raise the remainder. (Smaller parishes deal in smaller numbers, but the proportions are usually the same.)

A major problem for the PTA is collecting tuition. Amazingly, people who are better off, that is, those with nice houses or with summer homes, or who have two cars, are often slow to pay the monthly tuition. But that is the PTA's job, even if it involves personal visitation of other people's residences. The PTA, then, becomes an energetic fund-raiser, using parish facilities for multiple activities. Their dedication is ordinarily commensurate with their will to keep the school alive. In some towns, the lay leaders are fortunate, or skillful enough, to find a corporation or a bank to pick up the deficit.

Increasingly, dioceses cannot do this any more. Only a few years back, a diocesan interparish finance committee would grant as much as $250,000 per annum, to parish schools which made little or no effort to be self-sustaining. The "dole mentality" became a way of life for some pastors and religious, and for teachers, too, who wanted public school pay but not public school employment. Those days are gone!

Probably, the chief cost-saving factor is the pastor's genius at knowing "what" to hire, more than "who." Opening the rectory door, answering the telephone, mediating appointments for priests, relating to local shopkeepers, answering questions correctly and courteously, these are all vital public relations functions. Many a parish is done in by "the help" as often as by the wrong priest. Trained volunteers do not cost a great deal. The sections of a budget which really call for a pastor's close scrutiny are the cost of high-priced specialists, and taxes, diocesan or otherwise. Diocesan impositions (e.g., subsidy of poorer parishes) in many places have risen three hundred percent in twenty years.

One final point: Since the largest costs are often the result of replacing large machines (e.g., boilers) or repairing damaged goods (roofs, eaves, walls, gutters, etc.), preventative care is critical. Once or twice a year all such vital facilities should be surveyed. Neglect can damage interiors as well as exteriors. Oil distributors often provide insurance coverage, even on an emergency basis, for observed defects in day-to-day operations. If the local community lacks competent service shops (to examine the church roof, e.g.), the diocesan building office should be consulted. Buildings and machinery last a long time at minimal cost, if properly attended. A new pastor may spend hundreds of thousands of dollars cleaning up a mess in an unused parish building, simply because his predecessor ignored growing debris or concealed its condition from diocesan authorities.

Raising the Ante

Unlikely is the pastor who does not look upon fund-raising as one of his chief preoccupations. Some are joyful in the role ("People just like to give me money"). Others make it the work of their life. My first pastor paid off a depression debt of $300,000 in ten years, but was hated. Not only did the four money announcements per Sunday do him in, but taking up the collection himself by removing his vestments, whenever he wanted to "whoop it up" personally, was considered an outrageous and offensive act by most of the poor people who saw him do it regularly. Less odious, but mistaken, was the conduct of a very cultured pastor, who tarnished his reputation at the beginning of his term by taking his majestic presence into the pulpit at his first Midnight Mass, there with grand eloquence for forty-five minutes denounce the financial state of the parish he recently inherited. He never seemed to notice the stunned expressions on the faces of the fifteen hundred churchgoers who were not used to harangues of such a vulgar stripe.

The thing to be kept in mind is that good, indeed talented, priests can be trapped into doing untoward things on behalf of improving the parochial income. They may indeed succeed in inflating the parish bank account, but they injure the Church, and themselves in the process.

One pastor, a favorite with his peers, taught an interesting lesson about second collections, which almost everyone dislikes. He had just rejected an offer from his curate to run a bazaar because, he said, it was too much of a drain on the energies of the people, and of the priest in charge. But he was adamant about the importance of the second collection, even though this young priest reported the irritations of parishioners over that practice. Said the pastor: "Do you know what we receive in second collections annually? Ten thousand dollars! That pays for our heating. I'll cancel it, if you guarantee whatever shortfall we experience." As far as the curate was concerned, the second collection was a dead issue, except to remember the old man's reminder that, however much second collections may annoy envelope-users, they manage to attract an extra "little bit" from those whom more cynical pastors call the Church's "cheap Charlies."

But let us return to the substance. How can a pastor raise enough money to do all the things he feels he must do to make the Church work in his neighborhood, and simultaneously contribute to the solvency of his bishop?

If in olden days Catholics were never benefactors of their church as other religionists were it was because they were poor and raised large families. Today the reason may be that the newer generation prizes the size of their bank account or their assets more than their pastor's cry for help. John Paul II has made "consumerism" a rectory word, and it has validity, but there is probably little that a local pastor can do about it. Nagging the people sitting before them on Sunday morning about a cultural defect is likely to be counterproductive, especially if they know the criticism does not apply to them.

It would be better for a pastor to realize that a major part of the Church's contemporary economic problem is the result of a serious drop in Sunday Mass attendance about which local pastors can do something through personal contact, and by solid, ongoing Catholic catechesis.

The Shortcuts

We all know the parochial shortcuts to good bank balances — bingos, cake sales, flea markets, chance books. Older priests have participated in some of the most successful income-producing bingos of a lifetime, and they surely beget money. They sometimes also beget vulgar crowds and hordes of invading non-parishioners who do little to enhance the civic reputation of the local Catholic community. Following World War II, a pastor with a genius for city-wide organization raised $100,000 yearly from his bazaar and, though a priest of solid piety, spent most of his year getting it ready and cleaning up its mess. Many years ago, too, a creative pastor encouraged his parishioners to take out life insurance and make the parish the beneficiary. He did rather well.

While "games" of one kind or another are proper outlets for faithful Catholics working week after week on the Church's religious mission, and within this context are important instruments for creating fellowship and morale, they can also become ends in themselves, that is, pure money raisers. If the parish does not have the clerical or lay talent for undertaking these activities, all the pastor has to do is open the "Yellow Pages" of the local telephone company — under "Bingo," "Bazaar," or "Fund-Raising" — and he will find all the help he needs, for a price. He also has to make sure, of course, that the parish does better than his new professional helpmates.

The "periodic fund-raising campaign" is of a different genre. Unless it is a "Bishop's Appeal," for purposes which transcend the neighborhood, the parish campaign, normally intensive and prolonged, grows out of an emergency — a church fire, need for a better school, and (in the old days) the second most attractive reason for a campaign (after the church), a new convent for the nuns. When the need has such an emotional base, the campaign becomes a rallying point for parish involvement, especially if it is door-to-door, with a parishioner or the priest facing people (not just mail order). Recognizing the purpose, establishing the goal, calling out the workers, the weekly meetings with their inspirational talks and the coffee klatsches, the memorial gifts, the monthly pledges, the reports — and the finished product — bond a parish as few things do. Once a priest completes this experience (as long as he does not overdo it), he has memories that are lifelong. What a joy for a pastor to preside at a supper or at a good party for several hundred workers who have given him a half-million dollars — and a new church!

The Sunday Collection

But, when all is said and done, it is the Sunday offertory collection week after week which pays the bills, and builds the churches. One pastor may be lucky because he has the numbers, the right ethnic balance, and largely a middle-class membership that is traditionally generous to the Church. Today senior citizens are often the mainstay of solvent or prospering parishes. Another priest may work in a ghetto, among a poor ethnic group or others unaccustomed to American Catholic giving habits, with broken-down buildings besides, or perhaps with a vast complex whose heating bills alone are beyond the capacity of a declining population to afford.

In any case, however, every pastor faces the size, great or small, of his Sunday collection. Bills tend to mount in geometric proportion, but ordinary income only arithmetically. The artistry of the rector, or lack of it, becomes the dividing line between prosperity or depression. The pastor whose "people just love to give me money" probably earns his reputation, and his cash flow. "The Scrooge" usually deserves his own failure.

We also have a new phenomenon today — "priests on the dole," recipients of other pastors' earned income, courtesy of their bishop. Some never become self-sufficient; some never even try.

The Giving Situation

However, raising the weekly ante is not merely a matter of pleading. A priest's actions do speak louder than his words. Sunday chats on money are not wasted when pastors are good salesmen, with a gift for that kind of gab, and deft at making the argument that draws an extra five dollars out of the wallet. Yet it is what people see that develops in the pews the conviction that "their" money is being put to good use. The priest standing outside church on a Sunday morning, the coffee hours, the little tributes in parish halls to individuals and groups for services rendered — apart from the annual show or bus trip — all contribute to goodwill. But it is amazing how readily a new coat of paint (the right color, of course) gets an approving nod from the weekly pewholders.

Smart pastors use every spare dollar they can squeeze from the exchequer to doll up some part of the church or school month by month. Those who know what they are doing, or seek advice from someone who does know, will no doubt beautify the altar area first — a well-designed liturgical fall to grace the table of sacrifice, stylish candelabra to frame it, a beautiful crucifix to serve as backdrop to the event their people will share, and the best vestments that can be made or purchased (for a modest price), perhaps imported from Spain — to symbolize the special sacredness attached to Catholic worship. Liturgists, who write a lot, think that popular interest is focused on "participation," and that it is this which defines the post-Vatican Mass. Ministers, lectors, and singers have their place, more so since 1965, but it is the symbols of God's beauty reflected in the altar setting that inspire gratitude, and a modicum of awe.

What the pastor thinks should be done about the church, when it represents good thinking, applies also to other church buildings, especially to the school. Even people in the slums, often the very poor, prize cleanliness, neatness, newness. Some of the best-dressed children on Easter Sunday often come from the homes of parents who have difficulty making ends meet. Why should anyone be comfortable or satisfied walking into slummy buildings? Some buildings are old, some are new. The old ones are likely to be overdesigned and in need of repair. Their interiors, as well as exteriors, may need cleaning and simplification. On the other hand, new buildings, that often look like hospital wards, may require artistic touches. An old church, for example, may be over-ornamented in the Baroque or Rococo tradition, and in need of purification, if only by removing ugly or repetitious statuary, or by using paint to cover up what offends the modern eye. Church edifices erected later, often bare to the bone like many of those erected in Europe after World War II, can acquire warmth by the simple addition of some medieval artifacts, wood carvings of a saint or two, a new baptismal font or tabernacle — cut with style, of course.

It would be a foolhardy pastor who tampered with the basic internal design of a classic Gothic or Byzantine church, even to make points with modern parishioners. (Why any bishop would allow such defacement is the second mystery.) There are minor adjustments possible to bring the community closer to the altar, but these should be made only under the close (and wise) supervision of diocesan authorities.

The Appeals: Sincerity and Honesty Above All

Unquestionably, some fund-raising experts, including clergy, can get blood money from the "turnips" of their congregation, but may leave a less than sweet taste in the giver's mouth. But some priests have the undefinable talent to encourage giving without bitterness, and their sincerity and honesty probably have something to do with it. They undersell what they need, and they never ask for what they do not need.

Many fund-raisers of old were con men. They never told the people that their debt was paid as they continued their debt reduction collections anyway. One lady became so sick and tired of hearing about debt reduction year after year that one Sunday she walked into the sacristy with her checkbook, and pressed the pastor for the mortgage balance (which he said was $25,000). He was surprised when she wiped it out on the spot. He had been reducing the debt by only $1,000 a year, but collecting $30,000 annually toward the fictional end. Parishioners are not so easily seduced any longer by persiflage, and there are enough smart laity around to read between the lines of parochial balance sheets, which are now commonplace.

Obviously, the pastor should give a financial accounting once a year, at which time he rightly can encourage use of the weekly envelopes, and even tithing. Envelope-users, who often represent only a quarter of customary Mass attenders, carry the large part of the parish's burden and, granting variations from place to place, demonstrate the disparities in the pews, for example, five dollars per week per envelope-user versus fifty cents per nonuser. Promoting extensive envelope use, suggesting weekly contribution goals for various income levels (perhaps size of family, too), are guidelines best set with advice from lay members of the pastor's finance committee. An emergency may arise which would prompt the pastor to mount his pulpit a second time during the year to talk about money, but he becomes less persuasive the more he does it. Tithing, in the strict sense, is not a reasonable goal for many parishioners, given the nature of contemporary economic life. It was one thing during simpler days to set aside one-tenth of agricultural income for church support, but today a $50,000 annual gross income (the tithe then being

$100 weekly) is significantly less when taxes of one kind or another are deducted. Even one-tenth of net income may be hard on large families, for those who live where food prices or rents are high, not surprisingly in some ghettos. But tithing as a fixed percent of weekly income, recommended by the parochial finance committee, based on its sense of local possibilities, to which a family opts for itself, is sound policy. Such a norm, properly explained, helps parishioners judge their own performance against that of their neighbors, as the published list of contributors once did.

As to style, the pastor who is chatty, matter-of-fact, sincerely appreciative of the generosity of his people (especially of those sitting before him), has a better chance for a favorable response than the nagger. He can gain some points with his audience if he expresses reluctance to use shortcuts or pressure cooker tactics. Bingos by churches, like government sales taxes, are easy to administer, but both place an unfair burden on those least able to pay. It is desirable that the pastor identify with the struggles of his people to survive. Like government, the church pays its bills out of funds contributed by ordinary people, not from the outlays of the super-rich, whose numbers are always comparatively few.

In subtle ways the weekly bulletin carries his message throughout the year, particularly by reporting present income and costs, compared with a previous year. The bulletin can also keep the "norm of giving" (the tithe) before the consciousness of its readers. Of course, the parish publication must be attractive enough to earn readership.

The weekly bulletin is also used effectively by certain pastors to recommend that parishioners keep the church in mind when they complete their wills. In these days, many Catholics live long years, so much so that there is hardly any family remaining to be recipients of the bequest of monies earned with great difficulty, and harvested carefully. Such parishioners may think only of well-publicized causes when deciding on recipients. The truth is that the local parish, especially if it has been the center of worship and friendship over many years, is often a better object of such charity. It is a farseeing pastor who cultivates this interest. One successful cardinal, attributing the prosperity of his diocese to the generosity of his pastors, marvelled at the ability of another cardinal to build up the invested funds of his archdiocese through large benefactions from the estates of wealthy donors, many of whom were not Catholic. Ability was not the only factor in stimulating such generosity. Recognition of untapped local resources and solicitation of such funds on behalf of the church were the clinchers. Some clerics have that talent, others are poor fund-raisers because they are embarrassed at the very idea.

The Annual Collection

With good reason some pastors choose the first Sunday of October to make their annual financial report. Most of the repairing or redecorating of the parish church and other buildings occurs during the summer months. During this period the weekly collections fall to new lows. At the beginning of the fall season a pastor may deem it opportune to include in his review the cost of the new appointments, and the Sunday shortages during the summer months, suggesting the need for make-up by means of a one-shot "annual collection," to be conducted by mail between October and December. He asks each family to determine its own pledge to cover their own summer absences, or to help pay for the new improvements; and to send their contribution to the pastor personally at their own convenience during the forthcoming three month period. It is amazing how positively people respond to this kind of appeal, which has only common sense to justify it. Pastors report amounts between $20,000 to $40,000 of new money collected in this way. Of course, he should send a personal note of thanks to each benefactor.

The Second Collection

In addition to what has already been said on this subject, it is important to remind people that at least one second collection each month serves diocesan or papal purposes — the local seminary or the Holy Father's worldwide mission. Each of these collections has its own envelope, sometimes even a guest preacher. It is sometimes a matter of amusement when the outside speaker is so good at proclaiming the virtues of his cause that he walks away with a larger sum than the pastor receives in his offertory collection. This is symbolic, too, of the depths of generosity ready to be tapped when parishioners are properly motivated.

Since parishioners in many dioceses are taxed by the bishops each year to support poorer parishes, it is the practice of many pastors to set a second collection monthly to cover this forced outlay. To advise Catholics of their obligations to the poor is a good idea and, if the pastor says, "I need an extra $1,000 per month for poor parishes," he may come close to getting it in a well-defined second collection. In any event, all second collections, properly defined with advance notice, can serve a good purpose in spite of their annoying features.

They say that God writes straight with crooked lines, and at times it sure looks that way. There was a wonderful old pastor who took over a rundown parish and within ten years raised $750,000 to refurbish the plant and build a new school and a new convent. In his second ten years he deposited another $750,000 in the diocesan bank. One day, musing about his bishop's needs, the aging priest speculated aloud to his curates that maybe the parish should give all its savings to the poor bishop. He died the next day. The priest who took his place spent the entire $750,000 in two years merely to clean up the messes his predecessor's cataracts had never seemed to notice. "Poor Hughie," people thought. Still, poor bishop. But a very satisfied congregation came into being, since the new man credited "Hughie" with the foresight of anticipating the Second Vatican Council.

The Final Word: Stewardship

In December 1992 the National Conference of Catholic Bishops issued a pastoral letter entitled, "Stewardship: A Disciple's Response." Unquestionably, the rising deficits in diocesan administrations were the driving force in bringing this letter to fruition, but the Church's economic straits afforded bishops the opportunity of reminding Catholic people of a profound Christian truth: God owns the universe, and we are only his stewards, duty bound to handle our patrimony with care.

The author of Genesis (see Chapter 1) placed words in the mouth of God as he was reporting how God created the earth, the sun and the moon, the vegetable and animal kingdoms, and finally man and woman. At each step he had the Lord observing "that it was good." And, when beholding his finished products, the biblical writer described God's satisfaction as follows: "and indeed it was very good." And then the Creator placed all of his universe in the hands of our first parents to be caretakers on his behalf.

At a period of history when modern mankind tends to repeat the mistake of those first parents — to be as God, thinking that they own the universe, and thereby, unoriginally, to repeat the original sin — it is appropriate that bishops remind their people to render to God what is God's, by accounting for their stewardship, thinking about how we have used his creation, harnessed its resources, cultivated its fruitfulness, shared its benefits and, in the process, gave glory to him who made it all possible, especially the dignity of our human life. We praise God and we pray to God in thanksgiving for his gifts, and do penance for our failings. But if we, his people, are what the gospel says we are — "the salt of the earth" and "light of the world" (Matthew 5:13-16) — we honor the Lord by the work we do, by the care we give to his world, by our moderate use of creature comforts, by protecting our resources for the benefit of future generations, and by truly being our brother's keeper. And an important part of Catholic stewardship is taking care of the Church — a healthy reminder, unquestionably, to Catholics at this time.

Some commentators on the pastoral, including a few bishops, were not happy with the final product. Calling it too "vague," they criticized its lack of emphasis on finances, and on certain depressing facts of Catholic life — dioceses running out of money, church and school closings, low salary scales for lay employees, and the large pockets of alienated women and youth. While critics missed the central point of the pastoral, the incidental discussions did evoke pertinent facts, of use to every parish priest worrying about money: Catholics, with an average family income of $40,000 per annum, give $5.00 per week to the parish.

While regular churchgoers contribute three times more than anyone else, the median annual giving is $100. Half of the registered households in one study gave less than $2.00 per week. If we are stewards of the Church, we obviously should be doing better.

The Finance Committee and Parish Council

The two new dimensions to parochial administration to result from the Council, are the finance committee and the parish council. The first is a universal command of the new *Code of Canon Law* and binds all pastors everywhere; the second is recommended, but not mandated, unless the local bishop so decides. Both are advisory, not consultative, which means, in practice, that the pastor is free to reject their advice. If the process by which members of each group function is intelligently conceived, both can be helpful to the average pastor: the finance committee by providing sound counsel on fund-raising or on paring expenses, or by recommending business services that otherwise might not be available to him at low costs; the parish council as an instrument by which the pastor receives input on desirable or undesirable programs, counsel on major expenditures or radical departure from parish traditions, dealing with the bishop or chancery bureaus, etc.

In the past quarter-century, pastors and Parish councils have worked together rather well. (The finance committee should never be a problem, because the members are his direct appointees.) If the pastor supervises the election process for the parish council in the interest of proportionate representation of various population groups, rather than special interests, he will find himself the recipient of needed support, while the parish population acquires a sense that they share in the conduct of parochial affairs. Of course, it must be made clear very early, and at all times, that a parish council may not engage in activity contrary to the laws of the country or of the Church. In such a case, the pastor would have no option save to dissolve it.

If trouble within the parish council raises its ugly head, it may well be that the pastor was not alert, or there is a member or two who treat the parish as another political entity, subject to affirmative action procedures typical in modern America. Divisiveness in a parish is a serious matter, and must be dealt with resolutely. Presuming that the pastor has guaranteed all council members to be practicing Catholics, such difficulties are likely to be temporary. Occasionally, one pastor uses his council to intimidate the bishop and leaves his successor a group of malcontents intent on troublemaking. The newcomer has no choice but to dissolve it, and start all over.

By and large, however, the new instruments of parochial administration are boons, not only to the people, but to priests. As one learns the church from the inside, the other sees another perspective and, in most cases, all make lifelong friends. (These considerations apply as well to the diocesan pastoral council, if the bishop has one.)

Vicariates and Deaneries

Following the Council, what used to be called deaneries became vicariates — subdivisions of the diocese into workable units, whereby the diocesan bishop can better make his mind, and that of the Holy See, clear to priests at the level of their ministry. The bishop can then receive in return the counsel of those priests on subjects within their competence which are helpful to the ordinary in the administration of the diocese. While deans and deaneries continue to exist in some places, the new *Code* makes vicar and vicariates the preferable canonical terms. The motive for the new decentralization was partially to give auxiliary bishops an administrative, as well as a sacramental, role; but it also was an attempt to provide a semblance of shared responsibility to a Church which, by virtue of its hierarchical constitution, is somewhat centralized in a bishop ordinary or in the pope. The vicar also receives authority to give permissions, delegations, and dispensations hitherto reserved to the ordinary.

As designed, the vicariate (or deanery) system has obvious merits — simplifying administration, enhancing communication, encouraging priest participation in decision-making at the bishop's level. Presuming that the vicar truly represents the mind of a bishop in union with the pope, the advantages of the system are obvious, and require little further elucidation. When the bishop is faced with hard decisions about liturgy and the administration of the sacraments, about diocesan finances, opening or closing schools, creating or closing parishes, deciding priests' salary scales or welfare benefits, and so forth, information and advice from local priests through the vicariate/deanery is sensible, and an example of good ecclesial government at work; providing, of course, that "the vicariate voice" adequately represents priests at the county or area level, priests everywhere being notoriously inactive as political types.

No system is perfect and, since the Church is hierarchical, its machinery must be somewhat different from that which develops in a putative neutral political setting. In American political life nothing is sacred, nothing is final, so that precedents or standing decisions have no eternal value, and thus may be subverted whenever and however local groups decide that the time for negative resistance is opportune. Not so in the Church, where the givens include an established creed, cult, and code. The vicariate/deanery, therefore, is not an instrument for beginning the process by which papal or episcopal decisions, already finalized, can be reversed or overturned, for instance, on matters of faith or morals or universal Church law.

Due to the lack of specific guidelines, vicariate/deanery groups have sometimes been used to agitate against existing norms dealing with contraception, indissolubility, private confession and general absolution, first confession for eight-year-olds, altar boys and girls, etc. This is not their role. The bishop has personal responsibility to see that his administration reinforces episcopal or Roman decisions. But extended and freewheeling discussion of policies already determined — especially as it has to do with liturgy, sacraments, and norms of priestly life — gives the impression that these are still open questions, involving only differing opinions, with vicariate/deanery assemblies free to establish another way of

Catholic thinking and behaving. The impact on faithful parishioners of such bickering among priests is negative.

It is a matter of some scandal, too, that as an occasional pastor uses his parish council against the bishop, and an occasional bishop uses his presbyterate in its various parts against the general mind of his peers and/or that of the Holy See. It is noticeable, at times, how such dissidents use force of various kinds to thwart dissent from their dissent. This fractionalism has advanced neither Catholic unity nor piety. What is required, instead, is a uniform policy for the proper administration of ecclesial subdivisions.

The other downside of such a mechanism is the eternal time given over to talk without constructive purpose. John Cardinal Heenan of Westminster once complained, after the Council, that the Church now suffered from "the curse of assemblyism." Decisions postponed unduly, decisions watered down to placate special interests, decisions unenforced while decisions to reopen discussion of those already made are permitted, are all poor government, even in a democratic society. Its evil consists in the abdication of personal responsibility by public authority originally established to protect the common good of the society in question, in this case of bishops in union with the pope to protect the Church.

Endnotes

1. Robert I. Gannon, S.J., *The Cardinal Spellman Story* (New York: Doubleday and Co., Inc., 1962), p. 141.
2. The Paulist Press, Mahweh, NJ, has available a handy and short treatment, *Keeping Your Parish Financially Healthy*, by Harold B. Averkamp.

Chapter Seventeen

The Parish Priest as Diocesan Official

Clerics are bound by a special obligation to
show reverence and obedience to the Supreme
Pontiff and to their own Ordinary.

— Canon 273, *Code of Canon Law* (1983)

The diocesan bishop is to attend to presbyters with special concern and listen to them as his assistants and advisers; he is to protect their rights and see to it that they correctly fulfill the obligations proper to their state and that means and institutions which they need are available to them to foster their spiritual and intellectual life; he is also to make provision for their decent support and social assistance, in accord with the norm of the law" (cn. 384, *Code of Canon Law,* 1983).

The worst thing you can say, perhaps, about a parish priest is that he is parochial, that his interests are confined to his own little world, when in fact he belongs to a diocese and to the Universal Church. As applied to priests generally, the charge is calumny, of course, especially against those who know they must serve their bishop, the pope, and lots of people in between.

Getting along with others is a big American business. You can hardly enter a large supermarket without running into expensive paperbacks telling you how to understand yourself, or relate to your wife, to your dog, to the environment, as if human beings never knew how to do this before social scientists came along. Americans are also the most analyzed people in the world, and likely the most violent. The world of priests is much more irenic. While today an occasional priest is beaten up by a thug, they are pretty safe, especially if they wear their Roman collars, because they get along well with people and with each other, even with the young. Non-Catholics usually treat them with respect.

But life is not perfect. There are a few ugly priests, and some ugly laity. Common sense suggests that peace will more likely reign in the parish if they manage to stay out of each other's way. But, if they cross each other's path, it is the obligation of the priest, especially, to be civil. He should never say anything that makes the Church look bad. We deal here in personalities, so it is hard to be more specific than that. Some priests have the knack of controlling a malcontent with tact, or humor, or by virtue of office; others, like Saint Peter, sometimes put their foot in their mouth.

Priests are, or should be, "men of authority," after all, and can fall victim to the perils of office by arrogance, by patronization, or by not doing their job. By and large, however, these vices are not shared too often with parishioners, but may appear more frequently when they deal with each other, or with higher authority. The pastor who does not know how to use authority, or fails to use it at all, the younger priest who is selfish, spoiled, or congenitally rebellious, create problems for themselves, as well as for others. To make things easier, the guidelines for mutual relationships in a rectory must be clear, and become standard practice. If the older priest wants to be recognized as "Father," the youngster should not call him "Joe; " if the associate is a night person, the pastor should not expect wonders at 7:00 A.M.; if one is a do-er, the other a pray-er, they should manage a little respect for the difference. If the question is getting the work done, or a matter of faith and morals, agreeing to disagree is not a solution. In some of those situations, it may be necessary to involve the bishop. In other situations where the personalities are not precisely congenial, a little social distance helps, or a little suffering, either of which may be good for someone's soul. The same rule of thumb holds true for the relationships between priests and religious women.

One of the special thorns of our time is the popularity seeker, and the-peace-at-any-price priest. In earlier days there were bedrock understandings about faith and morals, about worship and the sacraments, supported and reinforced by those responsible for the discipline of the Church, according to its laws. Liking to be liked by any one individual did little harm. Not so today. The priest who curries favor by "tut-tutting" serious aberrations against Church teaching or policies in or out of the rectory, for the sake of one man's convenience, or a priest who freely says to a miscreant, "I would be glad to help you out with this, but the pope/bishop/ pastor won't let me," is fundamentally a troublemaker, no matter how compassionate others claim him to be. "Getting along with people" has its limits, if the price is undermining Christ's message or Church discipline. Prolonged silence in the face of grave evil has the same effect. The buck should not be passed upstairs, if stopping it at a lower level works; but upstairs it must go, when necessary, thus placing the solution in the hands of someone appointed to resolve problems of this kind.

Hullaballoos about getting along with the bishop are more serious, especially if one of the parties is a priest. Maybe it's the fault of some contemporary bishops that the subject is discussed at all, although the more likely reason is that the Catholic system, like secular society's, has broken down. In the absence of system, there are no rules to form the proper relationships between those who govern and those who are governed.

A lot of words, like "reverence" and "obedience" — or "law" and "order" — still surface in conversations, but, once the routine of institutional living has been sundered, role playing, as it used to be, becomes passé. It's hard to know in a given situation who really is running things.

Officials still hold office, to be sure, but in our time the influence of a "shadow" government looms everywhere. Civil society speaks of its "brain trusts," "industrial-military complexes," and "mafias." In the Church we hear of "curias," "creeping infallibilists," and the "reformers." Such groups exist in every society, but they gain independent power only after public officials have lost power to implement the demands of the common law. At such moments, the subgroup leaders arrogate to themselves legislative, judicial, or executive authority, sometimes by demonstrating that they will not conform to official rules, and manage somehow to pay no penalty for the rebellion.

This is about where a bishop is today — in a no-man's land between what the Church says he is and what the Church's internal enemies say they will let him be, if he behaves himself and stays out of their way in reconstructing a Church to their liking. The "shadow government" does not like John Paul for what he says, and less do they like the bishops he appoints. But disorder reigns as long as hierarchy only talks about obedience, and permits "bishop pretenders" to control Catholic infrastructures, on the promise that they will not make life too miserable for the faithful bishop. John Paul's appointees can hardly be comfortable in that role, although some are content with being mere facilitators.

Under the circumstances a good pastor should first "feel out" his bishop. The bishop's predecessors gave up ermine and the kissing of the ring years ago. They began to play the role of "regular guy," anticipating that their priests, and others, would not think less of their episcopal dignity or their authority. Those tradition-breakers overreacted to demands for change, and their successors have difficulty ever since with their runaway Catholic institutions, even their own bureaucracies. They also became victimized by media lords who gave special attention to religious leaders who seemed to mute the Church's otherworldly beliefs or moral absolutes. One bishop discovered he had a media fight on his hands if all he wanted to do was to suspend a bad priest. (Now we call it "administrative leave.") His friend next door walks into a diocese to find one of his parishes seized by disgruntled parishioners for a sit-in.

Some years ago at a national meeting, one bishop proposed that the episcopal body go on record in support of another bishop engaged in public controversy. The confrere rose to say no, it was his problem and he would resolve it. But as bishop number two told his friends later, "It's

271

not that I wouldn't have liked support, but I wasn't sure what I would get." A local bishop is never sure anymore of peer support for a tough, but right, decision.

Not all bishops are up to the martyrdom awaiting the best of them, or the final judgment staring the worst in the face. It was nice work to have, once upon a time, and you did not have to suffer very much to look good. There was of old a cardinal (not in New York), still something of a legend, who left his Chancery office every day at twelve noon, and never came back. Another cardinal blessed his cathedral flock every Sunday with such piety that the churchgoers just melted to their knees as he came near. Still another vacationed as often as he worked. Those days are gone forever.

Reverence and Obedience

These two words are the substance of what the Church has to say about the relationship between priests and their bishop. Reverence is the awe one feels in the presence — or near the presence — of God. Moses felt it at the burning bush, when he was told not to come any nearer (see Exodus 3:6). Mary Magdalene had a taste of it when, after the Resurrection, Christ told her, "Don't cling to me" (John 20:17). What belongs to God is "holy," "sacred," due to Christ especially, but also to him who represents Christ in a unique way, namely the bishop. The Church punishes severely anyone who places hands violently on a bishop (cn. 1374).

Obedience is what the Hebrew word suggests — being the servant of the Lord. In many places of Holy Writ, obedience, like fear of the Lord (another element in reverence), is the beginning of wisdom. And at ordination the priest promises obedience to the bishop.

This recital looks one-sided to a secularist, the one who disbelieves in the existence of anything "holy," and certainly in a "holy rule" (i.e., hierarchy). The secular offspring "cynic" debunks the use of the word "sacred" for anyone who, or any group which, exercises its juridical power to govern the lives of human beings. "Cynic's" substitute for legal power is "people power," reflected in a ballot box, a political party, in wealth or social position, in law enforcement, or social force — in anything except obedience to lawfully constituted superiors.

The prophets, and Jesus Christ, were not above using worldly weapons in a divine cause. And the promise of heaven and the threat of hell are also powerful enforcers of God's revealed word. By and large, however, for the effectiveness of its mission the Church relies on the faith of people in the "sacred" word proclaimed by a "sacred" person, to whom they commit obedience as the downside of reverence. No secularist understands that, nor would he tolerate it. But a priest's life, above all, is governed by bishops. Just as there is distance between God and his creatures, so there is distance between a bishop and members of his flock. Irreverence and disobedience are merely devices of half-believers to bring God, Christ, and the bishop down to the level of those whom they would govern, and eliminate the need of reverence. It is another example of the original sin: "We will not serve." Once either vice pervades the sanctuary, where priests reign as the dispensers of the mysteries of God, the Church is in serious trouble, because it means a house divided against itself. If parish priests are the transmission belt of the ecclesial machinery, then reverence and obedience to the bishop, and of the bishops to the pope, are the substance, after providence and grace, by which the Church moves and maintains its direction.

The other side of reverence for the bishop is his regard for the dignity of his subjects. That is why we have canon law, to specify the context of the relationship between bishops and priests. The Church's binding teaching is also part of the picture. A bishop is obligated to respect and protect the rights of his priests, and to treat them with scrupulous equity. One does not give evidence of irreverence or disobedience to his bishop, but when abiding by the Church's authentic teaching, the priest invokes canon law to protect his rights.

The Real World of Pastoring

Stress on virtue is a pipe dream or poppycock for cynics and skeptics. First, because seemingly it places all the burdens on people in the pews or on lower clergy. Second, because it enshrines privilege and power in the hands of a few triumphalists, an allegedly unworthy few at that.

Apart from the fact that critics rarely take their own unfitness into account, these arguments against virtue are snob arguments. Like the one against Christ — "From Nazareth?" said Nathanael. "Can anything good come from that place?" (John 1:46). All good societies presume civic virtue in most of their citizenry. They establish procedures for facilitating cooperation between rival but decent men and women, using strictures to restrain evildoers, who normally represent a tiny minority. By downplaying virtue, and exalting power (i.e., free choice detached from moral norms), the modern state has undermined its own claim to guard law and the commonweal. By aggrandizing what historically it has called vice (e.g., killing the unborn), it has set self-interest groups against each other. By hostility to transcendental religion, it has created an omni-competent state incapable of molding a good citizenry, and prone itself to oppressions and violences of various kinds.

The Church in earlier centuries had its moments of moral depravity in high places, due mostly to the corrupting influence of kings and princes. The modern period of Church history is not one of those. In times past, it often required schismatics and heretics to purge the Church of the worst vices in its clerical order, while most bishops and most priests today are good men. Saying this does not extirpate their humanness. Like fathers of any family, some are exemplary, brilliant, saintly, hardworking, successful; occasionally also ordinary, run-of-the-mill, poor leaders, worse governors, who would rather have somebody else clean up the messes they create. We can do without a few of those kinds of fathers, as many mothers (and Mother Church) know so well. But without bishops, there is no Church governance, and to bishops alone Christ has given the keys of the kingdom. Hence, it is they to whom reverence and obedience must be given, and it is we who must examine our own sinfulness before we withhold what we are obligated to render them in God's name.

Remember, too, it is the person of the bishop, not his accomplishments, we revere and respect. And because of that dignity the Church's law imposes on the bishop burdens few others would care to carry. For example, Canons 381ff. tells the bishop to do the following things:

- To care for all the faithful in his diocese, to be solicitous for non-Catholics and unbelievers.
- To be especially mindful of his priests and to provide for their care and support.
- To foster religious vocations.
- To preach himself, and supervise all other teaching.
- To set an example by his personal holiness.
- To say Mass for his diocesans.
- To preside over his cathedral.
- To make, execute, and adjudicate laws appropriate to diocesan needs.
- To promote the common discipline of the universal Church.
- To correct abuses in teaching, worship, and in the administration of property in his diocese.

- To foster various apostolates.
- To remain in his diocese eleven months of the year, unless excused by a just cause.
- To visit his diocese entirely within a five-year period.
- To pay bills and watch costs.
- To report to the pope personally every five years.

Without reverence and obedience from his pastors, and from priests generally, a bishop's work would be impossible.

This does not mean that difficulties cannot or do not arise, or that words like "reverence" and "obedience" require concrete defining. Much depends on what areas of Church life we mean when we undertake to demand that these virtues be acquired.

The Personality Question

"Only a mother could love him" has been said of many priests, not excluding a few bishops. We all come into the world with our special gifts, and along the way we acquire our own persona: lighthearted or dour, sanguine or choleric, aggressive or passive, compulsive or devil-may-care, well-organized or sloppy, very social or very private, good with people or good with things, great as a planner, inept as a doer, and so forth. The world can be grateful that there are as many personalities as people, and that part of the fun of living is finding out who can be our friends or happy coworkers, and who can make life as difficult for us, as we do for them.

No one suggests that our personalities be compatible with the bishop's, or that we become his chum, or his lackey. In a large diocese the personality factor rarely comes into play because priests and bishops rarely meet on a one-to-one basis. Most of what is required is mutual respect and cordiality. The big question, supposedly, is how much the bishop dominates his diocese and, therefore, sets the tone of his pastors' agenda; or how little, and why the diocese runs satisfactorily or amok. These are the things to know and it takes time to know them. Martinets like to micro-manage everything, glad-handers like to socialize, scholars do their own sermons, and saints may pray too much, unmindful that the diocese is on the verge of bankruptcy. One very nice bishop, early on, acquired the name "Sitting Bull" because he never seemed to do anything, until his pastors woke up one morning to find out they were about to get ten new high schools and three new hospitals.

It is the function of parish priests to learn to know the bishop. After all, he is the boss and, ultimately, his ways become theirs. Some personalities are incapable of adjusting to authority of any kind and spend most of their time agitating and, thereby, upsetting the diocese. Those who have not learned to obey should not be in positions of authority themselves.

Church Law, Church Policy, and Subsidiarity

When it is a matter of Church law, be it the *Code of Canon Law*, the Statutes of the Diocese, or the personal decrees of the bishop, the local parish priest has no choice but to obey, in some cases under the penalty of sin, or of suspension, or of removal from office. For the most part we deal here with issues already settled and about which there is no further room for discussion. (All statutory law is accompanied by unexpected dysfunctions, about whose ill-effects the bishop should be apprised. Dysfunctions are the price of having an orderly society.)

Church policy, on the other hand, has to do with planning, making decisions the bishop is free to make, determining priorities and procedures, setting guidelines. The policy is either settled, or is in the process of development. If it's settled, the priest is duty bound to respect it and accept it, certainly not resist it in public. If the issue is up for discussion, he is free, as any other Catholic is free, to take one side or the other. The matters about which the bishop seeks counsel, prior to a policy determination, may include liturgy (Latin Mass, general absolution, Eucharistic ministers, age of confirmation); education (opening or closing schools, textbooks, teachers' union, doctrinal dissent); social service (nursing care, hospital ethics, government regulations); parish life (terms for priests, authority of pastors, recommended apostolates, church renovations); extra-parochial matters (religious communities, Catholic colleges, Catholic press, media concerns); fiscal affairs (mergers, fund-raising, cost-cutting); etc.

Subsidiarity, an old Catholic principle of good governance, simply means that those decisions are best made by parish priests for their local community when they represent standard Catholic practice or legitimate initiative. These should be encouraged and supported by the bishop. Diocesan agencies should not micro-manage parishes, unless there is a compelling justification based on Catholic doctrine or the common good of the diocese.

The bishop ought to set the tone of his administration at the outset, making clear that what binds him binds his priests and what his general mind is on policy matters, about which he would like their counsel. It is a bishop's job to govern, and to command respect in the doing, even from those people who would do it differently if they held his office. While old-time bishops may have sat on their dignity too much, so much so that, after their consecration, they could be told, "You've heard the truth for the last time," newer bishops playing "hail-fellow-well-met" are sometimes not surprised to have some priest say: "I'm going to give you the truth, even if you're not smart enough to grasp it." It is more important for a bishop to be respected than liked or loved. And when a bishop is berated in private conversation, it is he who has lost control.

Reading the bishop's mind is a useful exercise in sacerdotal alchemy. If one does not know it, and can't guess at it, he ought to search out someone whom he knows who does. A chancellor, a vicar general, a seminary rector usually does. Some bishops think they are cute, and play their cards close to the vest, so that no one, not even their immediate staff, knows what goes through their mind. Priests generally do not respect this kind of a bishop. Better for him to say yes or no on altar boys or girls, general absolution, retirement of pastors, the local Catholic college, than have priests believe he has a hidden agenda. Better for him to appear to have opinions, strong opinions, too, looking for clarification or emendation, than to seem to be a prelate with his finger always out the window testing which way the wind is blowing.

But when the proper circumstance presents itself, the priest ought to tell the bishop what his best judgment understands as Catholic truth or what he thinks serves the interest of people's holiness best. A priest should conduct himself cautiously in public, carefully in private, but state his views respectfully. And he should never argue with his bishop, unless the bishop is his friend. If the bishop is his friend, he can say almost anything he wants, even at two o'clock in the morning. Bishops need friends like that. If the bishop is a relative stranger, or the priest lacks the bishop's experience, the priest should feel free to discuss, lay out his case, and withdraw. Never argue with a stranger, particularly at two o'clock in the morning.

Reducing this to the personal, and no counsel is much good unless it is strongly felt, the history-making bishops, to outsiders, have seemed to be men with a mind of their own. You never did not know where strong leaders stood. And depending on one's age at the time, or the circumstance of the meeting, a contesting priest could lose his head at any given moment of a disrespectful confrontation. But when the subaltern rose from the dust hours or days later, in which obviously he was the loser, the priest also knew he had been in the presence of a man, one who loved the Church as much as he did, and whose links to the core of Church well-being were closer. Strangely, too, on this or that occasion, when the priest was covered with a little "humus," he sensed he had not really lost the debate. Once in a while, he knew he won, even if the bishop took a week or a year to admit it. It is also good to learn that most bishops are smarter than their critics think, the good ones, that is.

There is only one other point to be made and that is about subsidiarity. In the past most bishops permitted most priests to do what they wanted, and the Church, not always glorified by the permissions, seemed to survive. Nowadays, many priests violate all kinds of norms and, while no permissions are given, the ecclesia suffers from a poor rectory lifestyle, confessions are rare or poorly timed, liturgical abuses of many kinds occur, and yet no one intervenes, in spite of what canon law says about correction. It is perfectly proper for the bishop to interpose himself into the life of a priest who would like to gut a Gothic church of its architectural fine points, who reorganizes the liturgy to exclude "God, our Father" and "Jesus, His Son," or who panders to the contraceptionists, or whose church is closed from Saturday to Saturday after the eight o'clock Mass.

However, priests who, in the renovation of their church, want to maintain the Blessed Sacrament in a prominent place, or a "confessional box" that guarantees privacy, or textbooks with an imprimatur that best reflects his best view of the Church, even if an assistant school superintendent thinks otherwise, who uses lay Eucharistic ministers only as substitutes for unavailable priests, or who wants an occasional Latin Mass, ought not be overridden by a chancery official, egged on or no by the bishop. Priests, good priests, that is, deserve elbow room.

The Errant Bishop

This is a section that could not have been written a generation ago, but the fact must be faced that today there exist bishops who not only bend the rules, but who do not believe in the present norms by which the Catholic Church is expected to live, and have its being.

What happens if a "good priest" works under such a bishop? Well, whatever else he does or does not do, he should be sure he knows what he is talking about. Second, he should bring his differences to the notice of the bishop and avoid, absolutely, any public brawling with his bishop. Third, if he is a pastor, he should give the bishop no reasons for removing him. Fourth, he should seek counsel from wiser clerics than himself, and from a bishop or two if he knows any. Fifth, he should resist the temptation of writing letters critical of his bishop, since they have a way of getting around. Priests who chronically complain about their bishops have relatively few fans, because some of them are unreliable witnesses of events. Others have an agenda that is inconsistent with universal Church policy, or their evidence against a bishop is a bad mixture of fact and fiction.

But, in a given case, a priest can be absolutely right. In such a circumstance he must keep his own counsel, take time to measure the "offenses" against universal norms and how they have unfolded, prepare a dossier of "case histories," preferably modest in quantity but classy in depth. When all other reasonable steps at reform or reconciliation have taken place, discuss the matter with a competent and trusted canon lawyer. Then, if the latter agrees that the issues are sufficiently serious, he should take the matter to a friendly bishop or to the metropolitan archbishop (via a suitable intermediary) and, as a final gateway to responsible conduct, to the apostolic pro-nuncio or to the appropriate Vatican cardinal (again, via the right intervenor, if he is not known personally).

The average priest is not responsible for the well-being of the diocese. That is the bishop's role, and that of the bishop's superiors. The Church has no need for a priest to play vigilante. Most observers understand the reluctance of higher authority to place a bishop of its own choice "on trial," and also understand the anxiety and frustration of would-be Savonarolas in the face of unduly delayed reform of obvious evil. Surprisingly, archbishops do not play the significant role in the oversight of their suffragan dioceses that some of their predecessors did. The new *Code of Canon Law* (cn. 436) may say that the metropolitan has "no other power of governance within the suffragan diocese," but this statement follows another declaration in the same law that says the metropolitan is competent to inform the pope about abuses in suffragan dioceses, and to visit the offender, if the Holy See agrees. Unless one believes that the episcopal club is so snug that not even the archbishop and the pope are interested in cleaning up abuses that go on over an extended period, then a prudent but complaining priest should proceed as if the judicial process, once initiated, will also proceed to its proper end, however slowly.

If all his efforts seem to be of no avail, then he should conduct his parish as best he can and leave the larger Church to God and to the pope. Then let him pray more fervently.

Vatican II's Decree on the Church (*Lumen Gentium,* No. 20) reads: "The Sacred Synod consequently teaches that the bishops have by divine institution taken the place of the apostles as pastors of the Church, in such wise that whoever listens to them is listening to Christ and whoever despise them despises Christ and him who sent Christ (Luke 10:16)."

May they be worthy of that trust, sufficiently so as to have the reverence and obedience of their priests.

Epilogue

The Church in the United States is still in better condition than that found in other parts of the Catholic world. We might wish that we had forty million worshipers regularly at Sunday Mass, rather than twenty, but American churchgoers, considering the way they have been trained, are unique in the Christian world. Not only for the depth of the piety manifested on the Church's festive occasions, but for the way their generosity continues to support the Church's mission throughout the world.

Our Church is a priestly Church. When it is at the peak of its effectiveness, parish priests are the ones likely to receive the credit, especially when their ministry is invigorated and reinforced by zealous coworkers in Catholic classrooms and agencies. The Church is and will remain a paternal Church, directed and protected by fathers who, when men of competence and quality, beget their own enthusiastic sons in Chist. On this evangelization will always depend.

It was easy to be a good priest in earlier days because the priest was looked upon as a sacred person, to whom respect was given, and reverence, too. Most of us rarely abused our status, but all intuited its special meaning. Priestly demeanor reflected the Church's understanding of this unique vocation, and people, even those who were not Catholic, treated us accordingly. American youth looked up to us, and boys flocked to follow our example. And the Catholic family prospered.

Undoubtedly, cultural forces are at work today to weaken the Church by denigrating anyone, or anything, that claims or is given sacred status. Not surprisingly, therefore, an attempt to level the priesthood has been underway for some time. "Take off the Roman collar," "Call him Joe," "The Church belongs to the laity," "Do away with celibacy," "Down with authority types," are the seeming endless cries of special interest groups whose agendas are other than what we hear John Paul preaching. As the pressures against the other-worldliness of the Church continue, most priests realize that the ultimate object of assaults on the priesthood are really aimed at moving the center of Christianity away from Jesus Christ, Son of God the Father, by first moving away from its vicars, namely priests. The proposed center of the "new Christianity" is to be none other than man.

So, priests of the morrow must be better than ever, men of high expectations, of firm resolve, hardworking, thick-skinned, obedient, and holy. And, unlike their predecessors, they may have to stand alone, like Christ did on Calvary. The reason they are likely to stand alone is that mobs, in and out of the contemporary Church, once they come face-to-face with the real Christ, are just as likely to call for Barabbas. Furthermore, sanctions normally aimed at evildoers are today commonly directed at faithful sons. Future priests must have unusually strong convictions about the Church and be willing to defend them in the public forum, like Peter and Paul did. They must be men of the people without being popularity seekers. They need to be discreet in speech, yet remain the Church's strong presence in every local community. It will be their conduct that speaks louder than well-chosen words. Their parishes, from canons to rubrics, must reflect the mind of the Church. Friends to their people they must be, but fraternization is carried on only within the context of their fatherhood. They speak with anyone, but are comfortable with those unprepared to listen to God's word. They keep an eye on evil without being intimidated by it, correct it without being inattentive to those in good faith, and are capable of doing what is possible, leaving the impossible to God. Effective parish priests are not cowed by petty tyrants nor are they fearful of bad-mouthing by enemies. In situations of a grave nature they take counsel with higher authority, as much to clarify their own thinking as to gain its insight. And they accept the firm decisions of higher authority with grace, and as a constituent element of their duty.

Faithful parish priests have confidence in the cause for which they dedicate their lives, are secure in their role and authority, modest in their rhetoric, cool under fire, available even to their enemies, wise enough to leave behind them a parish with more saints and near-saints, and more sinners struggling to reconcile, than they found on their arrival.

And to do all that is expected of them, they must daily go into their own little desert, preferably before the Blessed Sacrament, and communicate with their Lord and Master, to acknowledge their total dependence on God's Holy Spirit. *Domine, non sum dignus* is not just a statement of fact; it is a cry for help.

The meaning of the priestly life was rarely captured in words better than those used by Jean Baptiste Henri Lacordaire, O.P.:

"To live in the midst of the world without wishing its pleasures
To be a member of each family yet belonging to none
To share all sufferings
To penetrate all secrets
To heal all wounds
To go from men to God and God to men and bring them His pardon and hope
To have a heart of fire for charity
And a heart of bronze for chastity
Always to teach and forgive
To console and bless.
Merciful God, what an exalted life!
And it is yours, O priest of Jesus Christ."

Appendix One

Obligations and Rights of Pastors Under Canon Law

The following is taken from the Code of Canon Law, Latin-English Edition (1983) and is used by permission of the Canon Law Society of America.

Canon 528 — §1. The pastor is obliged to see to it that the word of God in its entirety is announced to those living in the parish; for this reason he is to see to it that the lay Christian faithful are instructed in the truths of the faith, especially through the homily which is to be given on Sundays and holy days of obligation and through the catechetical formation which he is to give; he is to foster works by which the spirit of the gospel, including issues involving social justice, is promoted; he is to take special care for the Catholic education of children and of young adults; he is to make every effort with the aid of the Christian faithful, to bring the gospel message also to those who have ceased practicing their religion or who do not profess the true faith.

§2. The pastor is to see to it that the Most Holy Eucharist is the center of the parish assembly of the faithful; he is to work to see to it that the Christian faithful are nourished through a devout celebration of the sacraments and especially that they frequently approach the sacrament of the Most Holy Eucharist and the sacrament of penance; he is likewise to endeavor that they are brought to the practice of family prayer as well as to a knowing and active participation in the sacred liturgy, which the pastor must supervise in his parish under the authority of the diocesan bishop, being vigilant lest any abuses creep in.

Canon 529 — §1. In order to fulfill his office in earnest the pastor should strive to come to know the faithful who have been entrusted to his care; therefore he is to visit families, sharing their cares, worries, and especially the griefs of the faithful, strengthening them in the Lord, and correcting them prudently if they are wanting in certain areas; with a generous love he is to help the sick, particularly those close to death, refreshing them solicitously with the sacraments and commending their souls to God; he is to make a special effort to seek out the poor, the afflicted, the lonely, those exiled from their own land, and similarly those weighed down with special difficulties; he is also to labor diligently so that spouses and parents are supported in fulfilling their proper duties, and he is to foster growth in the Christian life within the family.

§2. The pastor is to acknowledge and promote the proper role which the lay members of the Christian faithful have in the Church's mission by fostering their associations for religious purposes; he is to cooperate with his own bishop and with the presbyterate of the diocese in working hard so that the faithful be concerned for parochial communion and that they realize that they are members both of the diocese and of the universal Church and participate in and support efforts to promote such communion.

Canon 530 — The following functions are especially entrusted to the pastor:

    1° the administration of baptism;

    2° the administration of the sacrament of confirmation to those who are in danger of death, according to the norm of can. 883, 3°;

    3° the administration of Viaticum and the anointing of the sick with due regard for the prescription of can. 1003, §§2 and 3, as well as the imparting of the apostolic blessing;

    4° the assistance at marriages and the imparting of the nuptial blessing;

    5° the performing of funerals;

    6° the blessing of the baptismal font during the Easter season, the leading of processions outside the church and the imparting of solemn blessings outside the church;

    7° the more solemn celebration of the Eucharist on Sundays and holy days of obligation.

Canon 531 — Although another person may have performed some parochial function, that person is to put the offerings received from the Christian faithful on that occasion into the parish account, unless it is obvious that such would be contrary to the will of the donor in the case of voluntary offerings; after he has listened to the presbyterial council, the diocesan bishop is competent to issue regulations which provide for the allocation of these offerings and the remuneration of clerics who fulfill the same function.

Canon 532 — The pastor represents the parish in all juridic affairs in accord with the norm of the law; he is to see to it that the goods of the parish are administered in accord with the norms of cann. 1281-1288.

Canon 533 — §1. The pastor is obliged to reside in a parish house close to the church; in particular cases, however, the local ordinary can permit him to live elsewhere, especially in a house shared by several presbyters, provided there is a just cause and suitable and due provision is made for the performance of parochial functions.

§2. Unless there is a serious reason to the contrary, the pastor may be absent each year from the parish on vacation for at most one continuous or interrupted month; the days which the pastor spends once a year in spiritual retreat are not counted in his vacation days; if the pastor is to be absent from the parish beyond a week he is bound to inform the local ordinary of this.

§3. The diocesan bishop is to issue norms which provide for the care of a parish by a priest possessing the needed faculties during the absence of the pastor.

Canon 534 — §1. After he has taken possession of his parish the pastor is obliged to apply Mass for the people entrusted to him each Sunday and holy day of obligation within the diocese; if he is legitimately prevented from this celebration, he is to apply Mass on these same days through another priest or he himself is to apply it on other days.

§2. A pastor who has the care of several parishes is obliged to apply only one Mass for all the people entrusted to him on those days mentioned in §1.

§3. A pastor who has not satisfied the obligation mentioned in §1 and §2 is to apply as many Masses for his people as he has missed as soon as possible.

Canon 535 — §1. Each parish is to possess a set of parish books including baptismal, marriage and death registers as well as other registers prescribed by the conference of bishops or the diocesan bishop; the pastor is to see to it that these registers are accurately inscribed and carefully preserved.

§2. In the baptismal register are also to be noted the person's confirmation and whatever affects the canonical status of the Christian faithful by reason of marriage, with due regard for the prescription of can.1133, adoption, reception of sacred orders, perpetual profession in a religious institute, and change of rite; these notations are always to be noted on a document which certifies the reception of baptism.

§3. Each parish is to possess its own seal; documents which are issued to certify the canonical status of the Christian faithful as well as acts which can have juridic importance are to be signed by the pastor or his delegate and sealed with the parish seal.

§4. Each parish is to have a registry or archive in which the parish books are kept along with episcopal letters and other documents which ought to be preserved due to necessity or usefulness; all these are to be inspected by the diocesan bishop or his delegate during his visitation or at another suitable time; the pastor is to take care that they do not come into the hands of outsiders.

§5. The older parish books are also to be carefully preserved in accord with the prescriptions of particular law.

Canon 536 — §1. After the diocesan bishop has listened to the presbyterial council and if he judges it opportune, a pastoral council is to be established in each parish; the pastor presides over it, and through it the Christian faithful along with those who share in the pastoral care of the parish in virtue of their office give their help in fostering pastoral activity.

§2. This pastoral council possesses a consultative vote only and is governed by norms determined by the diocesan bishop.

Canon 537 — Each parish is to have a finance council which is regulated by universal law as well as by norms issued by the diocesan bishop; in this council the Christian faithful, selected according to the same norms, aid the pastor in the administration of parish goods with due regard for the prescription of can. 532.

Canon 538 — §1. A pastor ceases from office by means of removal or transfer by the diocesan bishop which has been done in accord with the norm of law, by resignation of the pastor submitted for a just cause and accepted by the same diocesan bishop for validity and by lapse of time if the pastor has been appointed for a definite period of time in accord with the prescriptions of particular law mentioned in can. 522.

§2. A pastor who is a member of a religious institute or a society of apostolic life is removed in accord with the norm of can. 682, §2.

§3. When a pastor has completed his seventy-fifth year of age he is asked to submit his resignation from office to the diocesan bishop, who, after considering all the circumstances of person and place, is to decide whether to accept or defer the resignation; the diocesan bishop, taking into account the norms determined by the conference of bishops, is to provide for the suitable support and housing of the resigned pastor.

Canon 539 — When a parish becomes vacant or when the pastor is prevented from exercising his pastoral office in the parish due to captivity, exile, banishment, incapacity, ill health or some other cause, the diocesan bishop is to appoint as soon as possible a parochial administrator, that is, a priest who substitutes for the pastor in accord with the norm of can. 540.

Canon 540 — §1. A parochial administrator is bound by the same duties and enjoys the same rights as a pastor unless the diocesan bishop determines otherwise.

§2. A parochial administrator is not permitted to do anything which can prejudice the rights of the pastor or harm parish goods.

§3. After he has fulfilled his function the parochial administrator is to render an account to the pastor.

Canon 541 — §1. When a parish becomes vacant or when the pastor is hindered from exercising his pastoral duty the parochial vicar is to assume the governance of the parish in the meantime until a parochial administrator is appointed; if there are several parochial vicars, the senior vicar in terms of appointment assumes the governance; if there are no parochial vicars, then a pastor specified by particular law assumes the governance.

§2. The person who has assumed the governance of a parish in accord with the norm of §1 is to inform the local ordinary immediately that the parish is vacant.

Canon 542 — The priests who have as a team been entrusted with the pastoral care of some parish or group of different parishes in accord with the norm of can. 517, §1:

1° are to be endowed with the qualities mentioned in can. 521;

2° are to be appointed or installed in accord with the prescriptions of cann. 522 and 524;

3° are responsible for pastoral care only from the moment of taking possession; their moderator is to be placed in possession of the parish in accord with the prescriptions of can. 527, §2; for the other priests a legitimately made profession of faith substitutes for taking possession.

Canon 543 — §1. Each of the priests who as a team have been entrusted with the pastoral care of some parish or group of different parishes is obliged to perform the duties and functions of the pastor which are mentioned in cann. 528, 529 and 530 in accord with an arrangement determined by themselves; all these priests possess the faculty to assist at marriages as well as all the faculties to dispense which are granted to the pastor by the law itself, to be exercised, however, under the direction of the moderator.

§2. All the priests of the team:

1° are bound by the obligation of residence;

2° through common counsel are to establish an arrangement by which one of them celebrates Mass for the people in accord with the norm of can. 534;

§3. In juridic affairs only the moderator represents the parish or parishes entrusted to the team.

Canon 544 — When one of the priests in the team mentioned in can. 517, §1 or its moderator ceases from office or when one of them becomes incapable of exercising pastoral duties the parish or parishes entrusted to the care of the team do not become vacant; however, the diocesan bishop is to name another moderator; the senior priest on the team in terms of assignment is to fulfill the office of moderator until another is appointed by the diocesan bishop.

Canon 545 — §1. A parochial vicar or several of them can be associated with the pastor whenever it is necessary or suitable for duly implementing the pastoral care of the parish; parochial vicars are priests who render their services in pastoral ministry as co-workers with the pastor in common counsel and endeavor with him and also under his authority.

§2. A parochial vicar can be assigned to assist in fulfilling the entire pastoral ministry on behalf of an entire parish, a definite part of the parish, or a certain group of the Christian faithful of the parish; he can also be assigned to assist in fulfilling a certain type of ministry in different parishes concurrently.

Canon 546 — To be validly named parochial vicar one must be constituted in the sacred order of the presbyterate.

Canon 547 — The diocesan bishop freely names a parochial vicar, having heard, if he judges it opportune, the pastor or pastors of the parishes for which he is appointed and the vicar forane, with due regard for the prescription of can. 682, §1.

Canon 548 — §1. The obligations and rights of the parochial vicar are defined in canons of this chapter, in the diocesan statutes, in the letter of the diocesan bishop and more specifically in the mandate given him by the pastor.

§2. Unless the letter of the diocesan bishop expressly states otherwise the parochial vicar is obliged by reason of his office to assist the pastor in fulfilling the total parochial ministry, except for the obligation to apply Mass for the people, and if circumstances warrant it, to substitute for the pastor in accord with the norm of the law.

§3. The parochial vicar is regularly to consult with the pastor on planned or existing programs so that the pastor and the parochial vicar or vicars can provide through their combined efforts for the pastoral care of the parish for which they are responsible together.

Canon 549 — Unless the diocesan bishop has provided otherwise in accord with the norm of can. 533, §3, and unless a parochial administrator has been appointed, the prescriptions of can. 541, §1, should be observed during the absence of the pastor; in this case the parochial vicar is bound by all the obligations of the pastor with the exception of the obligation to apply Mass for the people.

Canon 550 — §1. The parochial vicar is obliged to reside within the parish, or, if he has been appointed to different parishes concurrently, he is obliged to live in one of them; however, the local ordinary can permit him to reside elsewhere, especially in a house shared by several priests provided there is a just cause and such an arrangement does not hinder the discharge of his pastoral duties.

§2. The local ordinary is to see to it that some community of life is fostered between the pastor and the parochial vicars within the rectory whenever this can be done.

§3. The parochial vicar possesses the same rights as the pastor in the matter of vacation time.

Canon 551 — The prescriptions of can. 531 are to be observed concerning the offerings which the Christian faithful give to the parochial vicar on the occasion of his performing his pastoral ministry.

Appendix Two

Recommended Bibliography

Part I — The Parish Priesthood: Past and Present

Roger Aubert, ed., *The Church in a Secularized Society*, volume 5 of *The Christian Centuries*, 5 vols. (New York: McGraw-Hill, Inc., 1978).

Kenneth Baker, *Fundamentals of Catholicism: The Creed, the Commandments, Volume I* (San Francisco: Ignatius Press, 1982).

Louis Bouyer, Jean Leclerq, François Vandenbroucke, and Louis Cognet, *A History of Christian Spirituality*, 3 vols. (New York: Seabury Press, 1982).

The Catechism of the Catholic Church (Washington, DC: USCC [United States Catholic Conference], 1994).

Owen Chadwick, gen. ed., *The Pelican History of the Church*, 6 vols. (Baltimore, MD: Penguin, 1964).

Christian Cochini, *Apostolic Origins of Priestly Celibacy* (San Francisco: Ignatius Press, 1990).

Christopher Dawson, *The Making of Europe* (New York: Sheed and Ward, 1952).

Cardinal Henri De Lubac, *The Splendor of the Church* (San Francisco: Ignatius Press, 1986).

Patrick J. Dunn, *Priesthood: A Re-Examination of the R. C. Theology* (Staten Island, NY: Alba House, 1990).

John Tracy Ellis, *The Life of James Cardinal Gibbons, Archbishop of Baltimore 1834-1921*, 2 vols. (Westminster, MD: Christian Classics, Inc., 1987).

Joseph H. Fichter, S.J., *Parochial Schools* (Notre Dame, IN: University of Notre Dame Press, 1958).

Cardinal James Gibbons, *The Faith of Our Fathers* (Rockford, IL: TAN Books and Publishers, Inc., 1980).

Andrew M. Greeley and Peter Rossi, *Education of American Catholics* (Chicago: NORC, A Social Science Research Center, 1966).

Peter Guilday, *History of the Councils of Baltimore* (New York: Macmillan Publishing Co., Inc., 1932).

James Hitchcock, *Years of Crisis* (San Francisco: Ignatius Press, 1985).

George A. Kelly, *Keeping the Church Catholic with John Paul II* (New York: Doubleday and Co., Inc., 1991), and *Inside My Father's House* (Doubleday, 1989).

J. N. Kelly, *Oxford Dictionary of Popes* (New York: Oxford University Press, Inc., 1989).

M. David Knowles, ed., *The Middle Ages*, volume 2 of *The Christian Centuries*, 5 vols. (New York: McGraw-Hill, Inc., 1968).

Peter Kreeft, *Fundamentals of the Faith: Essays in Christian Apologetics* (San Francisco: Ignatius Press, 1988).

James M. Lee, ed., *Catholic Education in the Western World* (Notre Dame, IN: University of Notre Dame Press, 1967).

Gerhard Lenski, *The Religious Factor: A Sociological Study of Religion's Impact on Politics, Economics, and Family Life* (Westport, CT: Greenwood Publishing Group, Inc., 1977).

Albert J. Nevins, M.M., *Builders of Catholic America* (Huntington, IN: Our Sunday Visitor, 1985).

Aidan Nichols, O.P., *Holy Order: The Apostolic Ministry from the New Testament to Vatican Two* (San Francisco: Ignatius Press, 1991).

Marvin R. O'Connell, *John Ireland and the American Catholic Church* (St. Paul, MN: Minnesota Historical Society Press, 1988).

Cardinal Joseph Ratzinger and Vittorio Messori, *The Ratzinger Report*, trans. by Salvator Attanasio and Graham Harrison (San Francisco: Ignatius Press, 1985).

Rosemary R. Reuther and Eugene C. Bianchi, eds., *A Democratic Catholic Church: The Reconstruction of Roman Catholicism* (New York: Crossroad Publishing Co., 1992).

Gerald Shaughnessy, *Has the Immigrant Kept the Faith?* (New York: Macmillan Publishing Co., Inc., 1925).

Richard Shaw, *Dagger John: The Life of Archbishop John Hughes* (Mahwah, NJ: Paulist Press, 1977).

F. J. Sheed, *Theology and Sanity* (Huntington, IN: Our Sunday Visitor, 1978).

Part II— The Parish Priest and the Sacraments

On Preaching

Lawrence Boadt, *Reading the Old Testament: An Introduction* (Mahwah, NJ: Paulist Press, 1984).

Raymond Edward Brown et al., eds., *Jerome Biblical Commentary*, 1st edition (New York: Prentice Hall, 1986).

The Catechism of the Catholic Church (Washington, DC: USCC [United States Catholic Conference], 1994).

Michael Duggan, *The Consuming Fire: A Christian Introduction to the Old Testament* (San Francisco: Ignatius Press, 1991).

David N. Freedman, *Anchor Bible Dictionary*, 6 vols. (New York: Doubleday and Co., Inc., 1992).

Frank Gaebelein, ed., *Expositor's Bible Commentary, Volume 3* (Grand Rapids, MI: Zondervan Publishing Corp., 1992).

John Hardon, S.J., *The Catholic Catechism* (New York: Doubleday and Co., Inc., 1975).

Karl Keating, *Catholicism and Fundamentalism: The Attack on "Romanism" by "Bible Christians"* (San Francisco: Ignatius Press, 1988).

Peter Kreeft, *Fundamentals of the Faith: Essays in Christian Apologetics* (San Francisco: Ignatius Press, 1988) and *Yes or No? Straight Answers to Tough Questions About Christianity* (Ignatius Press, 1991).

Charles Miller, C.M., *Ordained to Preach: A Theology and Practice of Preaching* (Staten Island, NY: Alba House, 1992).

William G. Most, *Free From All Error: Authorship, Inerrancy, Historicity of Scripture, Church Teaching, and Modern Scripture Scholars* (Libertyville, IL: Prow Books/Franciscan Marytown Press, 1985).

Gerald O'Collins, S.J., and Edward Farrugia, S.J., *A Concise Dictionary of Theology* (Mahwah, NJ: Paulist Press, 1991).

Cardinal Joseph Ratzinger, *Introduction to Christianity*, trans. by J. R. Foster (San Francisco: Ignatius Press, 1990).

The Church's Confession of Faith: A Catholic Catechism for Adults, trans. by Stephen W. Arndt (San Francisco: Ignatius Press, 1987).

Claude Tresmontant, *The Hebrew Christ*, trans. by Kenneth D. Whitehead (Quincy, IL: Franciscan Press, 1989).

Bishop Donald W. Wuerl, Ronald Lawler, O.F.M. Cap., and Thomas Comerford Lawler, eds., *The Teaching of Christ*, 3rd ed., (Huntington, IN: Our Sunday Visitor, 1991).

On Worship and the Sacraments

Inos Biffi, *The First Sacraments*, trans. by Kevin Walsh (San Francisco: Ignatius Press, 1989).

Joseph M. Champlin, rev. ed., *Through Death to Life: Preparing to Celebrate the Funeral Mass* (Notre Dame, IN: Ave Maria Press, 1990).

Johannes Emminghaus, *The Eucharist: Essence, Form, Celebration* (Collegeville, MN: The Liturgical Press, 1978).

Environment and Art in Catholic Worship (Washington, DC: USCC [United States Catholic Conference], 1978).

Nicholas Halligan, O.P., *The Administration of the Sacraments* (Staten Island, NY: Alba House, 1963); *Sacraments of Initiation and Union* (Alba House, 1973); *Sacraments of Reconciliation* (Alba House, 1973); *Sacraments of Community Renewal (Holy Orders, Matrimony)* (Alba House, 1974); *The Sacraments and Their Celebration* (Alba House, 1986).

John Paul II, *Dominicae Cenae*; also *Inaestimabile Donum* (Boston, MA: St. Paul Books and Media, 1980).

Joseph A. Jungmann, S.J., *The Mass of the Roman Rite*, 2 vols., trans. by Francis A. Brunner (Westminster, MD: Christian Classics, Inc., 1989).

Liturgical Music Today (Washington, DC: NCCB [National Conference of Catholic Bishops] [c/o USCC], 1982).

Liturgy of the Hours (Washington, DC: NCCB [National Conference of Catholic Bishops] [c/o USCC], 1981).

A Manual for Church Musicians (Silver Springs, MD: The Liturgical Conference, 1964).

Hector Muñoz, O.P., *Will You Hear My Confession?* (Staten Island, NY: Alba House, 1982).

Music in Catholic Worship (Washington, DC: NCCB [National Conference of Catholic Bishops] [c/o USCC], 1983).

Adrian Nocent, *The Liturgical Year*, 4 vols. (Collegeville, MN: The Liturgical Press, 1977).

Thelma Nye, *An Introduction to Parish Church Architecture, 800-1965 A.D.* (London: Batsford Ltd., 1965).

James T. O'Connor, *The Hidden Manna: A Theology of the Eucharist* (San Francisco: Ignatius Press, 1989).

Paul Quay, S.J., *The Christian Meaning of Human Sexuality* (San Francisco: Ignatius Press, 1988).

Cardinal Joseph Ratzinger, *The Feast of Faith*, trans. by Graham Harrison (San Francisco: Ignatius Press, 1986).

On Marriage

Evelyn Billings and Ann Westmore, *The Billings Method* (New York: Ballantine Books, 1986).

Joseph M. Champlin, rev. ed., *Together for Life: Regular Edition*; also *Together for Life: Special Edition for Marriage Outside Mass* (Notre Dame, IN: Ave Maria Press, 1988).

Peter J. Elliot, W*hat God Has Joined: The Sacramentality of Marriage* (Staten Island, NY: Alba House, 1990).

Instruction on Respect for Human Life in Its Origin and on the Dignity of Procreation (replies to certain questions of the day) (Vatican City: Congregation for the Doctrine of the Faith, 1987).

George A. Kelly, ed., *Human Sexuality in Our Time: What the Church Teaches* (Boston, MA: St. Paul Books and Media, 1979).

John F. Kippley, *Birth Control and Christian Discipleship* (Cincinnati, OH: The Couple to Couple League, 1994).

Sheila K. Kippley, *Breastfeeding and Natural Child Spacing* (Cincinnati, OH: The Couple to Couple League, 1989).

John and Sheila Kippley, *The Art of Natural Family Planning*, 3rd edition (Cincinnati, OH: The Couple to Couple League, 1989).

John F. Kippley, *Sex and the Marriage Covenant: A Basis for Morality* (Cincinnati, OH: The Couple to Couple League, 1991).

Ronald Lawler, O.F.M. Cap., Joseph Boyle, Jr., and William E. May, *Catholic Sexual Ethics* (Huntington, IN: Our Sunday Visitor, 1985).

Charles A. McFadden, O.S.A., *Challenge to Morality* (Huntington, IN: Our Sunday Visitor, 1978).

Thomas J. O'Donnell, S.J., *Medicine and Christian Morality*, 2nd revised and updated version (Staten Island, NY: Alba House, 1991).

Paul Quay, S.J., *The Christian Meaning of Human Sexuality* (San Francisco: Ignatius Press, 1988).

H. Vernon Sattler, *Challenging Children to Chastity: A Parental Guide* (St. Louis, MO: Central Bureau, Catholic Central Union of America, 1991).

Herbert Smith and Joseph Dilenno, *Homosexuality: The Questions* (Boston, MA: St. Paul Books and Media, 1989).

Karol Wojtyla, *Love and Responsibility* (New York: Farrar, Straus and Giroux, 1981).

Michael Wrenn, *Pope John Paul II and the Family* (Quincy, IL: Franciscan Press, 1983).

On Humanae Vitae

Cormac Burke, *Authority and Freedom in the Church* (San Francisco: Ignatius Press, 1988).

John Ford, Germain Grisez, John Finnis, William May, *The Teaching of Humanae Vitae: A Defense* (San Francisco: Ignatius Press, 1988).

Germain Grisez, *The Way of the Lord Jesus: Christian Moral Principles, Volume 1* (Quincy, IL: Franciscan Press, 1983).

John Paul II, *The Role of the Christian Family in the Modern World, Familiaris Consortio* (Boston, MA: St. Paul Books and Media, 1982).

John F. Kippley, *Sex and the Marriage Covenant: A Basis for Morality* (Cincinnati, OH: The Couple to Couple League, 1991).

Daniel L. Lowery, C.S.S.R., *Following Christ: A Handbook of Catholic Moral Teaching* (Liguori, MO: Liguori Publications, 1983).

William May, *Contraception, Humanae Vitae, and Catholic Moral Thought* (Quincy, IL: Franciscan Press, 1983).

Cardinal Joseph Ratzinger et al., *The Catholic Priest as Moral Teacher and Guide* (San Francisco: Ignatius Press, 1990).

Part III — The Parish Priest and Evangelization

Catholic Teaching

Kenneth Baker, *Fundamentals of Catholicism: The Creed, the Commandments, Volume I* (San Francisco: Ignatius Press, 1982).

Lawrence Boadt, *Reading the Old Testament: An Introduction* (Mahwah, NJ: Paulist Press, 1984).

Raymond Edward Brown et al., eds., *Jerome Biblical Commentary*, 1st edition (New York: Prentice Hall, 1986).

The Catechism of the Catholic Church (Washington, DC: USCC [United States Catholic Conference], 1994).

Rodger Charles and Drostan Maclaren, *The Social Teaching of Vatican II — Its Origin and Development: Catholic Social Ethics, An Historical and Comparative Study*, 2nd edition (San Francisco: Ignatius Press, 1982).

Michael Duggan, *The Consuming Fire: A Christian Introduction to the Old Testament* (San Francisco: Ignatius Press, 1991).

David N. Freedman, *Anchor Bible Dictionary*, 6 vols. (New York: Doubleday and Co., Inc., 1992).

Frank Gaebelein, ed., *Expositor's Bible Commentary, Volume 3* (Grand Rapids, MI: Zondervan Publishing Corp., 1992).

John Hardon, S.J., *A Modern Catholic Dictionary* (New York: Doubleday and Co., Inc., 1980); *The Catholic Catechism* (Doubleday, 1975); *The Question and Answer Catholic Catechism* (Doubleday, 1981).

Karl Keating, *Catholicism and Fundamentalism: The Attack on "Romanism" by "Bible Christians"* (San Francisco: Ignatius Press, 1988).

Peter Kreeft, *Fundamentals of the Faith: Essays in Christian Apologetics* (San Francisco: Ignatius Press, 1988) and *Yes or No? Straight Answers to Tough Questions About Christianity* (Ignatius Press, 1991).

William E. May, *An Introduction to Moral Theology, Revised Edition* (Huntington, IN: Our Sunday Visitor, 1994).

Charles Miller, C.M., *Ordained to Preach: A Theology and Practice of Preaching* (Staten Island, NY: Alba House, 1992).

William G. Most, *Free From All Error: Authorship, Inerrancy, Historicity of Scripture, Church Teaching, and Modern Scripture Scholars* (Libertyville, IL: Prow Books/Franciscan Marytown Press, 1985).

Gerald O'Collins, S.J., and Edward Farrugia, S.J., *A Concise Dictionary of Theology* (Mahwah, NJ: Paulist Press, 1991).

James Pritchard, ed., *The Harper Concise Atlas of the Bible* (New York: HarperCollins Publishing, Inc., 1991).

Peter M. J. Stravinskas, ed., *Our Sunday Visitor's Catholic Encyclopedia* (Huntington, IN: Our Sunday Visitor, 1991).

The Church's Confession of Faith: A Catholic Catechism for Adults (San Francisco: Ignatius Press, 1987).

Claude Tresmontant, *The Hebrew Christ*, trans. by Kenneth D. Whitehead (Quincy, IL: Franciscan Press, 1989).

Bishop Donald W. Wuerl, Ronald Lawler, O.F.M. Cap., and Thomas Comerford Lawler, eds., *The Teaching of Christ* (Huntington, IN: Our Sunday Visitor, 1991).

Catholic Spirituality

Wilkie Au, S.J., *By Way of the Heart: Toward a Holistic Christian Spirituality* (Mahwah, NJ: Paulist Press, 1990).

Jordan Aumann, O.P., *Christian Spirituality in the Catholic Tradition* (San Francisco: Ignatius Press, 1985).

Ann Ball, *A Handbook of Catholic Sacramentals* (Huntington, IN: Our Sunday Visitor, 1991).

Louis Bouyer, Jean Leclerq, François Vandenbroucke, and Louis Cognet, *A History of Christian Spirituality*, 3 vols. (New York: Seabury Press, 1982).

Walter Brennan, O.S.M., *The Sacred Memory of Mary* (Mahwah, NJ: Paulist Press, 1988).

Jean-Pierre de Caussade, *Abandonment to Divine Providence* (New York: Doubleday and Co., Inc., 1975).

Charles J. Dollen, ed., *Traditional Catholic Prayers* (Huntington, IN: Our Sunday Visitor, 1990).

Charles J. Dollen, ed., *Introduction to the Devout Life: St. Francis De Sales* (Staten Island, NY: Alba House, 1992).

Thomas Dubay, *Fire Within: St. Teresa of Ávila, St. John of the Cross, and the Gospel* (San Francisco: Ignatius Press, 1989).

Thomas à Kempis, *Imitation of Christ*, trans. by John Rooney (Springfield, IL: Templegate Publishing, 1980).

Peter Kreeft, *Prayer: The Great Conversation* (San Francisco: Ignatius Press, 1991).

C. S. Lewis, *The Problem of Pain*; also *Mere Christianity* (New York: Macmillan Publishing Co., Inc., 1978).

Christopher O'Donnell, O. Carm., *At Worship with Mary: A Pastoral and Theological Study* (Collegeville, MN: The Liturgical Press, 1988).

Andre Ravier, S.J., *A Do-It-at-Home Retreat: The Spiritual Exercises of St. Ignatius* (San Francisco: Ignatius Press, 1991).

Cardinal Joseph Ratzinger, *Introduction to Christianity*, trans. by J. R. Foster (San Francisco: Ignatius Press, 1990).

William P. Sampson, S.J., *The Coming of Consolation* (Westminster, MD: Christian Classics, 1986).

Alberic Stacpoole, O.S.B., ed., *Mary's Place in Christian Dialogue* (Ridgefield, CT: Morehouse Publishing Co., 1983).

The Parish Experience

Bishop David Arias, *Spanish Roots of America* (Huntington, IN: Our Sunday Visitor, 1992).

Roy Barkley, *The Catholic Alcoholic* (Huntington, IN: Our Sunday Visitor, 1990).

William J. Bausch, *The Hands-on Parish: Reflections and Suggestions for Fostering Community* (Mystic, CT: Twenty-Third Publications, 1989).

Brian Benested, *The Pursuit of a Just Social Order: Policy Statements of the Catholic Bishops, 1966-80* (Lanham, MD: Ethics and Public Policy Center, 1982).

Thea Bowman, ed., *Families: Black and Catholic, Catholic and Black, Readings, Resources, and Family Activities* (Washington, DC: USCC [United States Catholic Conference], 1985).

William Consiglio, *Homosexual No More* (Wheaton, IL: Scripture Press Publications, Inc., 1991).

Jay P. Dolan, *The American Catholic Experience: A History from Colonial Times to the Present* (Notre Dame, IN: University of Notre Dame Press, 1992).

Bert Ghezzi, ed., *Keeping Your Kids Catholic: It May Seem Impossible But It Can Be Done* (Ann Arbor, MI: Servant Publications, 1989).

John F. Harvey, O.S.F.S., *The Homosexual Person: New Thinking in Pastoral Care* (San Francisco: Ignatius Press, 1987).

George A. Kelly, *Catholics and the Practice of the Faith* (Washington, DC: Catholic University of America Press, 1946); *Keeping the Church Catholic with John Paul II* (New York: Doubleday and Co., Inc., 1991).

Philip F. Lawler, *Operation Rescue* (Huntington, IN: Our Sunday Visitor, 1992).

Rawley Myers, *Journal of a Parish Priest* (Huntington, IN: Our Sunday Visitor, 1982).

The National Pastoral Plan for Hispanic Ministry, trans. by Marina Herrera (Washington, DC: NCCB [National Conference of Catholic Bishops] [c/o USCC], 1987).

Albert J. Nevins, M.M., *American Martyrs* (Huntington, IN: Our Sunday Visitor, 1987).

Joseph Nicolosi, Ph.D., *Reparative Therapy of Male Homosexuality: A New Clinical Approach* (Northvale, NJ: Jason Aronson, Inc., 1991).

Rosemary R. Reuther and Eugene C. Bianchi, eds., *A Democratic Catholic Church: The Reconstruction of Roman Catholicism* (New York: Crossroad Publishing Co., 1992).

Paul C. Vitz, *Censorship: Evidence of Bias in Our Children's Textbooks* (Ann Arbor, MI: Servant Publications, 1986).

Paul C. Vitz, *Psychology as Religion: The Cult of Self-Worship* (Grand Rapids, MI: William B. Eerdmans Publishing Co., 1977).

Paul Wilkes, *In Mysterious Ways: The Death and Life of a Parish Priest* (New York: Random House, Inc., 1990).

Michael J. Wrenn, *Catechisms and Controversies: Religious Education in the Postconciliar Years* (San Francisco: Ignatius Press, 1991).

The Family Apostolate

Clayton C. Barbeau, *The Father of the Family* (Huntington, IN: Our Sunday Visitor, 1990).

Evelyn Billings and Ann Westmore, *The Billings Method* (New York: Ballantine Books, 1986).

Rodger Charles and Drostan Maclaren, *The Social Teaching of Vatican II — Its Origin and Development: Catholic Social Ethics, An Historical and Comparative Study*, 2nd edition (San Francisco: Ignatius Press, 1982).

Ronda Chervin, *Feminine, Free and Faithful* (San Francisco: Ignatius Press, 1986).

H. P. Dunn, M.D., *The Doctor and Christian Marriage* (Staten Island, NY: Alba House, 1992).

John F. Kippley, *Birth Control and Christian Discipleship* (Cincinnati, OH: The Couple to Couple League, 1994).

Sheila K. Kippley, *Breastfeeding and Natural Child Spacing* (Cincinnati, OH: The Couple to Couple League, 1989).

Paul M. Quay, S.J., *The Christian Meaning of Human Sexuality* (San Francisco: Ignatius Press, 1988).

Donna Steichen, *Ungodly Rage: The Hidden Face of Catholic Feminism* (San Francisco: Ignatius Press, 1991).

Part IV — Parish Priests: Administrators and Diocesan Officials

Accounting Principles and Reporting Practices for Churches (Washington, DC: USCC [United States Catholic Conference], 1990).

Code of Canon Law: Latin-English Edition, trans. by The Canon Law Society of America Staff (Washington, DC: The Canon Law Society of America, 1983).

William A. Corbett, *Financial Guide for Catholics* (Huntington, IN: Our Sunday Visitor, 1989).

Robert L. Cord, *Separation of Church and State: Historical Fact and Current Fiction* (Grand Rapids, MI: Baker Book House, 1988).

James A. Coriden et al., eds., *The Code of Canon Law: A Text and Commentary, Study Edition* (Mahwah, NJ: Paulist Press, 1986).

James A. Coriden, *An Introduction to Canon Law* (Mahwah, NJ: Paulist Press, 1991).

Richard Hammar, *Pastor, Church, and Law Workbook* (Matthews, NC: Christian Ministry Resources, 1992).

The Handbook of Indulgences: Norms and Grants (New York: Catholic Book Publishing Co., 1991).

John Huels, *The Pastoral Companion: A Canon Law Handbook for Catholic Ministry* (Quincy, IL: Franciscan Press, 1986).

Russell Kirk, *The Roots of American Order* (Washington, DC: Regnery Gateway, Inc., 1992).

National Conference of Catholic Bishops Staff, *Complementary Norms: Implementation of the 1933 Code of Canon Law* (Washington, DC: USCC [United States Catholic Conference], 1991).

Richard J. Neuhaus, *The Naked Public Square: Religion and Democracy in America* (Grand Rapids, MI: William B. Eerdmans Publishing Co., 1986).

John T. Noonan, *The Believer and the Powers That Are: Cases, History, and Other Data Bearing on the Relation of Religion and Government* (New York: Macmillan Publishing Co., Inc., 1987).

Colman P. O'Neill, O.P., *Meeting Christ in the Sacraments* (New York: Staten Island, NY: Alba House, 1991).

Laurence J. Peter and Raymond Hull, *The Peter Principle: Why Things Always Go Wrong* (New York: William Morrow and Co., Inc., 1971).

Bernard A. Siegle, *Marriage: According to the New Code of Canon Law* (Staten Island, NY: Alba House, 1986).

Peter M. J. Stravinskas, ed., *Our Sunday Visitor's Catholic Encyclopedia* (Huntington, IN: Our Sunday Visitor, 1991).

Index

C

fund-raising 247, 254-263, 276

G

Gallup, George 61, 72, 223
Gallup poll 223
general absolution 51, 108, 122, 140, 147-149, 265, 276, 277
General Catechetical Directory 84, 142
General Instruction on the Roman Missal 105, 109
Gheon, Henri 85
Gibbons, Cardinal James 34
Gilder, George 237
going house to house 181
Goldsmith, Oliver 19
Goodbye, Mr. Chips 41
Greer, Germaine 234-235
Gremillion, Monsignor Joseph 72, 74
Grisez, Germain 28, 208
"Guidelines for the Renewal of Liturgical Life" 107
Guilday, Peter 32
guilt machine 143

H

hearing confessions 145
Heenan, Cardinal John 266
Hesburgh, Father Theodore 74
Hillenbrand, Monsignor Reynold 195
Holy Name 44, 191
Holy Order, Sacrament of 151-154
holy rule 28, 272
home study program 214
Human Life Foundation 131
Humanae Vitae 71, 124-135, 153, 225, 229, 238, 241
Humanae Vitae: A Generation Later 133

I

immigrants 171
inactive (Catholic) 72, 73, 188
Inestimabile Donum 107
infant baptism 135-136, 138, 175; *see also* Baptism, Sacrament of
interloping clerics 119
International Theological Commission 161
intrinsic reason for sexuality 127
Instruction on Infant Baptism 138

Ireland, John 159, 166, 170
irreverence 100, 144, 273
It Doesn't Take A Hero 78

J

Jesuits 41, 104, 193, 196; *see also* Society of Jesus
Jocist Movement 62
John XXIII 66, 102, 104, 141, 146, 198, 214; *see also* Roncalli, Angelo
    Giuseppi
John Paul II 9, 10, 15, 17, 21, 23, 51, 54, 55, 67, 72, 90, 91, 96, 101, 103, 107,
    132, 136, 160, 167, 177, 199, 206, 208-209, 212, 214, 218, 220, 222,
    223, 225, 227-228, 234, 235, 241, 255, 271, 281; *see also* Wojtyla,
    Karol
Joyce, Mary 236
Junior Holy Name Societies 211
Justice in the World 160

K

Keeping Costs Down 250-254
Kelley, Francis Clement 48
Kelly's Law 197
Kevane, Monsignor Eugene 90
Kippley, John 132, 231
Kisburg, Nicholas 168
Kung, Hans 70

L

Lactantius 177
Ladies of Charity 162
laissez-faire 37, 47
lay apostles 191
lay apostolate 80, 95, 194, 199, 241
lay catechists 176, 218
lay organization 79, 80, 194
Legion of Decency 61
Legion of Mary 185, 191, 193, 197-198, 200
licit marriage 118
Lincoln, Abraham 50
Liturgical Worship in the Absence of a Priest 218-220
Lucker, Bishop Raymond 17
Lumen Gentium 21, 24, 70, 101, 139, 280

M

magisterium 17, 51, 56, 57, 67, 68, 71, 89, 90, 91, 126, 163, 210
magisterium of the academe 66
magisterium of the hierarchy 66
Man and Woman in Christ 236
Marino, Father Ronald 176
marriage encounter 203, 204, 218, 231
marriage preparation 121, 122, 231
married deacons 110, 217-218
Mass, Sacrifice of the 18, 100-113, 205; *see also* Sunday Mass
matrimony 35, 106, 112-123, 124, 144, 223
Maynard, Theodore 170
McCarthy, Mary 15, 16
McIntyre, Bishop J. Francis A. 41, 250
Men and Marriage 237
Menninger, Karl 229
Michonneau, Abbé 61, 62, 67
minister 9, 14, 51, 56, 70, 71, 76, 95, 105, 106, 108, 110, 111, 117, 118, 132, 138, 150, 155, 163, 203, 204, 205, 211, 213, 215, 216, 218, 219, 258, 276, 278
ministerium 203
Ministry to Word and Sacraments 69
minority groups 110, 162
Minute Men 165-166
Missionary Spirit in Parish Life, The 61
Mitty, Archbishop John 79
mixed marriages 118, 215, 216
modernism 63
Momism 236, 237
Monaghan, Monsignor John Patrick 41, 158, 249
monotony 36
Moody, Father Joseph N. 148
morale problem 15, 16
motherhood 24, 87, 114-116, 133, 224, 228-229, 234, 235
motherhood, the office of 114
Moylan, Father John 41
multicultural 103, 169
Murphy's law 246
Murray, Father John Courtney 41

N

National Catholic Reporter 17, 29, 69, 81, 214

S

Spellman, Francis J. 113, 244-247, 266
"Stewardship: A Disciple's Response" 262
Strecker, Edward 236, 242
subsidiarity 276-278
Sunday collection 257
Sunday Mass 44, 45, 54, 62, 67, 75, 86, 87, 89, 100, 106, 109, 110, 115, 176,
    187, 188, 192, 213, 219, 228
Sword of the Spirit, The 62
Synod of Bishops 160

T

Third Council of Baltimore 33
Thomas, Father John L., S.J. 230
"To Teach As Jesus Did" 210
"transcendental" groups 203
Tridentine discipline 26
Tridentine Missal 105
Tridentine worship, 100

U

United States Catholic Conference 51, 71, 219, 220
Unknown Council 66
USCC 17, 74, 236

V

Vatican II 9, 10, 14, 15, 16, 17, 20, 24, 26, 33, 46, 50, 51, 53, 54, 61, 66, 67, 68,
    70, 72, 73, 74, 75, 77, 80, 85, 89, 90, 95, 96, 101, 103, 105, 106, 123, 125,
    136, 144, 146, 169, 193, 195, 196, 214, 223, 229, 280; *see also* Second
    Vatican Council
Vatican Two: The Conciliar and Post-Conciliar Documents 107
Vianney, Saint John 15, 85
Vicariates 264-266
Visiting the Sick 155
Visits to the Blessed Sacrament 108-109

W

Weigel, George 240
Whatever Became of Guilt? 229
Whatever Became of Sin? 229
Why Catholics Can't Sing 103
Willebrands, Cardinal Johann 216

Wiltgen, Ralph 66
Wojtyla, Karol 9; *see also* John Paul II
worshiping together 49
Wrenn, Monsignor Michael 8, 214, 220
Wylie, Philip 236, 242

Y

Young Christian Workers 213
young marrieds 226
Youth Ministry 206, 208-214

The following pages provided for your notes ...